AMAZING CONNECTIONS
Kemet to Hispanophone Africana Literature

AMAZING CONNECTIONS
Kemet to Hispanophone Africana Literature

Ian Isidore Smart

ORIGINAL WORLD PRESS
Washington, D.C. and Port-of-Spain

Original World Press
55 Edward Street, Port-of-Spain
Trinidad & Tobago

3306 Ross Place, N.W.
Washington, D.C. 20008

www.iansmart.com

Published 1996
Second Printing (paperback), 1998

Printed and bound in the United States of America

Library of Congress Card Catalog Number: 96-67809
ISBN 0-9641929-1-8
ISBN 0-9641929-2-6 (case)

Cover art by Wilcox Morris

For Buena Isidra,
for Monifa Isidra,
for Isidore, my father,
and for Isidore, my son;
for the million sons of Africa
who responded to the call
on October 16, 1995
in Washington, D.C.

Acknowledgements

I am greatly indebted to the impeccable scholarship and cordial collegiality of one of North America's great academicians, Henry J. Richards. His invaluable assistance has helped make possible yet another of my books. I am most grateful, too, to my colleagues and friends, the late Stanley A. Cyrus, may he rest in peace, Carol Beane, Mary A. Harris, and Effie Boldridge, who took the time to read and comment on my manuscript. Finally, my appreciation is great for those who helped with the proofreading: Wanda Sandle, Louis A. Hemans, Jean Purchas-Tulloch, and Charmaine Robinson; and for my sister, Maria, who, with her consuetudinary calm efficiency, rescued the index from my technological gaucheness.

CONTENTS

❒ Introduction ❒ 1

❒ 1 ❒
In the Very Beginning There Was Africa 11

❒ 2 ❒
Here Comes the Trickster 45

❒ 3 ❒
Here Comes the *Cimarrón* 79

❒ 4 ❒
Changó the *Cimarrón* 113

❒ 5 ❒
Cuminá as *Cimarrón* 145

❒ Epilogue ❒ 169

❒ Notes ❒ 175

❒ Works Cited ❒ 179

❒ Index ❒ 185

Introduction

Although there has recently been a veritable explosion of interest in the civilization of Pharaonic Egypt, the term "Kemet" means nothing to many scholars—perhaps not even to the majority. Raymond O. Faulkner's *A Concise Dictionary of Middle Egyptian* is greatly respected by contemporary Egyptologists. In the alphabetical order established by the experts the form *km* (all of these forms are, in fact, best-guess phonetic transcriptions) is the first to be found therein and is defined simply as "black." Immediately following it is the form *Kmt*, which is defined as "the Black Land, Egypt." Then follows *Kmt* with the meaning "Egyptians." Most interestingly, there follows after this the form *km* again, this time it is a verb with the meaning "total up to, amount to, complete." Furthermore, *km* is presented also as a noun meaning "completion" (286). Clearly, "complete," as both verb and adjective, is synonymous with "perfect," as both verb and adjective. The ancient Egyptians, then, named themselves and their land with a term the root meaning of which is both "black" and "perfect." Since the written forms of Egyptian took into account only the consonants, and since the vast majority of so-called Egyptologists appear to be ideologically committed to de-Africanizing *Kmt* and its civilization, there has been no systematic attempt to reconstruct the vowel system on the basis of scientific comparison with other African languages. Consequently, *Kmt* has been rendered in various ways: "Kemit," "Kamit," "Kimit," "Kemet," or "Khamit," "Khemit," etc. Our preference—and it is simply that, a preference or a taste—is for "Kemet." And the term "Kemet" for us has as its ultimate referent the entire classical civilization that emerged and flourished in the Nile Valley from the beginning of recorded history to the Greek invasion in the 4th century B.C.

With regard to the designation "Hispanophone Africana," suffice it to say at this point that it replaces "Afro-Hispanic." At the very end of this work we have presented the rationale for our preference, and the reader may wish to consult the first part of the "Epilogue" before proceeding any further.

□ □ □

A little over five years ago our Afrocentric, Pan-Caribbean study on the African-ancestored Cuban Poet Laureate was published. The work, *Nicolás Guillén, Popular Poet of the Caribbean*, charted a new course in the field of Hispanic literary criticism. The present volume is its necessary complement, for the focus of the literary analysis is brought to bear on two African-ancestored writers of fiction, Quince Duncan from Costa Rica and Manuel Zapata Olivella from Colombia. As the discussion will make clear, these two authors are worthy representatives not only of Hispanophone Africana writing, but also of Latin American and general Hispanic fiction.

The approach used in this present book seeks to be radically different. The Western academy as we know it today only came into being with the so-called Enlightenment, and, as we argue throughout the book (but especially on pp. 88-89), its principal goal is the shoring up of white supremacy. It is thus a fundamentally invalid enterprise which must be stood on its head, deconstructed. Sweeping approaches require sweeping strategies. To deconstruct the entire edifice, that is, to achieve what Blaise Pascal in his *Pensées* termed the "*renversement du pour au contre,*" the underpinnings must be exposed. This accounts for the expansive discussion of philosophical themes throughout the current volume.

Moreover, spirituality and theological thought absolutely undergird all expressions of African culture. A student of African civilizations, then, has to engage in theological speculation to make sense of her/his subject matter. Perhaps because of the profound African influence on Hispanic civilization, religion has been fundamental to Hispanic and Latin American literature. This religion has been Roman Catholicism, which still enjoys official or quasi-official status in Spain and in most Spanish American countries. The Mexican writer Juan José Arreola, for example, is one of the multitude of Spanish-speaking men of letters who see the culture of Roman Catholicism as the most significant metaphor in Hispanic letters. In our study we have entered in some depth and extension into ancient and traditional African spirituality and theological thought, as well as Roman Catholic theology. A book of a title such as ours could not have unfolded in any other way.

The title demands, too, absolute Afrocentricity in the elaboration of the arguments. This accounts for the frequent inclusion of and reference to the non-Spanish-speaking Americas, Afro-North America and the Caribbean in particular. Zapata Olivella in a most insightful discourse on the meaning of American civilization, *Las claves mágicas de América: (Raza, clase y cultura)* [The Magical Keys to America: Race, Class and Culture], declares:

> Al hablar, pues, de razas, clases y cultura en América, a menos que se peque de ingenuo o falaz, siempre debe arrancarse de la historia de las Antillas y del Caribe donde tuvo el encuentro violento de pueblos que al fusionar sus tradiciones y experiencas distintas, y validos de sus artes, ambiciones, dolores y sueños, construyeron una nueva sociedad. Utilizando un lenguaje del gusto de los comerciantes contemporáneos, valdría decir que América es un producto "made in" en el Caribe. (169)
>
> [When broaching the subject of race, class and culture in the Americas, one would succumb to naivete and fallacy unless one's theoretical framework were grounded in the history of the West Indies and the Caribbean. For that was the site of the violent encounter between peoples who, by fusing their distinct traditions and experiences, rooted in their peculiar esthetics, drives, sufferings and dreams, created a new society. To use the language dear to the contemporary world of commerce, it could be said that America is a product "made in" the Caribbean.]

Every reference to the Caribbean in this book is justified, if one were to respect the view of Zapata, and, as it turns out, of numerous others. Indeed, the reader will find that this justification is built into the very tissue of the arguments.

□ □ □

The first chapter, "In the Very Beginning There Was Africa," addresses, of course, the first element of the title, namely, Kemet. It establishes as forcefully as possible the basis for the proclamation that there are "amazing connections" between ancient Africa and the contemporary world of Hispanophone Africana literature. Essentially, this chapter examines the very ancient African roots of Roman Catholicism, one of the most significant cultural forces in Hispanic civilization. The new approach that our book presents leads to a reexamination of the concept of syncretism, for it is precisely through this concept that traditional Eurocentric scholarship has framed the relationship between Africa and Roman Catholicism in the Hispanic world.

Our revision of the concept yields several clarifications with respect to the true role played by Kemet in the formation of Roman Catholic doctrinal and liturgical tradition. The discussion of this topic relies on the biblical scholarship of Walter Arthur McCray, author of *The Black Presence in the Bible*. We are also greatly indebted to the archeological expertise of John G. Jackson and the school of Afrocentric researchers whose unofficial dean would be Ivan Van Sertima, and to the bona fide British Egyptologist, E. A. Wallis Budge. The amazing presence of ancient Africa in Roman Catholicism is evinced especially in the characteristic Roman position with respect to the Madonna and to the saints. In the context of the better understanding of syncretism, an understanding that eschews white supremacist biases and adheres rigorously to the historical data, the cultural significance of New World carnivals is considerably enhanced. The second part of this first chapter seeks to unmask the false ideological presuppositions of Latin

American literary (and cultural as well) history by focusing on the massive errors introduced by the influential nineteenth century Argentine political thinker Domingo F. Sarmiento. Since his intellectual mischief was effected principally through his "civilization and barbarism" model, it is precisely on this very axis that the false edifice of his racist ideology is turned on its head. It is the compellingly logical approach to the history of human civilization by Cheikh Anta Diop, the twentieth century intellectual giant from Senegal, that is used to deconstruct Sarmiento. Diop's major contribution in this respect is made through a work entitled, *Civilization or Barbarism: An Authentic Anthropology*.

Chapter Two is "Here Comes the Trickster," and, as the title announces, it examines the literary significance of the Trickster figure. The well-known contemporary literary theoretician, Henry Louis Gates, Jr., provides the scholarly base for this examination. Gates has contributed impressively to the academy's understanding of the traditional African roots of contemporary African American culture. These roots are traced in and through the figure of the Signifying Monkey, an African American version of the traditional Yoruba Trickster figure, Legba. And Gates's fundamental text on the subject is precisely, *The Signifying Monkey: A Theory of African-American Literary Criticism*.

The exploration of Gates's ideas leads to our consideration of the centrality of laughter and humor in African and neo-African literature throughout the ages. Following this lead we revisit the topic of Islamic Africa's massive influence on the development of culture and civilization in the Iberian Peninsula. A disinterested study of the relationship of the Moors to what are generally considered to be typically Hispanic cultural expressions suggests a radical revision of certain cherished assumptions. Our discussion touches on such cultural elements as music, food, and architecture. However, faithful to our specific focus in this book, we entered with some detail into the matter of the possible African roots of the quintessentially Hispanic genre, the picaresque novel. Our presentation unveils a clear connection between the *pícaro* and the trickster. Our earlier essay, "The Trickster *Pícaro* in Three Contemporary Afro-Hispanic Novels," had opened the door to precisely this line of analysis.

Gates's literary theorizing on Legba dovetails with other contemporary theological, literary, and sociological theories emanating from the Caribbean. Chapter Three, "Here Comes the *Cimarrón*," begins with a review of the contributions made by Kortright Davis, a Caribbean theological scholar, in his first book *Emancipation Still Comin'*. In that book he argues compellingly that the emancipatory quest for the West Indian spirit is rooted in the Christian religious tradition. Davis privileges the term "emancipation" over "liberation," because of the peculiarly Caribbean resonances it evokes.

Not unmindful of the gaps in Gates and Davis, our discussion in the first subsection—"The Ancient African Connections"— of the third chapter, makes explicit connections between contemporary *cimarronaje* and the powerful Yoruba ancestor figure, Shango. Traditional Yoruba religious thought is rooted in ancient Africa, and Shango is a quintessential liberator figure consonant with ancient African spirituality. Just as Legba could be considered the Trickster figure par excellence, Shango could be viewed as the *cimarrón* par excellence. We then undertake a survey of the manifestations of *cimarronaje* in Caribbean letters using theoretical constructs of Frantz Fanon, Selwyn R. Cudjoe, and Patrick Taylor to complement those of Davis and Gates. In this line of development we were guided by Zapata Olivella's insight referenced in the opening pages of the Introduction. For if the Caribbean is the seed from which the Americas sprung, then the African element is the soul force of the entire complex. The focus on literary expression from the Caribbean irrespective of the language used is not misplaced, even in a book on Hispanophone Africana literature. The Africana element is the essential one, the linguistic vehicle is accidental.

With the subtitle, "The Caribbean Carnival Connection," the second part of Chapter Three dwells at some length on representative samples of Pan-Caribbean literary expressions. Carnival is a cultural phenomenon through which the emancipatory thrust of Caribbean and circum-Caribbean culture is articulated. It is thus another significant connecting element for the neo-African literary expressions of the Americas. The carnival link is best appreciated through the analysis of such forms as the Cuban *son*, the Colombian *vallenato*, and the Trinidad and Tobago kaiso. For this analysis we referred principally to Alejo Carpentier's essays on the *son*, to Rito Llerena Villalobos's book on the *vallenato*, and to Raymond Quevedo's (Atilla the Hun) and Hollis Liverpool's works on kaiso. The literary samples that are examined are taken from both verse and prose forms and come from the works of Guillén, Earl Lovelace, Aimé Césaire, Gerardo Maloney, and Lorna Goodison. There is some consideration, as well, of the work of Nelson Estupiñán Bass and Gabriel García Márquez, among others.

Chapter Four, "*Changó* as *Cimarrón*," presents a literary analysis of Manuel Zapata Olivella's major novel, *Changó, el gran putas*. The presentation includes a revision of the concept of magical realism as introduced by Alejo Carpentier. A holistic unbiased approach to this very popular Latin American literary trend reveals its glaring white supremacist underpinnings. Analogous flaws are unmasked in the poetic movement initiated by Luis Palés Matos that has been labelled *negrista*, "Afro-Antillean," or "Afro-Cuban." Charles S. Finch's book, *Echoes from the Old Darkland*, provides the scholarly base for our presentation of the amazing connections between Olivella's *cimarrón* figure, Shango, and the wonderful world of Kemetic mythology.

For Quince Duncan the *cimarrón* figure is not Shango but *Cuminá*, a fully Caribbean and fully Hispanophone, and hence perfectly Hispanophone Africana literary symbol. This idea is the basis of Chapter Five, "*Cuminá* as *Cimarrón*." Complementing the preceding one, this fifth chapter presents a literary analysis of Duncan's fiction. Again, it is necessary to revisit Carpentier's magical realism, placing it in its proper perspective as an exclusionary, esoteric approach, like romanticism from which it came and existentialism to which it is intimately connected. Magical realism is contrasted with negritude, which is inclusionary and collectivist, and seeks to plunge into the throbbing heart and soul, the *sous-réalité* of the sweaty black masses. Some stylistic similarities are shown to exist between Duncan's fiction and that of the Latin American writers of the "boom," Carlos Fuentes and

Mario Vargas Llosa, for example. Duncan, like these authors, is heavily indebted to William Faulkner.

The theoretical speculations of Chapters One and Two bear their full fruit in the last two chapters, and especially in Chapter Five, which argues for the profound Kemetic mythological roots of Duncan's literature with its uncannily insightful rendition of the Wosir (Osiris)/Heru (Horus)-Auset (Isis)-Set tragic tangle in full contemporary Hispanophone Africana garb. The considerations in this chapter help to shed light on some deeper meanings of the "African origin of civilization," to use the terminology articulated in the very title of Cheikh Anta Diop's ground-breaking work.

□ □ □

Quince Duncan and Manuel Zapata Olivella, brilliant creative Hispanophone Africana voices from Costa Rica and Colombia respectively, are as worthy representatives of the entire enterprise of Latin American fiction as an Alejo Carpentier, a Gabriel García Márquez, a Carlos Fuentes, a Juan José Arreola, or a Mario Vargas Llosa. This book brings most of the strictly literary analysis to bear on fiction because in our earlier book on Nicolás Guillén we initiated this kind of Afrocentric analysis in the poetic genre. Indeed, when it comes to examining the African connections—still an uncommon preoccupation—the scholarly community is first inclined to turn its attention to poetry, which necessarily includes drama, for poetry has always been the language of drama. Our emphasis on fiction in this book is thus timely. Obviously, too, Duncan and Zapata are not the only important African-ancestored prose writers from contemporary Latin America. Richard L. Jackson, the veritable dean of Hispanophone Africana literature scholars, in his classic, *Black Writers in Latin America*, makes this abundantly clear. He highlights fiction writers such as Adalberto Ortiz, Arnoldo Palacios, and Juan Pablo Sojo. There exists too, for example, Henry J. Richards's impressive work on the literary giant from Ecuador, Nelson Estupiñán Bass. However, Duncan and

Zapata are the pioneering creative souls who, as our book will show, have taken the lead, not just among African-ancestored writers, but for all of contemporary Latin American fiction.

At this juncture some reader may still be wondering what Kemet has to do with contemporary Latin American fiction. This is, of course, precisely the point, the question our book answers. We encourage the reader, then, to continue reading. Our book is a part of the exploding Afrocentric discourse that has emerged from the contemporary academy. This discourse brings holism, wholesomeness to the academy. It brings inclusiveness and multiculturalism. It constitutes an act of liberation.

1

In the Very Beginning There Was Africa

Some two decades ago John S. Mbiti opened his ground-breaking study, *African Religions and Philosophy* (1969), with the bald statement that Africans "are notoriously religious" (1). Much earlier, in fact, as many as three decades prior to the appearance of Mbiti's book, Melville J. Herskovits, in *The Myth of the Negro Past* (1941), had begun awakening academe, or certain circles therein, to the reality of the profound African religious and cultural influence on the Americas. He was himself following the lead of the master of the Eurocentric New World Africanists, the Cuban, Fernando Ortiz Fernández (1881-1969). In the wake of Herskovits, it became quite common for anthropologists, ethnomusicologists, and linguists to take seriously the so-called African cultural retentions in the so-called New World. Studies emerged on Haitian voodoo, on Cuban *santería*, on Trinidad and Tobago Shango, on Brazilian *candomble*, on Jamaican Pukumina, Kumina, and Rastafarianism.[1] The Barbadian poet, historian, and essayist, Edward Kamau Brathwaite, produced a watershed article, "The African Presence in Caribbean Literature," on the subject. Then, as Chapter Two will present in some detail, during the decade of the eighties, the African American critic, Henry Louis Gates, with "The Blackness of Blackness: A Critique of the Sign and the Signifying Monkey," his signature essay in the collection, *Black Literature and Literary Theory* (1984), brought to the center of focus in highbrow North American academic circles the pivotal role of traditional religion in the development of all aspects of African American literature and culture.

Théophile Obenga, a scholar of significant stature, has a somewhat different slant. Excerpts of an English version of one of his works have been published as "African Philosophy of the Pharaonic Period 2780-330 B.C." in *Egypt Revisited* (1989), edited by Ivan Van Sertima. Therein Obenga argues as follows:

> Thus, *philosophy* in the strictest sense of the word, was practiced in Ancient Egypt. Texts such as the preceding [the Bremmer Rhind Papyrus] sufficiently prove this fact. The exegetes are mistaken to interpret all the important Egyptian texts as religious documents left behind by their authors to make their religion understood. When discussing Ancient Egypt it is always "religion" and never "philosophy" which is mentioned. This fault can only be attributed to the interpreters of the Egyptian texts. African Egyptologists must react against this generalized tendency which may well be the result of an unadmitted and yet dangerous bias. Ancient Egyptians thought about being, life, and death. Let us not reduce their important writings to the single dimension of the "sacred," the "religious." Let us exercise enough critical judgement to see them in another light from now on. (307)

Obenga's slant is a necessary one in the current climate of the academy, where atheistic secular humanism is the order of the day. But, it is important to consider that this is not the only order possible, nor is it the best of possible orders. The Roman Catholic Church, for example, mandates a thorough grounding in philosophy for all of its priests. The Roman Catholic theologian par excellence was St. Thomas of Aquinas, who was as much a philosopher as he was a theologian. Obenga's words strike a note of caution, bringing a clarity of focus. In the final analysis, however, the line between philosophy and theology is too blurred to be really meaningful.

Amazingly, with this wealth of data and analysis, the mere tip of which was referenced above, the true center of the question has not really been broached. In this matter, as is frequently the case, Western academic tradition has exhibited a profound compartmentalization, forming a pattern of hardened ivory towers often in intimate physical contact but totally independent of, and even perniciously hostile to, one another. Out of this wilderness of disconnected probings, there have emerged from time to time by way of exception some wholesomely holistic voices. The French scholar Count Constantine Francis Chassebeuf de Volney, in the eighteenth century, for example, declared the following with reference to Black Africa or African Ethiopia, as he would have put it: "There a people, now forgotten, discovered, while others were yet barbarians, the elements of the arts and sciences. A race of men now rejected from society for their *sable skin and frizzled hair*, founded on the study of the laws of nature, those civil and religious systems which still govern the universe."[2]

In the contemporary period several other giants of integrity have surfaced. George G. M. James is one such. In 1954 he dared take the logical step forward with his *Stolen Legacy: The Greeks were not the authors of Greek Philosophy, but the people of North Africa, commonly called the Egyptians*. Before James's work came to the attention of even the limited circle of African-centered intellectuals, Cheikh Anta Diop began to energize the field with his uncommon brilliance. Yosef ben-Jochannan, somewhat vociferously, has been proclaiming the connection for decades. So have Chancellor Williams and John G. Jackson. Their example has been followed by a host of others in the last two decades: Ivan Van Sertima, Asa Hilliard, Molefi Asante, Wayne B. Chandler, Walter Arthur McCray, Beatrice Lumpkin, Runoko Rashidi, and Cain Hope Felder, to name a few. In 1987 Martin Bernal joined the ranks of these enlightened ones.[3] Even the likes of Mbiti, Herskovits, Brathwaite, and Gates, for many reasons, stopped short of making these connections. Penetrated through and through by the delimiting parallelism of academe, they missed the point made by the scholars who could have provided the necessary missing links, scholars who did not just see an occasional flash of light but lived for the most part illumined by the constant glow of historical veracity and intellectual honesty. Indeed, while Herskovits, Mbiti, and even Brathwaite were probing gingerly at the rim of this reality, those other stalwart "black" scholars (all are

African ancestored with the exception of Bernal, and, interestingly, he is also one of the most accommodating to the Eurocentric status quo) had penetrated to the core and were basking in the light of the tremendous truths. They would be happy to share them, but have been largely shut out of the high places of academe.

Diop has to be credited with turning the tide in favor of a reexamination of the cherished white supremacist assumptions of the academy. A scholar of such incredibly impeccable credentials could not be marginalized. Mercer Cook's translation and edition of Diop's *The African Origin of Civilization: Myth or Reality* (1974) went far towards giving respectability and a hearing to the disparate voices of holism. Diop's posthumously published English version of *Civilization or Barbarism: An Authentic Anthropology* (1991), a work of truly classic dimensions, has signalled the dawning of an entirely new era for all of academe.

Enlightened by the new holism, each of the various branches of humanistic studies has to be reconfigured. This present book seeks with careful and hopefully unpretentious scholarship to address the seemingly pretentious task of reshaping the approach to the analysis of scribal literature in Spanish in the specific area that was once designated as "Afro-Hispanic Literature." We have opted to replace the designation "Afro-Hispanic" with "Hispanophone Africana." The reasons for this will become clear as the book unfolds, and this specific question is addressed in our "Epilogue." The reader who carefully follows our presentation will, we believe, be furnished with a wealth of detailed evidence and copious demonstration of the massive African influence not only on the work of a small number of relatively unknown "black" writers, but on all of Hispanic letters, indeed, on all of human literature. At this stage in the development of knowledge, it is easier and more "politic" to focus this demonstration on so-called "black" writings. However, as our argument develops, the simply massive range of African presence will become clear to the reader.

□ □ □

Syncretism

The so-called process of syncretism has been one of the linchpins of the accepted approach to the phenomenon of what used to be called African cultural survivals in the New World. It can therefor serve as the point of deconstruction for this approach. The elements that were supposed to have merged through syncretism were the African—barbaric and pagan—primitive religious theory and practice and the civilized, Christian—principally Catholic—doctrine and liturgy. Thus, the simple-minded Africans, always slaves, in their dim-witted religiosity were presumed to have taken such purely external elements of Catholicism as the iconography, the physical arrangement of the place of worship and liturgical patterns in general, and to have married them to their traditional pagan religious theory and praxis. So Shango, the so-called god of thunder, is worshipped under the guise of or through an iconographic representation that is exactly the same as that of Saint Barbara or of Saint George. Analogously Oshun, one of Shango's wives, goddess of the sea, is represented as one of the Catholic Madonnas—the Virgin Mother of God. Also, the African religious ceremonies employed altars, for example, that closely resembled the sensually bedecked altars of pre-Vatican 11 Catholicism.

The theory of syncretism fits admirably the experiential data available to even the most casual observer. However, it rests on an endemic and wholly spurious Eurocentrism. Perhaps the most flagrant subverting of this treasured academic fiction occurs in the very title of one of ben-Jochannan's works, *African Origin of the Major "Western Religions."* With the documentation that is now generally available, and that has always existed hidden away in the darkest corners of the Western academy, a credible case can be made that the Catholicism the "unlettered" slaves were thought to have, with open-mouthed and dim-witted awe, grossly misappropriated was, in fact, being claimed as one of their intellectual offspring by a sophisticated African population, well-schooled in the mysteries of religion. As was indicated in the Introduction, no treatment of any aspect of African or even Latin American culture can ignore the centrality of religion or spirituality. This writer is not a theologian, but simply a scholar of common sense; so that whereas the discussion advanced in this section focuses on issues that are essentially theological, the position presented is merely a personal opinion and nothing more. As regards liturgy, anyone familiar with the Bible will have been struck by the fact, for example, that David danced a prayer on at least one occasion. Dance as a form of worship was practiced by Africans before David's time and still is normal for them. It is common in the so-called Judeo-Christian tradition for holy people to enter into a trance when they pray. Trancelike states induced by meditation or music have been normal components of African liturgies from the earliest times to the present day. Ancient Africans used incense as part of their worship. The central acts of worship for ancient Africans were the sacrifice of a symbolic animal—the shedding of its blood which waters, propitiates—and the ritual eating of the slain victim, and continue as such in many African liturgies. Ancient Africans offered grain (bread) and wine (in place of blood) as sacrificial items. Modern Africans still offer food to their departed ancestors. The Catholic Church shares with ancient and modern Africans these and other important central liturgical elements. Of course, the Catholic Church distinguishes itself in and through its claim of being the Body of Christ. Whereas this Christness is not seen as culture-specific, the liturgical elements are. This proposition needs to be explored.

The central liturgical act for Catholics is the Mass, which theological tradition posits as essentially a memorial in a very special sense of Christ's redemptive act, his passion, death, and resurrection. To illustrate some of the historical antecedents of this liturgical practice the following passage from a famed British Egyptologist E. A. Wallis Budge, *Osiris and the Egyptian Resurrection*, (1911) is useful:

> It is impossible to state when and where the first shrines in honour of Osiris

> were built in Egypt, but it is tolerably certain that his most ancient shrine . . . was at Abydos . . . and that the cult of the god was firmly established . . . at the beginning of, if not before, the Dynastic Period. . . . The cleaning and preservation of his shrine were, no doubt, committed to the care of a special body of men, who thus became his priests, and received the offerings made to him, and made arrangements for his festivals and for the performance of the annual play, in which his sufferings, death, and resurrection were acted. (2: 1-2)

The preceding is an account of one of the earliest forms of organized religious worship. It occurred in Africa, and, in the sense that in every detail it is consistent with the religious worship of Africans of every age, including our contemporary epoch, it is quintessentially African. Fascinatingly, there is an incredible similarity between the Kemetic ritual practice and the central liturgical act of the Catholic religion.

It is important to consider certain details with regard to the Kemetic roots of Catholicism. Wosir, whose name was deformed into Osiris by the Greeks, was the greatest ancestor of the Egyptians. He was murdered and his body mutilated by Set, his brother, from whose name, interestingly, the word "Satan" is said to be derived. The Greeks corrupted the name of Wosir's faithful sister/wife Auset into Isis (and, as will be presented in our discussion in Chapter Five, Wosir could be seen, too, as the *son* of Auset). Auset resisted the seductive and eventually murderous wiles of Set (also her brother) and was able, with the guidance of Jehuti, Thoth to the Greeks—symbolized by the Ibis bird—to gather together the scattered parts of Wosir's body for burial with appropriate honors. Once appropriately buried, Wosir went on to reign forever in the afterworld, but not before, somehow or another, again with Jehuti's help, begetting a son, Heru (Horus for the Greeks), who would eventually avenge his father's death. The Osirian religion of ancient Egypt is by all accounts the oldest of man's organized monotheistic religions. This is the religion from which the biblical Jews borrowed so massively in order to form their own religious system. It was the religion of Moses's father-in-law Jethro, a priest of Midian (Exodus 3:1). It was the religion that in a special way informed the life-style and doctrines of the

Essenes, a Jewish monastic brotherhood to which John the Baptizer belonged.

In reference to this religion, Budge claims that: "The ancient Egyptians worshipped their ancestral spirits and the gods, who, it seems, were developed from them, with sacrifices and offerings, with prayer, and, perhaps, by the wearing of amulets" (1: 247).

The spirits or gods were honored daily through prescribed services performed by the appropriate priest. It is reasonable to assume that the annual memorial mystery play in honor of Wosir must have developed from these daily services. These services were essentially the same as the ones performed for living dignitaries, and involved bathing, anointing with oil or perfume, dressing, and feeding. Now, since the spirits could not partake of material food—all of these substantial gifts were disposed of by the priests, having become the property of the temple/shrine—the priest had to *transmute* the food, "giving it such a nature that the deceased might feed upon it" (1: 254). The offerings, or most likely a representative token thereof, were brought into the inner sanctum of the temple/shrine and placed on an altar, a "stone or wooden tablet." Budge continues: "And it must be remembered that the altar was believed to possess the power of transmuting the offerings which were laid upon it, and of turning them into spiritual entities of such a nature that they became suitable food for the god Osiris and his spirits" (1: 264).

It was through the utterance of the appropriate formulae by designated priests that the transmutation was effected, for the Egyptians, like all Africans, were thoroughly imbued with a sense of the power of the word. Budge claims that "according to Egyptian views, the world and the things in it came into being as the result of the utterance of a word" (1: 266). Further on in this chapter the Egyptian ideas on the creation of the universe will be discussed, bearing out the validity of Budge's claim, and drawing attention to the great similarity to the so-called Judeo-Christian complex of beliefs. In fact, anyone even remotely familiar with the New Testament will think instinctively of the first chapter of the Gospel according to John: "In the beginning was the Word."

Finally, one more set of details must be considered. Budge

asserts: "In the earliest times we find him [i.e. Wosir] identified with the spirit of the growing crop and the grain god, and he represented the spirit of vegetation in general. His chief assistant was his wife Isis, who taught men to prepare the grain which her husband had given them, and to make the flour into bread" (2: 18-19). The Egyptians were the first to make wine from grapes, and very early on in their history wine replaced blood as the appropriate offering to the spirits and to God. In plain language, then, the preceding may be summarized as follows. At the Catholic Mass bread and wine—two very powerful religious symbols of ancient Africa—are transmuted, changed, "transubstantiated" into the Body and Blood of Christ, through the words of consecration, a powerful "miraculous" formula pronounced by a priest. The Mass is a "memorial" which acts out, makes present, relives the passion, death, and resurrection of Christ.

Jackson in one of his earlier books, *Christianity before Christ*, and certainly in his masterful latest book, *Man, God, and Civilization*, makes much of the documented fact that there existed at least sixteen "saviors" before Jesus the Christ. He cites from Charles H. Vail's *The World's Saviors*, which "records the stories of miraculous births of fifteen other saviors, who lived before the Christian era. The names of these world's saviors are Krishna of India, Gautama of India, Horus of Egypt, Tammuz of Babylonia, Mithra of Persia, Zoroaster of Persia, Quetzalcoatl of Mexico, Bacab of Yucatan, Huetzilopochtli of Mexico, Freyr of Scandinavia, Attis of Phrygia, Bacchus of Greece, Adonis of Syria, Yu of China, Jesus" (*Man, God* 123).

A slightly different list is provided by Kersey Graves, who in *The World's Sixteen Crucified Saviors* very conveniently provides a chronological context by giving the dates of the "reputed deaths" of these figures. "The list is as follows: Krishna of India (1200 B.C.), Sakia of India (600 B.C.), Tammuz of Syria (1160 B.C.), Wittoba of the Telingonese (522 B.C.), Iao of Nepal (622 B.C.), Hesus of the Celtic Druids (834 B.C.), Quetzalcoatl of Mexico (587 B.C.), Quirinius of Rome (506 B.C.), Prometheus of Greece (547 B.C.), Thulis of Egypt (1700 B.C.), Indra of Tibet (725 B.C.), Alcestos of Greece (600 B.C.), Attis of Phrygia (1170

B.C.), Crite of Chaldea (1200 B.C.), Bali of Orissa (725 B.C.), Mithra of Persia (600 B.C.)" (135-36). There is, clearly, no certainty nor even rigid conformity in the presentation of this extraordinary data. Jackson himself, somewhat incoherently, makes further reference to Vail's book—just thirteen pages after the quote that appears on p. 123 in Jackson, p. 19 in our text—to report the following: "Vail gives a list of twenty-three savior gods who died and arose from the tomb. The names of these ancient gods, as given by the Reverend Vail, are Krishna, Wittoba, Indra, Bacab, Quetzalcoatl, Prometheus, Mithra, Bacchus or Dionysus, Baldur, Samheim or Bal-Sab, Tien, Aesculapius, Marsyas, Artemes, Melkarth, Sandan, Hyacinth, Marduk, Osiris, Tammuz or Adonis, Attis, Bel Merodach, Jesus" (*Man, God* 136). Jackson immediately refers his readers to pp. 81-135 of Vail's work for "details concerning the list of ancient saviors named above" (136).

Even allowing for the fact that Vail's first list of sixteen saviors is based on patterns of similarity in the accounts of their miraculous birth stories whereas the later list of twenty-three is based on such patterns in the accounts of their miraculous death and resurrection stories, there are disquieting inconsistencies. A significant amount of work needs to be done in collating and analyzing the data before any serious scholar can make any reasonable determinations about the validity of the claim that Jesus the Christ was just one of a long line of miracle workers who claimed to be the Son of God. In any case, if this claim were found to be valid, it would enhance rather than vitiate the central tenet of Christianity, that Jesus is the Alpha and the Omega, the one and only Son of God. The other figures might be, with absolute intellectual consistency, considered simply precursors.

Within the epistemological constraints of this body of knowledge there are elements that are of profound relevance and validity for our analysis. One such element is posited as follows by Jackson: "In Indian art, Krishna is depicted as a man of black complexion, and the name Krishna literally means *the black*." He further declares that "In early Christian art, Jesus is almost invariably represented as black-skinned. . . . In discussing the black complexion of Krishna, John M. Robertson noticed, 'He thus in the first place comes into line with black deities of other faiths, notably the Osiris of Egypt, to say nothing of the black manifestations of Greek deities and of the Christian Jesus'" (*Man, God* 132). Jackson, who appears to be of no religious persuasion, advances the claim that the historical Jesus Christ was black, and he cites what he views to be conclusive evidence. The claim is, of course, stunningly relevant.

William Arthur McCray, in *The Black Presence in the Bible*, is another scholar who, on the strength of the documentation presented in the Bible, comes to the conclusion that "The Old Covenant-Messianic community was Black, the Messianic line was Black, and the Messiah Himself was Black" (1:129). He reaches this startling conclusion through an exhaustive examination of the biblical texts, an examination that is careful and quite compelling. Abraham is listed in the Table of Nations as a descendant of Shem, but his place of origin was Ur of the Chaldees. "Ur," McCray asserts, "was probably the most powerful Sumerian city of its era" (1:123), and the Sumerians, he contends on the basis of internal biblical evidence and independent external archeological findings, were Black people. McCray continues:

> Among the nations in which Abraham lived during his sojourn we find the Canaanites (Genesis 12:6), the Perizzites (13:7), the Philistines (21:34), the Egyptians (12:10), and the Hittites (Genesis 23) [all Hamitic peoples]. It is clear from Genesis 14:14,15 that Abraham's household included servants who were not home-born. They probably were Egyptians who became a part of his group while he dwelt in Egypt, as did Hagar. . . . Joseph [one the significant Hebrew ancestors] . . . married the Egyptian Asenath, the daughter of Potiphera, priest of the city of On or Heliopolis. From this union two children were born, Ephraim and Manasseh (cf. Genesis 41:45, 50-52). These sons of Joseph became ancestors of the tribes of Israel bearing their names; two explicitly Black tribes. (1:123)

McCray points out that only "140 persons . . . made the trek with Jacob from Canaan [a land of black people] into Egypt." They left 400 years later a mighty multitude. The leader of that great throng of the "children of Israel" had himself formed a union with an identifiably and apparently black, woman, Zipporah "the Cushite" (1:123-24)—whose father, Jethro, was referred to earlier. The multitude who left Egypt finally settled in another land of black people, Canaan.

"The genealogical line through which the Jewish Messiah was to come was ethnologically Black," asserts McCray. He illustrates this assertion through what he refers to as "the implicit Blackness as well as through specific Black persons who appeared in this line." Judah, through whom came the line of the Messiah, "married Canaanite wives . . . Bathshua and . . . Tamar . . . (Genesis 38:7ff; 1 Chronicles 2:3,4)" (1:124). Citing 1 Chronicles 2:1ff, McCray traces the line from Perez, Tamar's son to David. The Bible indicates how the line flows from David to Joseph, the husband of Mary who was the Mother of Jesus. In this post-Davidic line appears Hezekiah, who:

> According to Zephaniah 1:1 . . . was the great-great-grandfather of the prophet Zephaniah. . . . Hezekiah was the fourteenth king of the southern kingdom of Judah, the kingdom through which the Messianic line continued. [Now] Zephaniah says his father was named "Cushi," "son of Gedaliah, son of Amariah, son of Hezekiah" (1:1). Thus, the Messianic line proceeding from Hezekiah contained a pronounced degree of Blackness, demonstrated in the Cushite ethnicity of Zephaniah's father. (1:125)

McCray then looks specifically at the genealogical information on Jesus Christ given in the Gospel of Matthew, focusing on the Blackness of "three of the four women who are noted [there] as being ancestors of the Lord!" (1:126). Tamar the first of these three, whom he indicates is implicitly identified in Genesis 38 as a Canaanite. Rahab, the second woman, is mentioned in Joshua 2:1-21 and 6:17-25. She, too, was a Canaanite, and she bore a son, Boaz, who was an ancestor of Jesus. The third woman, Bathsheba, is demonstrated by McCray to have been black as well. She was the wife of Uriah the Hittite, and her story "is recorded in 2 Samuel 11" (1:127). McCray supposes that Bathsheba was of the same ethnicity as her husband, and "It is widely known and accepted that the Hittites were a Hamitic people" (1:127). The child David fathered through her was Solomon.

Of course, McCray deals with the objection that Joseph was not the physical father of Jesus. He does so by pointing out that both

Mary and Joseph belonged to the "house of David." "Further," he contends, "it may not be unreasonable to assume that Mary's bloodline may also have been influenced through Solomon, the son of Bathsheba and David" (1:128).

For the finale of his presentation McCray relies on the arguments and documentation provided by "William Mosley, *What Color was Jesus?*. . . pp. 12ff., 19ff.," and by Joel Augustus "Rogers . . . *Sex and Race: Negro-Caucasian Mixing in All Ages and All Lands. Vol 1 - The Old World* . . . Appendix to Chapters 1 to 1X - Part 11 'The Black Madonna and the Black Christ,' pp. 273-283" (1:176). On the word of these two scholars he makes the following declaration: "Of course, there is also the extra-Biblical evidence which affirms, among other things, the Blackness of Christ Jesus. For instance, the earliest portrayals of Christ Jesus in art show Him and His mother Mary as Black in actual skin color" (1:129).

Needless to say, after hundreds of years of tilting towards a militantly Eurocentric approach to biblical exegesis, one would almost require a photograph of the historical Jesus to debunk the accretion of misconceptions, even deliberate lies. However, the cumulative effect of the evidence and arguments both biblical and extrabiblical, from believers as well as unbelievers, is staggering. Even the most avid adherent to the Eurocentric view must take pause at such an overwhelming collection of hard data and compelling speculation, especially when just plain common sense impels one to reject the conventional wisdom that the land of Palestine in the time of Christ was peopled almost exclusively by types who bear striking resemblances to contemporary European Jews. Indeed, even after two thousand years of turbulent history the people who are in any real sense native to Northeast Africa—what has been deliberately mislabeled the "Middle East" with a view to obfuscating the data—are brown and black.

Returning to Jackson's claim in *Man, God, and Civilization* as to the existence of, as he puts it, "Christianity before Christ," there is yet another forceful element in his presentation. It relates to the "story of the savior-god Bel of Babylonia . . . for here we have a documentary source of unquestioned authenticity in the form of an ancient cuneiform tablet, now in the British Museum" (125). The tablet in effect contains the script for a Passion Play that predates the Christian era by, it is believed, about two thousand years. Jackson continues: "The English translation of the cuneiform record referred to above is reproduced here: (1) Bel is taken prisoner; (2) Bel is tried in the Hall of Justice; (3) Bel is smitten; (4) Bel is led away to the mount; (5) with Bel are taken two malefactors, one of whom is released; (6) after Bel has gone to the mount the city breaks out into tumult; (7) Bel's clothes are carried away; (8) Bel goes down into the mount and disappears from life; (9) a weeping woman seeks him at the gate of burial; (10) Bel is brought back to life" (125-26). The parallels between the preceding and the Gospel account of the Passion, Death, and Resurrection of Jesus Christ are nothing short of stunning. The documentation appears to be unassailable, for, as Jackson asserts, there exists in the British Museum a tablet that must be assumed to be authentic. Furthermore, this datum is consistent with a veritable multitude of data and with a line of interpretation that are incontrovertible. It is particularly significant to consider that ancient Babylon is present-day Iraq, and that the founders of the earliest civilization in that part of the world were listed in the Table of Nations in Genesis 10 as being among the sons of Ham. This information is corroborated by extrabiblical archeological evidence and will be further examined later on in this chapter.

It is a fact that Roman Catholicism has been characterized, in the face of the outright hostility and derision of many other Christian groups, by its steadfast devotion to the Holy Mother of God, the Blessed Virgin Mary. Hispanic literature, from the very earliest period, has reflected this feature of the religion that is still today the state religion in many Spanish-speaking countries. The most impressive, best known, and, indeed, representative manifestation of this Mariological dimension is the work of the thirteenth century poet Gonzalo de Berceo. His *Milagros de Nuestra Señora* [Miracles of Our Lady], for example, reflect the special flavor of the profound devotion coupled with an almost irreverent familiarity that characterizes mainstream Hispanic literature in its treatment of the Mariological and all other religious themes. Of the other major religions only Islam comes close to Catholicism in its special reverence for the Virgin Mother, and, clearly, the historical links between Hispanic Roman Catholicism and Islam are deep.

There is clear evidence, however, that the early Christian Church, even before the existence of Islam, appropriated the widespread devotion to Auset, the holy mother of Heru (Horus) and unimpeachably faithful wife of Wosir, bringing it into the new Christian ambit by replacing her with the Virgin Mother of Christ. Budge in *The Gods of the Egyptians* asserts that "it is clear that the early Christians bestowed some of her attributes upon the Virgin Mary. There is little doubt that in her character of the loving and protecting mother she appealed strongly to the imagination of all the Eastern peoples among whom her cult came, and that the pictures and sculptures wherein she is represented in the act of suckling her child Horus formed the foundation for the Christian figures and paintings of the Madonna and Child" (2:220). On the temporal, natural, level this might be considered a purely political strategy on the part of the nascent Church. Obviously, there accrued significant political benefit for the new organization, for it thereby potentially wooed into its fold millions of people throughout the entire African, Afroasiatic, and European regions of Western civilization. Indeed, it is not without significance that it was at the Council of Ephesus that Mary was declared Mother of God. This was the same city of Ephesus that had once risen up in riot against St. Paul's preaching of the Gospel because it feared that the new religion would diminish the importance of the great mother goddess, manifested in her Roman version as Diana, to whom the city was particularly devoted, and from whose devotion the local silversmiths derived financial benefit (*Acts* 19: 23-41). In fact, when four centuries later, in 431 A.D., the Christian church seemed to have finally replaced the pagan "mother goddess" by declaring Mary, Mother of God, the people of Ephesus again took to the streets, this time in celebration of their "victory."

On the other hand, it could obviously be argued with considerable validity that Jesus the Christ was the culmination of a long chain of preparation that in the biblical account began with the events in the Garden of Eden. Furthermore, Wosir (Osiris) is historically the first of the pre-Christ figures who have undoubtedly existed. He is, moreover, the most important. It is then appropriate that Auset (Isis) and Heru (Horus) should also be incorporated fully into the new order that Jesus the Christ represents: Auset as the Virgin Mother of God and Heru as a conflation with Wosir, for Heru is, even in the writings and traditions of Kemet, frequently indistinguishable from Wosir, and his name, in fact, according to Charles S. Finch in *Echoes from the Old Darkland*, means begotten of Auset (75).

Now Auset, like all of the other "gods" and "goddesses" of Kemet was always represented as black. Budge affirms that in Rome, for example, "Splendid buildings and temples were set up in her honour, filled with Egyptian objects, obelisks, altars, statues, lavers, etc., which were brought from Egypt with the view of making the shrines of the goddess to resemble those of her native country" (*Osiris* 2: 286). In pursuit of this verisimilitude it was common throughout the ancient world, even outside of Africa proper as well as Northeast Africa, for Auset's priestesses to be African women. Certainly in her icons she is represented as a black woman. It is incredibly significant that when the early Christian church acting for the first time as a world-class political organization remade Auset into a Christian symbol, it was pleased to have her as black woman. In fact, Jackson on parallel track asserts that the earliest representations of Christ, even in Rome, were as a black man—consistent with the tradition of the crucified saviors. Hence the earliest icons of the Christian Madonna and child were simply rebaptized examples of the preexisting iconography of Auset and Heru. This is the only logical explanation for the proliferation of the so-called black Madonnas throughout the world, even in the contemporary period. The patron saint of Poland, the native country of the reigning Catholic Pope, John Paul 11, is Our Lady of Czestochowa, one of the many black Madonnas.[4]

In many aspects of its doctrine, then, even in those that are most fundamental and characteristic, the Roman Church simply incorporated preexisting peculiarly African elements. The data indicate that in the first centuries of its existence the Church incorporated the iconography that African peoples had used for millennia to represent Auset, one of their most revered ancestors. This African religious symbol became a Christian one, initially without need of any external modification whatsoever. The process is representative and appears to have paralleled exactly what transpired consequent on the introduction of millions of Africans to the Americas over the last five hundred years. The modern version of the process has been given the label "syncretism." It is reasonable to use the same label to identify the earlier Europeanization of an original African religious symbol. Whatever about the label, it should become clear that modern "syncretism" occurred because there was a true and profound connection between the Catholicism practiced by the European oppressors in Latin America and the native religious systems of the incoming Africans. The point has to be made that whereas even after five centuries Eurocentric scholars are still ignorant of this connection, Africans coming to the New World understood it well.

Modern "syncretism" in its most striking form identifies not only the Virgin but the saints as well with African "deities." Along with "syncretism" much has been made of the "ancestor worship" tradition of the Africans who came to the Americas in the last five hundred years. It must be clear to the reader by now that Auset, Wosir, and Heru were, in fact, ancestors of the inhabitants of Kemet. In our later discussion, it will be shown that for the Yoruba people Shango exactly parallels Wosir of the people of Kemet. Shocking as it may appear at first consideration, it is without any doubt that Catholicism is as much an "ancestor worship" religion as are the traditional and ancient religions of Africa. It is truly incredible that so many Christians miss the central importance of "ancestor worship" in their religion. Jesus the Christ is nothing for a Christian unless he is both God and man. And his humanity is presented in the Bible essentially in terms of his genealogy, that is, his humanity is legitimated by tracing his line back to the first ancestor, the common ancestor of all men, Adam (the African). He is thus a true brother to us all.

In Catholicism saints are ancestors. Since there is less emphasis on the carnal connectedness, the new importance being given to the spiritual ties of brotherhood in Jesus the Christ, these ancestors are seen as ancestors in the spirit rather than in the flesh. However, their role and function exactly correspond to those of the ancestors in ancient and traditional African religions. They are the links between the living, still weighed down by the chains of the flesh, and the utterly transcendent spiritual order, that is, in a marvelously mysterious way, God Himself. The saints, like the ancestors, are higher up on the chain of being, and through interaction with them the living are helped to fulfill their destiny and to disengage themselves gradually from the burden of matter, so that when their time comes to shuffle off the mortal coil, the separation will be easy and (super)natural.

Fundamental to Catholicism is the doctrine of the Communion of Saints, which asserts that all the faithful, living and dead, exist in a marvelous and real union that is the Mystical Body of Christ. The full implications of this doctrine are accessible only to theologians, however any scholar of good faith will immediately recognize its relationship to the principle of vitality that is supposed to characterize African ancestor worship religions. The ancestors are not dead, they live on, increasing, in fact, in vitality. For vitality is transcendence. The saints have not died. Actually, no Christian—nor any human being for that matter—ever really dies. In the eyes of the unbelievers, the dead are asleep and have reverted to nothingness. In the eyes of the Christian, physical death is merely the shuffling off this mortal coil and the passing on to true transcendence, to true and (super)natural life, for life is eternal.

When the "ancestor-worshiping," enslaved, New World Africans realized that the enslavers, a group of apparent humanoids—albeit lacking in melanin and in some of the basic manifestations of civilization—practiced a religion that involved the veneration of the living dead and that had a liturgical tradition with roots in a common antiquity, they must have felt a profound sense of relief. For they realized that herein existed a common bond, and any bond would be useful in their struggle against the unspeakable barbarism of the savage oppressor. Since Africans have from the beginning of recorded history understood the insignificance of matter vis-a-vis the spirit, their art has never been slavishly representational of the base reality grasped through the five senses. Hence, for example, it was simply not a problem to use a base pictorial representation of Saint Barbara as a symbol of Shango. Their artists and even the common folk were accustomed to see not the vulgar externals but the inner transcendence of things. This is how so-called "syncretism" worked for the first Africans forced into barbaric servitude in the post-1492 "New World." This is how it continues to work for many Africans in the Americas. Apparently, it has been impossible—and ultimately understandably so—for Eurocentric scholars to fathom this.

It is important to signal one of the consequences of this new understanding of syncretism. Although scholars generally have not explicitly examined the "syncretic" elements of New World carnivals, it is clear that the African-inspired carnivals of the Americas are universally assumed by scholars to have been derived from a preexisting cultural phenomenon that was essentially European. Nina S. de Friedemann, a Colombian anthropologist considered to be one of the leading experts on that nation's "Blacks," is a prime exponent of this historical incompleteness. She begins one of her more important articles, "Perfiles sociales del carnaval en Barranquilla (Colombia)" [Social Profiles of Carnival in Barranquilla (Colombia)], with this declaration: "El carnaval, una tradición occidental, tiene una profundidad histórica que se remite a celebraciones rituales de propiciación de dioses protectores del agro en Grecia y Roma, antes de la aparición del cristianismo" (127). [Carnival, a Western tradition, has a deep historical base that is rooted in ritual celebrations to propitiate certain gods who were patrons of agriculture in Greece and Rome, before the advent of Christianity].

An objective examination of the clear data leads, however, to quite the contrary of this universally accepted assumption. Clearly, the mechanism for memorializing the transcendent events in the life of Wosir has been the driving force of African religious celebrations, literally, from time immemorial. This is the principle that, many centuries before the birth of Jesus Christ, generated the "Passion Play" devoted to Bel of Babylonia. This is the principle that generated the celebration of the mystery plays in the holy towns of Egypt, notably in Abydos and Dendera. Budge reports on the act of the Wosir play that was "the greatest," as follows:

> This act . . . represented the "coming forth" of Osiris from the temple after his death . . . . A solemn service was performed in the temple before the body was carried from it, and offerings were eaten sacramentally, and then the procession set out for the tomb. When it reached the door of the temple it was received by a mighty crowd of men and women who raised the death-wail, and uttered piercing shrieks and lamentations, and the women beat their breasts. Many of the men in the crowd were armed with sticks and staves, and some of them pressed forward towards the procession with the view of helping the god, whilst others strove to prevent them. Thus a sham fight took place, which, owing to the excitement of the combatants, often degenerated into a serious one. (*Osiris* 2:6)

Those who know what carnival in the Americas is about recognize immediately that the scene described above is a quintessentially carnivalesque one. In fact, it includes a description of an element that is fundamental to the traditional Trinidad and Tobago carnival, namely, the stickfight, played out in a dramatic annual ritual that involved masses of people dancing and singing in procession through the streets. The warrior element has persisted and attained preeminence in all New World carnivals (as the discussion in Chapter Three brings out). This is an adaptation in reaction to the barbaric nature of the new civilization. The element that was central to the original Egyptian celebration was one of renewal, regeneration, of the king or of the leadership principle. The celebration took place during the five days outside of time, that is, outside of the 360-day year. Wosir is above all else a "god" of rebirth, a promise of universal resurrection. Furthermore, later descriptions of the closely related ritual for Auset strongly suggest that the participants in this Osirian drama also wore disguises; that is, they were masqueraders.

It is reasonable to affirm that the Osirian mystery plays are the source of the theatre for the Greeks and thus for Western civilization. A convincing argument can be presented to support the theory that the Latin carnival, a Christianization of preexisting "Roman" religious rites, had its source, too, in ancient Africa.

Budge and others report that Egyptian religion was extremely popular in the entire ancient world and throughout all of pre-Christian Europe: "In the fourth century before Christ Athens was a kind of centre of the Egyptian religion. . . . In Rome, in the first century before Christ, Isis was regarded as one of the principal goddesses of the city. . . . From Rome, the capital, the cult of Isis naturally spread to the provinces, and thence, little by little, to Germany, Switzerland, Spain, Portugal, Gaul" (2:285-86). There were two important festivals for Auset in the Rome referred to above, one in November and the other in spring. Budge reconstructs this spring festival, providing the following description: "At the head of the great procession came men who were dressed to represent a soldier, a huntsman, a woman, and a gladiator. These were followed by men dressed as magistrates, philosophers, fowlers, and fishermen" (2:296-97).

In the face of this kind of evidence, the honest scholar must conclude that not only carnival, but drama itself had its origin in ancient Africa. There is an ignorance that is always indictable, a view crystallized in the saying: ignorance of the law is no excuse. A scholar who purports to explicate the artistic expression of the "Black poet" Nicolás Guillén would be expected to be aware of the argument for the African origin of carnival. Indeed, ignorance of this area of academic inquiry is neither innocuous nor irrelevant. Vera Kutzinski is a scholar who claims expertise in Afro-American literature, yet totally misses the basic Africanness of Guillén's use of carnival. This, in spite of the title she gives to her long essay on the Cuban poet, "The Carnivalization of Poetry: Nicolás Guillén's Chronicles," that appears in *Against the American Grain* (131-235). Kutzinski's error springs from her uncritical reliance on the Eurocentric theories of the modern day masters, Mikhail Bakhtin and Jacques Derrida, for example. The former especially had elaborated significant disquisitions on carnival and parody, indictably ignoring the massive and decisive African contributions to those cultural phenomena.

□ □ □

Civilization and Barbarism

Syncretism has been one of the important axes of analysis by Eurocentric experts on Latin American culture. The dichotomy civilization/barbarism has been another such cardinal axis. It is important at the outset of this literary study to reexamine the use and significant consequences of this dichotomy in the development and critiquing of Latin American literature and culture. The Argentinean thinker and political figure Domingo Faustino Sarmiento (1811-88) articulated in the most direct and most influential fashion the relevance of the dichotomy to Latin American civilization. It is his formulation that has survived and even today impacts on the academy. Most of his theory on the matter is contained in a strangely structured work, the first edition of which bore the quaint, confusedly convoluted title: *Civilización i barbarie—Vida de Juan Facundo Quiroga, i aspecto físico, costumbres, i ábitos de la República Arjentina, por Domingo F. Sarmiento* [Civilization and barbarism—life of Juan Facundo Quiroga, and physical features, customs, and habits of the Argentine Republic, by Domingo F. Sarmiento].

The formulation of the title, of course, most fittingly mirrors the crude, tendentious content. The work first appeared in 1845 as a series of political tract essays in Chile during the writer's exile there, and was published within months in its entirety as a book. The first part, by way of introduction, is a historicosociological interpretation of the Argentine republic. The second part is a biography of Juan Facundo Quiroga (1790-1835), for the author the quintessential Argentine political figure. The third part is an unabashed political pamphlet denouncing Manuel Rosas, the first of a long series of despotic national leaders who would afflict not just Argentina but all of Latin America, a direct consequence of the monumental upheaval wrought by European conquest, genocide, colonization and postcolonization.

Part One is of most interest at this point. It is a classic work of wrongheaded, simplistic, racist, Eurocentric analysis. It presents Argentine society as formed from a struggle between civilization, that emanates in its purest form from Europe and is centered in the Argentine cities, and barbarism, which emanates in its purest form from the native Argentine reality where the very topography—vast expanses of flat land—the flora, the fauna—of which the native Americans are simply an element—are a constant inducement to barbarism. There are two kinds of European civilization, one is retrograde, conservative and is associated with Spain, the ex-colonial power. The other is superior, progressive, and more generically European. The most perfect national ethos would be ground out through the interaction of these forces, resulting in a synthesis that would benefit from the vitality of native Argentine barbarism, tempered by all of the enlightenment of the non-Hispanic, progressive, European civilization. Sarmiento is quite clear on the role of Africans in this schema:

> La raza negra, casi extinguida ya, excepto en Buenos Aires, ha dejado sus zambos y mulatos, habitantes de las ciudades, eslabón que liga al hombre civilizado con el palurdo; raza inclinada a la civilización, dotada de talento y de los más bellos instintos de progreso. . . . Las razas americanas viven en la ociosidad y se muestran incapaces, aun por medio de la compulsión, para dedicarse a un trabajo duro y seguido. Esto sugirió la idea de introducir negros en América, que tan fatales resultados han producido. (p. 15)

> [The black race, almost extinct now, except in Buenos Aires, has left its zambos and mulattos, city dwellers, a link that ties civilized man to the uncivilized; a race [the mulattos and zambos] inclined to civilization, endowed with talent and the finest instincts for progress. . . . The native American races live in laziness and demonstrate an inability, even under compulsion, to engage in hard and consistent work. This reality gave rise to the idea of introducing blacks into Americas, which has produced such devastating results.]

Sarmiento is, of course, simply reflecting the current European ideology in its implausible combination of racism and romanticism. There is an abiding fascination with the noble savage of the American hinterland, but only as an exotic material engine to drive European intellectualism that was somewhat effete but essentially intact. Africa was simply beyond the pale of humanity. Africa is merely a point of reference, a synonym for the antithesis of civilization. At one juncture, speaking of the government of Rosas, Sarmiento characterizes it as a "sistema de asesinatos y crueldades, tolerables tan sólo en Ashanty o Dahomey, en el interior de Africa" (47) [system of assassinations and cruelties, tolerable only in Ashanty and Dahomey, in the heart of Africa].

Sarmiento was profoundly impressed with North America, the United States in particular, which he saw as the model republic where the vitality of the New World wedded the vision and intelligence of the Old to produce a superior form of civilization. As a political figure—he would go on to become president of his country—he did everything in his power to copy the United States of North America's civic systems. He used as his governing principle the dictum: "poblar es civilizar" [to populate is to civilize]. This spawned a policy of encouraging unbridled European immigration. Most of these Europeans turned out to be down-and-out Italians, but they were Europeans, and this was all that mattered.

Sarmiento's analytical framework imported from Europe is still immensely popular with Latin Americans. Every generation of thinkers that has emerged since his has framed its frenzied quest for identity in almost exactly the same terms. At the turn of the last century Latin America sought to achieve authentic cultural independence for the first time—almost a century after achieving apparent political independence. Mesmerized by the Sarmiento ideology, that generation of writers and thinkers confused independence from direct Spanish influence with cultural authenticity. Hence the *modernismo* movement, spearheaded by the Nicaraguan Rubén Darío (1867-1916) of monumental literary importance, is nothing more than a slavish imitation of European artistic models, but in advance of and thereby obviating Spain's traditional mediation. The fervor of so-called creative self-expressiveness was matched by the insistence of essayists on defining the peculiar Latin American ethos.

Ariel (1900), by the Uruguayan essayist José Enrique Rodó (1871-1917), is one of the best samples of this wave of self-defining writing. It is an apologia for the intrinsic merit of the more humanist and idealist culture of the Latins as contrasted with the pragmatic spirit of North America. Like Sarmiento, Rodó does not question for a moment the centrality of European/Western cultures and civilizations. The Argentine Carlos Octavio Bunge's speculations on Latin America lead him to unabashed racism along the lines of Sarmiento. Even in México's José Vasconcelos (1881-1959)—proponent of the concept of *La raza cósmica* [The Cosmic Race]—there is little real respect for any of the "marginal" cultures and civilizations. His famous "raza cósmica" is merely a slightly more exotic and better tanned version of the typical European. *Modernismo* and its sequel *posmodernismo* provide the dominant motif for Latin American culture and civilization until the 1920s.

It is through the novel that Latin America's culture has had its greatest impact on twentieth century humanity. The Colombian Gabriel García Márquez, who won the Nobel Prize for Literature in 1982, is one of the best known writers in the world. The Western academy has intensely studied and, in fact, to some extent created the "boom" in the Latin American narrative. In both the creative and the critical aspects of this significant area of Latin American culture Sarmiento's line of approach has dominated. The development of the twentieth century novel is presented as a struggle between civilization and barbarism. According to this schema, up until the end of the nineteenth century, the raw barbaric energies of the indigenous factors—climatic conditions, flora and fauna, according to Sarmiento's conception—remained unaffected by the civilizing European presence. This presence, again according to the Sarmiento conception, was confined to the few urban enclaves. The *modernismo* movement, which was largely a poetic expression, was touted as permitting some degree of native self-expression, but its independence was simply in appearance.

It was the monumental upheaval of the Mexican revolution, a product, according to this notion, of the inevitable rumblings of the barbaric natural forces that are peculiarly *americano*, that triggered the first truly independent *americano* literary expression, namely, the novel of the Mexican revolution, quintessentially represented by Mariano Azuela's *Los de abajo* (1916). Once unleashed, the forces sought the only channels available, the European literary tradition: the genres, styles, conventions, etc, in so far as this was possible. The resulting distortions and evolutions were aesthetically successful, and the process continued. The first generation of twentieth century Latin American novels was established on the principles and approaches that made for the Mexican novel of the revolution. These approaches still bear the stamp of Sarmiento's misguided musings.

At one of the many aesthetic moments of truth in Azuela's relatively short novel, a character presented by the narrator as a "poeta romántico" (128) [romantic poet] pours forth this characterization of the revolutionary process:

> ¿Villa? . . . Obregón? . . . ¿Carranza? . . . ¡X . . . Y . . . Z . . .! ¿Qué se me da a mí? . . . ¡Amo la Revolución como amo al volcán que irrumpe! ¡Al volcán porque es volcán; a la Revolución porque es Revolución! . . . Pero las piedras que quedan arriba o abajo, después del cataclismo, ¿qué me importan a mí? . . . (128)
>
> [Villa? . . . Obregón? . . . Carranza? . . . X . . . Y . . . Z . . . ! What's it to me? . . . I love the Revolution like I love an erupting volcano! The volcano because it's a volcano; the Revolution because it's a Revolution! . . . But that some particular stones end up on top or below, after the cataclysm, what do I care? . . .]

Alberto Solís, a more moderate voice, echoes these sentiments in an unforgettable utterance: "¡Qué hermosa es la Revolución, aun en su misma barbarie!" (72) [How beautiful is the Revolution, even in its very barbarism]. The socioeconomic process is reduced to the inherently beautiful unspoiled barbarism of Sarmiento's Argentine flora and fauna. Thus the Colombian José Eustasio Rivera's (1889-1928) *La vorágine* [the vortex], published in 1924, sets up a fundamental opposition, a primordial struggle between the barbarism of the local topography, climatic conditions, flora and fauna of the Amazon, and local man (European) as the representative of civilization. Unfortunately, at this early stage, man loses, and the novel ends with the dramatic declaration: "¡Los devoró la selva!" (261) [The jungle devoured them].

The very title of the novel, *Doña Bárbara* (1929) by the

Venezuelan Rómulo Gallegos, reveals its indebtedness to the Sarmiento schema. In this novel the forces of local topography, climatic conditions, flora and fauna have a human manifestation, in the person of the main protagonist, a woman called Barbara (the Spanish adjective *bárbaro/a* means "barbaric"). She seeks to gobble up the representatives of Europe's civilizing force, all males, interestingly, as surely as the *selva* had devoured their peers in *La vorágine*. However, she is ultimately stopped by an uncommon male, Santos Luzardo, by name and nature the representative symbol of European enlightenment. Santos's achievement signals the beginning of a new phase, one of felicitous Eurocentric syncretism.

While the dominant minority in Latin America sought its cultural salvation through Sarmiento's formulations, even those few brave souls who concerned themselves fully with the condition of native Americans in themselves and not just as elements of the exotic fauna, still succumbed to the basic assumptions of the racist schema. For the native Americans were considered an entity apart, their world was treated in the appropriate non-mainstream movements, the *indianista* and the more empathetically focused *indigenista* novel. The prime example of this latter is *El indio* (1935) by the Mexican Gregorio López y Fuentes. At its best the *indigenista* current joined the mainstream in the protest or sociological novels like the Ecuadorian Jorge Icaza's *Huasipungo*, (1934) or *El mundo es ancho y ajeno* (1941) by the Peruvian Ciro Alegría (1909-1967). When, in the twenties and thirties, some concern—passing or otherwise—with the plight of the poor "Indians" became almost fashionable among the intellectuals and literati, there emerged a parallel interest in the equally "irrelevant" Africans from Latin America. All of the so-called Afro-Antillean, Afro-Cuban, *negrista*, and even the Negritude expressions have to be considered, then, in their true contexts, as absolutely marginal to the Latin American cultural mainstream.

The Latin American novels of the "boom" are really those of the third generation, in which the evolutionary process envisaged by Sarmiento reaches its peak, bringing to completion the phase initiated by Santos Luzardo's victory over Doña Bárbara. The intervening second generation of novels was not all that powerful, for the focus had switched to the unfamiliar reality of the human psyche in the mostly European urban enclaves. A good example of this would be *El hermano asno* (1922) by the Chilean Eduardo Barrios, a psychological novel studying the problem of celibacy among members of a Franciscan monastery. Juan Carlos Onetti, a Uruguayan, has created existential novels unfolding in the La Plata region, the most European in Latin America. He could be considered to belong to this second generation, but he manages to inject into his narrative a sufficient dosage of the raw "American" barbarism to justify its candidacy as a third-generation "boom" narrative. So, too, does the work of the Argentinean novelist Eduardo Mallea, *Todo verdor perecerá* (1941), for example. With the works of a García Márquez, the blending of civilization and barbarism attains a marvelous peak. The world of Macondo, site of most of the action in García Márquez's fictional universe, is a wonderful place where the magic of "American" native barbarism is just barely tempered by the order and reason of European civilization.

Providentially, Diop's magnum opus, *Civilization or Barbarism*, appeared in its first English version in 1991—the original French version was first published in 1981—just in time to put the final nails in the coffin of the defunct racist schema. The timing is perfect, for it comes at the very dawn of the second half of the millennium of the imposition of European barbarism on the Americas. The English-speaking world was first introduced to Diop's work through the translated edition, significantly entitled, *The African Origin of Civilization: Myth or Reality*. It is not by chance that another magnum opus of another great seeker of the hidden facts, John G. Jackson, should have as its title: *Man, God, and Civilization*. All of these titles were foreshadowed by the pivotal work of Chancellor Williams, *The Destruction of Black Civilization*. The preoccupation of these thinkers with the concept of civilization should be by now understandable to the reader.

These diligent African-ancestored scholars have effected the Pascalian *renversement du pour au contre* on the entire edifice of the schema that has shaped post-colonial Latin American creative and critical writing. They have made it abundantly clear that Africa is the very cradle of humanity, in the sense that Homo sapiens sapiens first emerged in Africa and, indeed, resided there exclusively for 90,000 to 110,000 of the approximately 130,000 to 150,000 years of his existence (Diop, *Civilization*, 60). According to Diop's masterfully scientific presentation, Cro-Magnon, the first non-African species of modern man, appeared in Europe only 20,000 years ago. This phenomenon resulted from the "Invasion of Europe by the Grimaldi Negroid from Africa, 33,000 years ago" (53). Spain was precisely the point of contact then, as it has been ever since, between Africa and Europe (a topic that will occupy several pages in Chapter Two). Indeed, Diop asserts that the current Basque people are the direct descendants of these original Cro-Magnons, the original Europeans (18). Rejecting the widely disseminated speculation, Diop demonstrates that "the Caucasus is in no way the cradle of the White race" (35). He further affirms that the Asiatics are the last group to evolve. Indeed, according to his documentation the "present Chinese type" first appeared "around 6000 B.C." and the "Nipponese type: Neolithic, perhaps around 5000 or 4000 B.C." (53).

Diop's schema is corroborated by much of the historical data that is emerging of late. Conventional wisdom had it that man first created a high civilization in Mesopotamia, in the land of the Tigris and Euphrates, two of the rivers cited in the creation account of Genesis. That this belief is erroneous becomes quite clear when one simply examines the data. In the first place, the creation account in Genesis 2 locates the Garden of Eden between four, not two rivers, namely, the Pishon that encircled the land of Havilah; the Gihon that encircled the land of Cush; the Tigris that flows east of Ashur; and the Euphrates. The exegetical note in *The Jerusalem Bible* (1966) claims that the Pishon and Gihon rivers are unknown and that "the two 'lands' named are probably not the regions designated elsewhere by the same names" (7). On this matter Cain Hope Felder, one of the scholars whose nonhegemonic reading of the sacred text has led to a more liberating vision, affirms in *Troubling Biblical Waters*: "The oldest mention of Ethiopia in the Bible occurs in Genesis 2:13, which is part of the older version of the creation story . . . usually dated around 950 B.C. The Jahwist writer speaks of a river Gihon 'which flows around the whole land of Cush/Ethiopia' as part of his description of Eden. . . . The probability is that the Gihon River refers to the Nile River" (23). It seems quite plausible that the Pishon and the Gihon were the two major branches of the Nile, and thus the land of Eden circumscribed by the Blue and White Nile and the Tigris and Euphrates would be coterminous with the world that was best known to the people of the Bible.[5]

Then, even granting the commonly averred white supremacist fantasy that the height of Mesopotamian civilization predated the height of Egyptian civilization by a few hundred years, the indications are that the original civilizers of Mesopotamia (also known as Sumer and Shimar) were Africoid.[6] Diop, in *The African Origin of Civilization,* presents a collection of powerful arguments. He points out that "it is in Egypt that we encounter, with mathematical certainty, humanity's most ancient historical date" (100). He is referring to the date 4236 B.C. when it is known that the calendar was definitely in use in Egypt. He indicates that at this historical period there is nothing in Mesopotamia but some "sun-dried bricks made of clay that rain transformed into a mass of mud" (100). In any case, the archaeological as well as anthropological evidence compel the conclusion that Mesopotamia was "a belatedly born daughter of Egypt" (106).

The very Bible, which has been blasphemously misused as the source of justification for so much Eurocentric racist doctrine, makes it quite clear that the Babylonians were Hamitic, that is, Negroid. In fact, in the Table of Nations given in Genesis 10, the only individual to be particularly singled out is Nimrod the Babylonian, one of the sons of Ham (see Genesis 10: 8-12). Indeed, amazingly, Shimar, said to be Sumer, and Ashur are indicated here to be part of Nimrod's empire. This coheres with the nonbiblical data and interpretations that would place Babylonians, Sumerians, Elamites among the Africoids of the world.

When the myth of a non-Africoid preeminent Babylon falls through, racist "scholars" try to resort to a preexisting Asiatic civilization. The Peking Man mythology was created for this purpose, and Diop is quite firm in his rejection of that fantasy as well, affirming that

> It appears . . . that the most ancient *Homo sapiens* of Europe, as far as the borders of Asia, were Negroids, if one adheres to an objective analysis of the facts. When we move to Asia, the old Asia of the Orientalists, what strikes us, contrary to all expectations, is the extremely recent appearance of *Homo sapiens sapiens*. The carbon 14 analysis done by the Chinese themselves helped establish that Ziyang Man—estimated by scholars to be 100,000 years old—dates from 7500 + 130 B.P., or 5500 B.C. . . .
>
> So all the usual Eastern chronology falls apart with the advent of radiometric methods of dating. (*Civilization* 52-53)

Thus his schema of the appearance of present-day man, already referred to, concludes with the following:

> Arrival of Australians in Australia, 30,000 to 20,000 years ago.
> Appearance of the first Paleosiberian (according to Thoma), 20,000 years ago.
> First *Homo sapiens* in China, 17,000 B.C.
> Appearance of the present Chinese type, around 6000 B.C.
> Appearance of the Nipponese type: Neolithic, perhaps around 5000 or 4000 B.C. (53)

Furthermore, Runoko Rashidi, a young scholar of the contemporary Nile Valley School, in his essay anthologized in Van Sertima's *African Presence in Early Asia*, asserts on the basis of his study of the historical evidence that "The pronounced cultural developments of the Indus Valley complex, with its vast extensions into Central Asia and peninsular India, where its legacy remains distinct, owe their origins to Asia's early black presence." This original Indian civilization, he asserts, attained its height "from about 2200 B.C. to 1700 B.C." (34). Everywhere the scholars go in their pursuit of the origins of human civilization they appear to unearth some group of Africoid original peoples who have been credited by the locals with first bringing civilization.

There is no escaping, then, the African origin of civilization. Indeed, as the creators and the consumers of the dominant Eurocentric mythologies seek to usher in the second half of the millennium of Europe's ravishing of the Americas, the new school of Afrocentric scholars led by Van Sertima have begun to assert with credible documentation that even the idea of Columbus being the first nonnative American to come to the "New World" is just another myth to be debunked. Van Sertima's work, *They Came Before Columbus* (1976), nearly two decades in advance, raised a cry of alarm against the canonization of the racist fantasies that were to be paraded interminably before the unsuspectingly passive, uncritical consumers of print and electronic media output in 1992. Furthermore, the final refuge of the fantasizers has been foreclosed on with a careful presentation and examination of all of the relevant data. Claiming a disinterested realism that is assumed to be self-evidently benevolent, some Europeans of good will turned their focus in 1992 to the celebration of the positive results of that devastating collision between Europe and America. The most important of these "goods" is, for some, "The Evangelization of America."

If Quetzalcoatl were indeed one of the sixteen or so Christ figures who predated the historical Jesus Christ, then the concept of the Christ came to America even before Christianity existed. Furthermore, the Christianity that came to America in 1492 differed in many nonessential but politically significant respects from "The Way" instituted by the historical Jesus Christ. It was employed as one of the useful arms in the arsenal of those committed to an unspeakably vicious policy of genocide and plunder, unparalleled in the history of mankind. Indeed, had the European Christians of 1492 heeded the message of the original evangelizers, to be all things to all men, they would have discovered and built on the concept of Christ that by all accounts was already glimpsed by the many highly developed cultures in the "New World." After a careful consideration of the evidence, the true man or woman of goodwill can only view 1992 as a watershed, the most promising opportunity to reverse and remedy the process, to reconstruct the Americas.

□ □ □

The thrust to deconstruction is of more profound significance than even Jacques Derrida suspected. All psychologically and culturally healthy persons of African ancestry experience the need to undertake this deconstruction of the governing paradigms of so-called Western civilization. These paradigms are posited on the destruction of African civilizations and are founded consciously and unconsciously on untruths or half-truths. The preceding pages have attempted to make the case for the necessity to deconstruct the Eurocentric hegemonic worldview that has shaped us all. The rest of the book will endeavor to effect precisely such a deconstruction by constructing an African-centered analysis of specific literary works produced by African-ancestored writers from Latin America. This analysis will, by very definition, remove these works from the dark margins to which they have been relegated by Eurocentric literary scholars and transport them to the wonderful new center of focus. Since this center is attained through a purified or liberated epistemology, that is, one not conditioned by the need to justify the unacceptable, it follows necessarily that it will be richer, wider, and deeper than the current center of focus for the academy.

2

Here Comes the Trickster

In Chapter One we demonstrated, through the works of several experts, the central importance of African religious thought to all aspects of culture. This has been seen clearly by many writers, although Théophile Obenga, a scholar of significant stature, has a somewhat different slant, which was presented as well. The emphasis on religion and spirituality was the central burden of Edward Kamau Brathwaite's pivotal essay, "The African Presence in Caribbean Literature," and the list of scholars includes other eminent names such as John S. Mbiti and Melville Herskovits. In my book, *Central American Writers of West Indian Origin: A New Hispanic Literature* (1984), the centrality of African religious thought to the aesthetic of the contemporary Costa Rican writer, Quince Duncan, is the subject of Chapter Five. Even against this background the very recent work of the renowned African American literary critic, Henry Louis Gates, Jr., represents a significant step forward, for it brings the discussion of African religious thought to the attention of the mainstream of the North American academy.

It must be indicated from the outset that Gates's analysis is ultimately limited by the severe constraints of Eurocentrism. Locked hopelessly into the myth (in the worse sense of that term) of African orality, he does not acknowledge that it was in the heart of Black Africa that mankind first invented writing and literature. This notwithstanding, his insights are of considerable significance and spring from his analysis of a very misunderstood novel, *Mumbo Jumbo*, by one of the many *bêtes noirs* of contemporary American literature, Ishmael Reed. The critic's case was made in an essay, "The Blackness of Blackness: A Critique of the Sign and the Signifying Monkey," in the intriguing collection under his editorship, *Black Literature and Literary Theory* (1984). Later he developed it into an entire book, *The Signifying Monkey: A Theory of African-American Literary Criticism* (1988). For Gates, *Mumbo Jumbo* "is a novel about writing itself—not only in the figurative sense of the post-modern, self-reflexive text but also in a literal sense" (*Black Literature* 298). A central figure of this perplexing novel is the detective, PaPa LaBas, engaged in the consuming quest for the Text of Jes Grew:

> Unlike Jes Grew, PaPa LaBas does indeed speak. He is the chief detective in hard-and-fast pursuit of both Jes Grew and its Text. PaPa LaBas's name is a conflation of two of the several names of Esù, the Pan-African trickster. Called 'Papa Legba' as his Haitian honorific and invoked through the phrase 'eh là-bas' in New Orleans jazz recordings of the 1920s and 1930s, PaPa LaBas is the Afro-American trickster figure from black sacred tradition. His surname, of course, is French for 'over there', and his presence unites 'over there' (Africa) with 'right here'. He is indeed the messenger of the gods, the divine Pan-African interpreter, pursuing, in the language of the text, 'The Work', which is not only *Vaudou* but also the very work (and play) of art itself. PaPa LaBas is the figure of the critic, in search of the text, decoding its telltale signs in the process. (*Black Literature* 300-01)

The above is one of the more illuminating passages of this remarkable essay, in which, using the language of the canonized literary theories, Gates establishes a central aesthetic connection between a contemporary North American literary expression and traditional African religion/culture in both its Old World and New World manifestations. Indeed, as our discussion in Chapter Four will highlight, the "là" of "là-bas" is particularly expressive, its resonances reaching the very core of what appears to be the exclusively European literary tradition, for this is the same "là" that Charles Baudelaire pronounced in his stirring poetic voice of the nineteenth century.

The connection on which Gates focuses is the "Signifying Monkey," of which he says: "Perhaps only Tar Baby is as enigmatic and compelling a figure from Afro-American mythic discourse as is that oxymoron, the Signifying Monkey" (*Black Literature* 286). He continues, making the claim that "Signifying is a trope that subsumes other rhetorical tropes, including metaphor, metonymy, synecdoche and irony (the 'master' tropes), and also hyperbole, litotes and metalepsis. . . . In black discourse 'signifying' means modes of figuration itself. When one signifies, as Kimberly W. Benston puns, one 'tropes-a-dope'. The black rhetorical tropes subsumed under signifying would include 'marking', 'loud-talking', 'specifying', 'testifying', 'calling out' (of one's name), 'sounding', 'rapping' and 'playing the dozens'" (*Black Literature* 286). African American popular culture is by this analysis tied inextricably to its source, traditional African culture/religion. As obvious as this connection may appear to be, its assertion represents a quantum leap for many intellectuals, including African-ancestored North American scholars.[1]

The link between popular African American culture and Haitian *vaudou* is the true centerpiece of Gates's theorizing. Those who have studied the works of African-ancestored writers from the rest of the Americas will be uplifted by this direction in Gates's thought, for they would be familiar with the contemporary Martinican poet Aimé Césaire's supremely insightful reference to Haiti in a work that is still considered the manifesto of "Négritude," *Cahier d'un retour au pays natal/Return to My Native Land*: "Haiti où la négritude se mit debout pour la première fois et dit qu'elle croyait à son humanité" (67) "Haiti, where Negritude stood up for the first time and swore by its humanity" (66). Ishmael Reed was clearly convinced of the validity of this insight, asserting through the reliable narrator that Haiti is the "miasmatic source" (64) of Jes Grew. And Jes Grew may be defined quite adequately in the terms once employed by Léopold Sédar Senghor to explain his concept of negritude: "La négritude est le patrimonie culturel, les valeurs et surtout l'esprit de la civilisation négro-africaine" [Negritude is the cultural patrimony, the values and above all the spirit of Black African civilization].[2] It is an indefinable something that one catches and without which black cultural expressions could not be created. It comes from Haiti, so that, as Reed's reliable narrator in *Mumbo Jumbo* affirms: "When an artist happens upon a new form he shouts 'I Have Reached My Haiti!'" (64).

It is through Haiti that Esu-Elegbara, the Yoruba "god," orisha, *loa*, *ntr*, power, is metamorphosed into Papa Legba and then installed as the driving force of the literary expression—in the first instance oral—of African Americans. In the book, as distinct from the essay, Gates devotes an entire chapter, "A Myth of Origins: Esu-Elegbara and the Signifying Monkey," to exploring how the Yoruba divinity developed into the Signifying Monkey of African Americans. He first attempts an unearthing of the theology of Esu and makes the following fascinating series of connections: "The Fon call Legba [Esu] 'the divine linguist,' he who speaks all languages. . . . Yoruba sculptures of Esu almost always include a calabash that he holds in his hands. In this calabash he keeps *ase*, the very same *ase* with which Olodumare, the supreme deity of the Yoruba, created the universe. We can translate *ase* in many ways, but the *ase* used to create the universe I translate as 'logos'" (*Signifying* 7).

Gates with this assertion has made a connection the full significance of which he appears to ignore. He further on states that

> One of the many Yoruba creation myths lists Esu as the primal form, the very first form to exist. Before Esu assumed form, only air and water existed. Air (*Olorun*) moved and breathed and became water (*Orisanla*). Air and water interchanged to become liquid mud. The dos Santoses describe what happened next:
>
> From this mud, a swelling or small mound was raised, the first matter endowed with form, a reddish, muddy rock. Olorun admired the form and breathed over the mound, blowing his breath into it and giving it life. This form, the first form of existence, laterite rock, was Esu, or rather a proto-Esu, Esu the ancestor of Esu Agba, the Esu who was to be the king of all his descendants or Esu Oba or also Esu Yangi, on account of his association with laterite (which is called yangi). (*Signifying* 36)

It is almost unbelievable that Gates would not have been intrigued by the similarity of this creation story not only with the biblical account, but also with the teaching of *The Holy Qur'ān* with respect to how man was made by God:

> Man We did create
> From a quintessence (of clay). (Sūrah 23:12)

Any exposure whatsoever to classical African civilization would have led Gates to the seminal cosmogony developed in the Nile Valley before historical time began. Almost a half century ago George G. M. James brought to light in *Stolen Legacy* one of the most compelling articulations of this cosmogony, the Memphite Theology, which he describes as

> an inscription on a stone, now kept in the British Museum. It contains the theological, cosmological and philosophical views of the Egyptians. . . . It is dated 700 B.C., and bears the name of an Egyptian Pharaoh [Shabaka, the Nubian] who stated that he had copied an inscription of his ancestors. This statement is verified by language and typical arrangement of the text, and therefore assigns the original date of the Memphite Theology to a very early period of Egyptian history, i.e., the time when the first Dynasties had made their new capital at Memphis: the city of the God Ptah, i.e., between 4000 and 3500 B.C. (139)

The text is a very complex philosophico-theological statement, but is accessible to any contemporary scholar who would take the time to study humankind's classical language, the language expressed through the hieroglyphs of Kemet. For the vast majority commentary and exegesis are absolutely necessary, and James, whose work was first published in 1954, is one of the more reliable of the commentators. He reconstructs the text of "Part 1" of the document as follows:

> The Primate of the Gods Ptah, conceived in his heart, everything that exists and by His utterance created them all. He is first to emerge from the primeval waters of Nun in the form of a Primeval Hill. Closely following the Hill, the God Atom also emerges from the waters and sits upon Ptah (the Hill). There remain in the waters four pairs of male and female gods. . . . This arrangement in the Memphite Theology could only mean that the ingredients of the

> Primeval Chaos contained ten principles: four pairs of opposite principles, together with two other gods: Ptah representing Mind, Thought, and creative Utterance; while Atom joins himself to Ptah and acts as Demiurge and executes the work of creation. . . .
>
> (b) Creation was accomplished by the unity of two creative principles: Ptah and Atom, i.e., the unity of Mind (nous) with Logos (creative Utterance). . . . .
>
> (e) The elements in creation were Fire (Atom), Water (Nun), Earth (Ptah or Ta-tjenen) and Air. (139-41)

For Obenga the text is a statement by the philosopher-priests of Memphis, capital city of the Old Kingdom, showing "the mechanism of creation." He continues:

> The heart *(h3ty)* and the tongue (*ns*) are mere images used to express abstractions: reason and speech, the Spirit and the Word.
>
> It is through thought and the spoken word that Atum (The All-in All), all the other gods, and all of their creations are given life.
>
> The authors of the text were searching for the initiating principle of creation, of genesis, of intelligence and of the order that underlies the universe. It is a commendable exercise in contemplation, to understand the design behind the birth of the cosmos, behind human existence. This more than two thousand years before the Greek and Hebrew civilizations. (312)

Esu of the Yoruba creation myth cited earlier corresponds essentially with one of the creative principles of the Memphite Theology, the Logos or executing principle that is immanent in the Primate God who is the preexisting formless Chaos out of which everything came. In the Memphite Theology this creative principle, the effecting Logos, is a person distinct from Ptah, the conceiving mind (nous). In both accounts the original substance of reality is seen as a hill or mound. In the Yoruba account it is a mound of mud. In the original Kemetic, the hill emerges out of primeval waters, and this is not inconsistent with its being a mound of mud.

The most reliable archeological evidence establishes the chronological primacy of Nile Valley civilization, carefully indicated in our first chapter. The coincidences, then, between the Yoruba cosmogony and those of both Christianity and Islam can be understood and explained only through reference to the common source out of which they emerged, namely, classical African civilization, the civilization of Kemet. This is precisely the point that Gates misses in his analysis. It is the point that Eurocentric investigators are trained to ignore.

The ancients understood the creative power of the dialectic, that creation is a dialectic. In the very beginning there was the One, Ptah who was somehow not One but Two, *nous* and *logos*, that is, Ptah was there and then Atom, as James puts it, "sits upon Ptah (the Hill)." And then there are those "four pairs of male and female gods (the Ogdoad, or unity of Eight-Gods)" who remain in the primordial waters, the *Nun* (James 140). These gods are male and female because the sexual dichotomy is seen as the fundamental and certainly the creative one par excellence. This is why, for the Yoruba, Esu is an extremely complex "figure of mediation and of the unity of opposed forces" (*Signifying Monkey* 6). In light of Gates's style of formulating theory, it must be pointed out that preoccupation with "indeterminacy," "mediation," "deconstruction," "the dialectic," and the "dialogic" has been the hallmark of African culture from the dawn of recorded history. Gates, elucidating further this aspect of Yoruba thought, continues:

> Ifa is the god of determinate meanings, but his meaning must be rendered by analogy. Esu, god of indeterminacy, rules this interpretive process; he is the god of interpretation because he embodies the ambiguity of figurative language. . . . Esu decodes the figures.
>
> If Ifa, then, is our metaphor for the text itself, then Esu is our metaphor for the uncertainties of explication, for the open-endedness of every literary text. . . . If Esu stands for discourse upon a text, then his Pan-African kinsman, the Signifying Monkey, stands for the rhetorical strategies of which each literary text consists. . . . The figure of writing appears to be peculiar to the myth of Esu, while the figure of speaking, of oral discourse densely structured rhetorically, is peculiar to the myth of the Signifying Monkey. (*Signifying* 21)

Legba is, as Gates is at pains to point out in his earlier essay, a Trickster standing at the crossroads between this world and the world beyond, he is a messenger between the two. In Yoruba mythology he is "the master of style and the stylus, phallic god of generation and fecundity, master of the mystical barrier that separates the divine from the profane world." It is by his very tricks that he mediates between the two worlds, two poles of the inherent, irreconcilable contradiction of the human condition. "The figure of Esù can stand . . . as our metaphor for the act of interpretation itself" (*Black Literature* 287). Developing this idea further along in the book, Gates attempts to account for how the figure of Esu evolves into that of the monkey. There are several versions of the Yoruba mythos that explains the invention of writing and of interpretation. He claims: "It is the presence of the monkey in the Yoruba myth, repeated with a difference in Cuban versions, which stands as the trace of Esu in Afro-American myth, a trace that enables us to speculate freely on the functional equivalence of Esu and his Afro-American descendant, the Signifying Monkey" (*Signifying* 13-14). And he concludes: "The roles of Esu and the Monkey, in several accounts of the myth, are crucial. For reasons extremely difficult to reconstruct, the monkey became, through a displacement in African myths in the New World, a central character in this crucial scene of instruction" (*Signifying* 15). Since Yoruba people have significantly influenced the culture of Brazilians, Cubans, Haitians, Trinidadians, Gates's analysis and data on the evolution of Esu into the Signifying Monkey of African Americans is extremely instructive, an example of Pan-African or Afrocentric scholarship.

Man has been described in the Thomistic philosophical tradition, half jokingly but all in earnest, as an "animal risible." The Yoruba philosophical tradition, a quintessentially African one as our analysis has been at pains to point out, evinces a similar approach to the essential definition of the human animal. Neither angels nor brutes indulge in laughter, a peculiarly human or anthropomorphic activity. Janheinz Jahn in his decades old *Muntu: The New African Culture* (1961), which fits perfectly into the latest wave of cultural studies currently sweeping the Eurocentric academy, presents a vision and analysis of this matter, based on his study of Bantu philosophy. He asserts on the authority of the African sages he consulted that "'man' has not only the power of the word, but also the power of laughter. Laughter is a special kind of flowing; in neo-African poetry it is repeatedly associated with a river" (139). Man stands fundamentally at the crossroads of the cosmos, as the seventeenth century, Roman Catholic, French philosopher-theologian Blaise Pascal put it with such succinct power, he is "un rien entre deux infinis" [a nonentity between two infinites]. He is a being in fundamental contradiction, half animal and half angel: a rational animal, an impossible and unworkable combination—some would say—or a miraculously harmonious blend—as others would assert—of two diametrically opposed principles: matter and spirit.

Esu is the loa ("god," orisha, *ntr*) who best symbolizes the human condition. He is the mediator, the guardian of the crossroads, the portal through whom man must pass in order to experience the supernatural. Thus he is the first loa to be greeted and summoned forth in all of the ceremonies. He is the "lame old man on a crutch" according to the tellingly apt description of the poet Edward Kamau Brathwaite (*The Arrivants* 174). The same poet has incorporated the authentic Haitian opening salutation into his own verse, ending the poem "Negus" as follows:

> *Att*
> *Att*
> *Attibon*
>
> *Attibon Legba*
> *Attibon Legba*
> *Ouvri bayi pou' moi*
> *Ouvri bayi pou' moi* . . . (*The Arrivants* 224)

Gates correctly reasons that "Exú in Brazil, Echu-Elegua in Cuba, Papa Legba in the pantheon of the *loa* of *Vaudou* in Haiti, and Papa La Bas in the *loa* of Hoodoo in the United States," are symbols par excellence of literariness (*Black Literature* 286).

Literature and, indeed, all art, like laughter, are peculiarly human activities, products of beings caught in the middle between two opposing principles. African and neo-African philosophies make this connection and concretize it in the symbolism of Esu, the messenger, the mediator, the bridge. As the messenger/mediator, Esu connects the two poles of the inherent, irreconcilable, primordial contradiction of the human condition. His response is literature *and* laughter, for the mediator is essentially a trickster:

"These trickster figures, aspects of Esù, are primarily *mediators*: as tricksters they are mediators and their mediations are tricks" (*Black Literature* 286). Laughter and literature are two sides of the same coin. Contemporary philosophers like the virtually prototypical existentialist Albert Camus glimpsed at this powerful insight. For, on the one hand, literature is an essay at giving expression to the undecipherable, the mysterious, the enigmatic. On the other, laughter is really only an acknowledgement of the irreconcilable contradiction. And the Mexican writer, Juan José Arreola creates a masterful metaphor for his craft declaring prophetically: "Yo también he luchado con el ángel" [I too have wrestled with the angel]. As a writer he engages in an "operación metafísica y muscular" [metaphysical and muscular operation] that is, in effect, a "batalla irremisiblemente perdida" (33) [battle irredeemably lost]. Esu, then, as Gates sees so clearly, is the *pícaro*/trickster, a "signifying monkey," a "smartman," who utters enigmatic statements, one who essentially provokes laughter. He is the inveterate player or joker.

Roger D. Abrahams, especially in *The Man-of-Words in the West Indies*, demonstrates as well as any other scholar a thorough understanding of the quintessential role of the trickster/joker/smartman in Caribbean, a "neo-African," culture. He sees the joker figure precisely as the inveterate player, zealous of his reputation, the ruler of the crossroads. Abrahams does not appear to make an explicit connection between Esù and the joker. He does, however, come close when he reports that Nansi, a trickster figure, is a "*bruck-up*," a stutterer, an "in-between" character (164, 170). He thus has physical characteristics exactly analogous to those of Legba, the "lame old man on a crutch," his limping or crippled state being, as Gates lucidly indicates, a symbol of indeterminacy (*Black Literature* 287). The connection has to be inferred, especially when the question of the crossroads is taken into consideration. Abrahams's joker, like Legba, is the lord of the crossroads. According to Abrahams, the joker dominates the forces of chaos, creativity, conflict. He is the reverser of order, of household values. However, the controlled, ritual release of his forces, in wakes, carnival, joking, and all forms of "playing," acts out for the community the basic drama of the human condition, that is, the contradiction, the constant menace of absurdity—to use the language of existentialism. This acting out helps the community to deal with death and other such problems, scandalous demonstrations of the fundamental contradiction, manifestations of the menace of absurdity. Abrahams declares:

> But in the actual operations of the group, nonsense provides the major motive for a number of important ceremonial entertainments such as wakes. In wakes, license for making nonsense is given so that the social confusion of death may be articulated, brought playfully into the open, played out. Licentious play brings the group together and allows it to rehearse confusion and embarrassment in a context that is under control. On such occasions nonsense is a community focus in channeling creative energies in socially useful directions. (81)

Joking, or nonsense, is an important philosophical activity. True art would be impossible without it, therefore literature would be impossible without it. Abrahams's empirically based research confirms, then, the more theoretical assessments of his fellow anthropologist and outside observer of African and neo-African cultures, Jahn. Most importantly, the theses of both are consistent with reality as seen by members of the culture group. Furthermore, at the level of strict philosophical speculation, the interplay between Esu and chaos mirrors the primordial process by which Atom, Ra, Ptah, or the Existing One harnessed the creative potential of *Nun*, chaos.

The joker/trickster/"smartman" is highly regarded in Caribbean culture. Abrahams argues for St. Vincent that "friendship among the Vincentians is a joking relationship" (95). It is this writer's observation that in his native land, Trinidad and Tobago, "giving fatigue or picong," that is, joking, forms the basis of many if not most relationships between men. This basic aspect of Trinidad and Tobago culture, a neo-African culture, is a fundamental source of scandal for V.S. Naipaul, an insightful and truly brilliant commentator on the society of his native Trinidad and Tobago, but a man blinded by frequent bouts of confusing emotionalism. He rightly sees the importance of trickery or, what he calls in his impeccably elegant English, "picaroon" behavior. However, he completely misunderstands its origin and misinterprets its systemic significance. In *The Middle Passage*—the title itself is iconoclastically ironic in light of the views expressed—he presents the case of a notorious "smartman," Valmond "Fatman" Jones, who promoted with great fanfare the visit to the island and a show by the famed African American recording artist, the late great Sam Cooke. However, Mr. Jones "flew unexpectedly to Martinique . . . 36 hours before his singing idol was booked to perform before a sell-out crowd at the Globe Cinema, Port-of-Spain."[3] The visit and show, of course, did not materialize, and, naturally, the ticket holders were not reimbursed. Naipaul's commentary on the incident begins with the following passage:

> Three youths were talking about this affair one afternoon around a coconut-cart near the Savannah.
>
> The Indian said, 'I don't see how anybody could vex with the man. *That* is brains.'
>
> 'Is what my aunt say,' one of the Negro boys said. 'She ain't feel she get rob. She feel she pay two dollars for the *intelligence*.' (82)

But Naipaul's basic instinct guides him through the cloud of bias, and he dimly intuits the systematic validity of the "picaroon" society: "To condemn the picaroon society out of hand is to ignore its important quality. And this is not its ability to beguile and enchant. For if such a society breeds cynicism, it also breeds tolerance, not the tolerance between castes and creeds and so on — which does not exist in Trinidad anyway — but something more profound: tolerance for every human activity and affection for every demonstration of wit and style" (82). Naipaul was not far from the heart of the matter. One could reasonably conjecture that he himself shared some of the admiration enshrined in the: "*That* is brains."

The Caribbean is awash with "smartmen." Their presence is systematically related to profound cultural values. The more extreme cases of the "Fatman" type are as much a part of the system as the daily and more clearly benevolent manifestations discussed by Abrahams. The "smartman," even when his antics are unequivocally criminal, induces laughter, and laughter, even in the case of "Fatman," is therapeutic: "I don't see how anybody could vex with the man." Indeed, the "Fatman" style of picaroon behavior derives essentially from the therapeutic trickery practiced by enslaved Africans. So the tricks potentially can achieve two important effects: in some cases a mitigation of the absurdity on the immediate, material plane, and, in every case, relief is provided on the psychological plane. In both cases laughter is involved.

In this writer's earlier book on the Cuban poet, specifically in the chapter entitled "The Smartman," it was asserted that Nicolás Guillén understood the basic importance of laughter and, either consciously or unconsciously, structured his art on theoretical underpinnings consistent with the ones just outlined. The figure of the "smartman" stands as the most apt symbol for the irony and humor, the *choteo*, or in Trinidadian parlance, the "picong," that are fundamental in Guillén's poetry. This ironic humor is of unquestionably African origin and is thus thoroughly Caribbean/West Indian. The poem "Llegada" ["Arrival"] that initiates the poet's statement of his new beginning, the book, *Sóngoro cosongo* (1931), ends with a declaration of the final victory, a strong poetic declaration that "we shall overcome," "we are somebody." This declaration is couched in terms that reveal the deep underlying significance of laughter in African and neo-African cultures: "nuestra risa madrugará sobre los ríos y los pájaros" (Guillén 1: 116) [Our laughter will rise before dawn over the rivers and the birds]. It is most interesting that Frantz Fanon, another famous West Indian intellectual from the island of Martinique, would have used the very same trope in elaborating his vision of the final victory. In his classic work, *The Wretched of the Earth*, referring to the second phase of his three-phase process of the awakening and commitment to struggle of a native artist or intellectual, he describes this intermediate phase as one in which "We spew ourselves up; but already underneath laughter can be heard" (179).

Many other instances are cited in our book referenced above to make the case of the importance of the "smartman" or "trickster" or "Signifying Monkey" in Guillén's art.[4] For example, the poem

"Cuando yo vine a este mundo" [When I came to this world], from the collection *El son entero*, contains further elucidation of the importance the poet attaches to laughter. The third strophe reads:

> Otros lloran, yo me río,
> porque la risa es salud:
> lanza de mi poderío,
> coraza de mi virtud.
> Otros lloran, yo me río,
> porque la risa es salud. (1: 235)
>
> [Others weep, I laugh,
> because laughter is health:
> the lance of my power,
> the breastplate of my virtue.
> Others weep, I laugh,
> because laughter is health.]

The catchy "son" rhythm encodes a profoundly philosophical statement, but of a characteristically homespun, popular, variety. The assertion of the importance of laughter highlights a systematic cultural value, and again Jahn, in *Muntu*, provides the most useful analysis of this aspect of neo-African and African civilizations. The passage is lengthy but illuminating:

> And laughter itself, this special *Kuntu* force, is closely related to the word, to Nommo, for 'man' has not only the power of the word, but also the power of laughter. . . . Laughter is a special word, it liberates and throws off one's bonds, it is unbound like a river. 'A river rises in the heights,' writes the Ecuadorian Adalberto Ortiz in his novel *Juyungo*, 'and goes into the depths. It carries gold and silver and mud and glass, always different, never tiring, full of goodness. It is a prolonged Negro laugh on the dark face of the forest.' And the Cuban Nicolás Guillén writes: 'To you, tropics, I owe that childlike enthusiasm of running, laughing over mountains and clouds, while an ocean of sky is shattered in innumerable star-waves at my feet!' And his countryman Marcelino Arozarena sings: 'Laughs, river, not of water, river of teeth, not a boat road, but warm laughter seasoned with peppers and water teeth, as we do it at home, as my wit is seasoned with the salt of your tears.' Laughter becomes Nommo, the power word itself, in the verse of the North American poet Paul Vesey: 'and my raining laughter beats down the fury . . .' And in the revolutionary verses of Césaire: 'Yes, friends, your untamed laughter, your lizard laughter in their walls, your heretics' laughter in their dogmas, your

> incorrigible laughter, your whirlpool laughter, into which their cities fall spellbound, your time bomb laughter under their lordly feet, your laughter will conquer them! Laugh, laugh, till the world, conquered by your laughter, falls at your naked feet!' (139-40)

To Jahn's list could profitably be added references to Duncan. Gerardo Maloney (born 1945), a Panamanian poet, is of Anglophone Caribbean ancestry like Duncan. And, like his fellow Central American, Maloney uses laughter as a manifestation of hope and triumph over adversity as is demonstrated by the poem, "Arturo King," from his first collection *Juega vivo* (1984). The title of the book could be translated as "play it smart," "keep your wits about you," "be a smartman," and clearly declares the centrality of Legba, who is the "Signifying Monkey," the "trickster," the "mamaguyer," or the "smartman." The poem opens with the lines:

> Arturo King
> había tomado a pecho
> su apellido y no su nombre.
>
> [Arturo King
> took quite seriously
> his surname if not his given name.]

These lines create in the reader/hearer the expectation of being regaled with some engagingly humorous anecdote at the expense of "the King." The work is indeed saturated with a heavy irony aimed at Arturo and his human frailty, which turns out to be the transcendental dethronement that is representative of the experience of all oppressed, dispossessed people. Arturo begins the enterprise of life with a heady enthusiasm that is reflected in his wardrobe and in his bearing:

> Se hizo entusiasmado,
> de varios zapatos de tacones,
> tres nuevos pantalones,
> camisas de colores,
> pomadas y perfumes
> con olores a flores.
> Un rostro de alegría

> y un caminao
> tranquilo y elegante.
>
> [He was excited about
> various pairs of platform shoes,
> three new pairs of pants,
> colored shirts,
> flower-scented perfumes
> and pomades..
> A beaming face
> and a strut that was
> cool and fine.]

The poem ends devastatingly:

> Con la ilusión perdida
> y la realidad, hecho lucha
> día a día
> vive alejado ahora de su trono. (33)
>
> [With his illusions shattered
> and his reality reduced to a
> day-to-day struggle,
> he lives now far removed from the throne.]

Harsh as it is, Maloney's humor is ultimately not negative, and above all it works on the same principles as those which have informed African and African American poetry throughout their secular existence, those of signifying or, in Trinidad and Tobago parlance, "giving fatigue," or "giving picong," or "mamaguying." The laughter evoked in Maloney, as in all cases when the mechanisms are used in accordance with their pristine purity, springs from love and is ultimately salutary.

The Puerto Rican playwright, Francisco Arriví, employs the same kind of "mamaguying" as do Guillén, Maloney, and all of those countless millions of "smartmen," "mamaguyers," "signifyers," givers of "picong," "fatigue," *choteo*, etc. In the play, *Vejigantes* (1956), for example, he constructs the plot basing himself on the stinging popular saying: "¿Y tu abuela, dónde está?" [And your grandmother, where is she?] that is flung in the face of so many "wannabes" to bring them back to the harsh reality of their African ancestry.[5] Representative of his literature, this work seeks to correct through "mamaguying" the defeatist self-image Puerto Ricans of African ancestry have allowed themselves to adopt.

One of the greatest of the literary "mamaguyers" is undoubtedly the Ecuadorian Nelson Estupiñán Bass, author of the classic, *El último río* (1966), the English translation of which was published in 1993 as *Pastrana's Last River*. His protagonist, José Antonio Pastrana, takes to new depths of absurdity the self-hatred that afflicts African-ancestored people. He dramatically ascends the social ladder from being a dirt-poor ex-soldier to become an important captain of industry through his tremendous energies, but with venture capital obtained through a brashly executed scheme. The scheme is the simple one of faking that he is robbed of a sum of money he is charged with delivering. Pastrana cleanses himself and, in a sense, establishes a credible claim to the stolen funds by enduring a brutal whipping inflicted by the local police in an attempt to extract a confession and thereby recover the money. His rise to the top is crowned by his elevation to the position of governor of his native province, one in which the African-ancestored population constitutes the majority. With consummate art Estupiñán "signifies" on Pastrana, turning him into a "total ass," a man ridiculous to the extreme, a negrophobic Negro. He is one who converts his environment into the symbolic glass of milk, but by doing so he becomes the fly therein. He has everything painted white, the walls, the furniture. He dresses in white, and he surrounds himself with white—or a reasonable facsimile thereof—employees, associates, and lovers. He even concocts a plan to import one hundred foreign white boys to impregnate the black women of his province and thus, to improve the race (*mejorar la raza*). When the author has had his fill of regaling us, he orchestrates Pastrana's conversion to a more or less healthy Afrocentrism.

□ □ □

The Trickster in Traditional Hispanic Letters

If it is accepted that "signifying" or "mamaguying" are central to the aesthetic of African-ancestored Americans, and that this cultural reflex came down through the generations, literally from the beginning of recorded history, it is only to be expected that it would manifest itself wherever African peoples were influential in creating a cultural milieu. It is a matter of historical record that African peoples called Moors are chiefly responsible for shaping what we view today as typical Spanish and Portuguese cultures. Writers like Stanley Lane-Poole are very clear, eschewing neither stridency nor rhapsody, on the matter. Speaking in his 1886 work, *The Story of the Moors in Spain*, of the civilization introduced into the Iberian Peninsula by the Moors, he affirms: "When we remember that the sketch we are about to extract from the records of the Arabian writers, concerning the glories of Cordova, relate to the tenth century, when our Saxon ancestors dwelt in wooden hovels and trod upon dirty straw, when our language was unformed, and such accomplishments as reading and writing were almost confined to a few monks, we can to some extent realize the extraordinary civilization of the Moors" (129-30).

This is the kind of information that John G. Jackson, in his introduction to the 1990 reedition of Lane-Poole's classic, summarizes as follows:

> Cordova was the most wonderful city of the tenth century; the streets were well-paved, with raised sidewalks for pedestrians. At night, ten miles of streets were well illuminated by lamps. (This was hundreds of years before there was a paved street in Paris or a street lamp in London.) Cordova, with a population of at least one million, was served by four thousand public markets and five thousand mills. Public baths numbered in the hundreds. This amenity was present at a time when cleanliness in Christian Europe was regarded as a sin.
>
> Moorish monarchs dwelt in splendid palaces, while the crowned heads of England, France, and Germany lived in big barns, lacking both windows and

> chimneys, with only a hole in the roof for the emission of smoke.
>
> . . . In the tenth and eleventh centuries, public libraries in Europe were nonexistent, while Moorish Spain could boast of more than seventy, of which the one in Cordova housed six hundred thousand manuscripts. Christian Europe contained only two universities of any value, while in Moorish Spain there were seventeen great universities. The finest of these were located in Almeria, Cordova, Granada, Juen, Malaga, Seville, and Toledo. (no pagination)

It is a matter of general knowledge that algebra, algorithm, Arabic (of course) numerals were introduced to Europe through Moorish Spain. Beatrice Lumpkin in "Africa in the Mainstream of Mathematics History," claims: "But one book, more than any other, was the vehicle for introducing Europe to Muslim algebra and Hindu-Arabic numerals and arithmetic, I-Khowarizmi's *Al-jabr wa'l muqabalah.*' From the author's name we get the common mathematical term 'algorithm.' From the title, *al-jabr*, we get the modern term, 'algebra'" (74).

It is also a matter of general knowledge that Aristotle's works and the so-called classics of the Graeco-Roman world were *introduced* to Christian Europe through Moorish Spain. However, the Western academy, impervious to certain objective truths because of its racist ideology, automatically de-Africanizes the Moors. Thus, when, in courses on the history of philosophy, Catholic seminarians in the sixties were taught that the "Arabic" philosopher Averroes had a profound effect on the development of Scholastic philosophy and on Saint Thomas Aquinas, there was absolutely no indication that this powerful philosophical figure, "Abu-Al-Walid Mohammed ibn Mohammad ibn Rashd . . . was," as Wayne Chandler reveals, "an African who lived in Spain" (168). Lane-Poole is, then, one of those voices that from time to time rise above the clouds of white supremacist bias.

Lane-Poole ends his remarkable book on a note that might appear to strike a strident cord of anti-Hispanicism. Referring to the final defeat of the Moors culminating in their deportation back to Africa, he asserts:

> The deportation was not finished till 1610, when half a million of Moriscos were exiled and ruined. . . .

> The misguided Spaniards knew not what they were doing. The exile of the Moors delighted them . . . . They did not understand that they had killed their golden goose. For centuries Spain had been the centre of civilization, the seat of arts and sciences, of learning, and every form of refined enlightenment. . .
>
> The Moors were banished; for a while Christian Spain shone, like the moon, with a borrowed light; then came the eclipse, and in that darkness Spain has grovelled ever since. The true memorial of the Moors is seen in desolate tracts of utter barrenness, where once the Moslem grew luxuriant vines and olives and yellow ears of corn; in a stupid, ignorant population where once wit and learning flourished; in the general stagnation and degradation of a people which has hopelessly fallen in the scale of the nations, and has deserved its humiliation. (279-80)

Those who have made a close study of Hispanic culture immediately associate the peculiar musical form from Andalusia, the *cante hondo*, with what is essentially Spanish. Not many years ago, one of the great scholars of Hispanic letters and culture, Wilfred Cartey, pointed out to this author the amazing similarity between the Spanish *cante hondo* of incontrovertible Moorish provenience and the traditional music of the Mandingo griots. The haunting melodies sung almost a capella in a grating, intensely dramatic voice that borders on the monotonous, and accompanied by the equally stark and stirring music of a stringed instrument—guitar for the Spanish, kora for the Mandingo—are clearly closely related. There is also an equally evident similarity between the flamenco dance of the same Andalusian culture and the traditional rumba dance of the Cubans. Both dances represent the age-old contest between man and woman, and one of their more obvious common motifs is the use of the handkerchief (*pañuelo*). The dish enjoyed throughout West Africa and known as "Wolof rice" is particularly dear to natives of The Gambia, some of whom consider it a national dish (*plato típico)*. It is, however, indistinguishable from the *plato típico* par excellence of Spain, namely, *paella*.

The data offered in the preceding paragraph bear further assessment by an appropriate specialist. However, an exactly analogous pattern of similarity can be documented in the area of literature, the specialty of this author. Lane-Poole in his almost rhapsodic recording of the documented glories of tenth century

Cordova, and apparently without himself realizing the full significance of his asseverations, declares that

> as for the graces of literature, there never was a time in Europe when poetry became so much the speech of everybody, when people of all ranks composed those Arabic verses which perhaps suggested models for the ballads and canzonettes of the Spanish minstrels and the troubadours of Provence and Italy. No speech or address was complete without some scrap of verse, improvised on the spur of the moment by the speaker, or quoted by memory from some famous poet. The whole Moslem world seemed given over to the Muses; Khalifs and boatmen turned verses, and sang of the loveliness of the cities of Andalusia, the murmur of her rivers, the beautiful nights beneath her tranquil stars, and the delights of love and wine, of jovial company and stolen meetings with the lady whose curving eyebrows had bewitched the singer. (147)

Lane-Poole was apparently influenced by the same Muses, but the Moorish Andalusia he describes as drunk with the music of poetry, in the words of Baudelaire in his "Enivrez-vous" [Get drunk] from *Petits poèmes en prose* [Little Prose Poems] "toujours ivre . . . . de poésie" (125) [always drunk . . . on poetry], closely resembles Port-of-Spain at carnival time certainly, and, some would argue, all the year round. The same state of constant inebriation on music ("toujours ivre") apparently characterizes the folk of that region in Colombia—on the Caribbean coast—where the musical form called the *vallenato* originated. This is certainly what Rito Llerena Villalobos is at pains to demonstrate in *Memoria cultural en el vallenato* [Cultural Content in the *Vallenato*]. The universal urge to grace speech with "some scrap of verse, improvised on the spur of the moment by the speaker, or quoted by memory from some famous poet" manifests the same cultural reflex that Chinua Achebe reports on with the unforgettable declaration in the opening pages of *Things Fall Apart*: "Among the Ibo the art of conversation is regarded very highly, and proverbs are the palm-oil with which words are eaten" (10).

Lane-Poole concedes only that the "Arabic verses . . . perhaps suggested models for the ballads and canzonettes of the Spanish minstrels and troubadours of Provence and Italy" (147). Martha K. Cobb, a contemporary Afrocentric scholar, goes much further in her essay, "Afro-Arabs, Blackamoors and Blacks: An Inquiry into Race Concepts through Spanish Literature," which is anthologized in Miriam DeCosta Willis's, *Blacks in Hispanic Literature*. Cobb introduces the subject of Antar in the following manner:

> One of the most distinguished Afro-Arabs, honored and well known in the Eastern world. . . . His full name was Antar Ibn Shaddad al'Absi. . . . son of a Black woman from the African continent and a Berber Arab, Antar was renowned as a warrior, poet, and the ideal representative of a chivalric code which, according to the legends that followed his death, he formulated. His *Mo'allaqua* or "Praise Song," which hung in the Mosque at Mecca, is considered a masterpiece, one of the seven golden odes of the Arab world. . . . It is also interesting to discover that Antar took pride in his Black pigmentation. (22)

Cobb reports that Antar died in 615 A.D., at a time when Europe was sunk deep in the ignorance and barbarism of the Dark Ages. His "praise song" verses then clearly predate the famed epic and lyric poetry of Europe—Rodrigo Díaz de Vivar, the historical El Cid, for example, hero of the first of the great epic poems in Spanish, died in 1099. On the death of Antar, "the tradition of Antar spread because his celebrated career and writings were perpetuated in song and story through the efforts of a group of storytellers and poets, his disciples, who called themselves Antaristas." Antar, the black knight in shining armor, was to the Islamic world what El Cid and Roland would become to the Spanish and French world respectively some four centuries later. And Cobb indicates expressly: "It was this Antarista tradition, brought to the Iberian Peninsula by the Moors, that formed the base of many European romances of chivalry and later influenced the development of the codes of chivalry in medieval Europe" (22).

In 1948 mainstream Hispanists found and accepted evidence that corroborated the insights and analyses of scholars like Lane-Poole and Cobb. A discovery was made in Cairo of twenty so-called *muwassahas*. These were poems written in Hebrew that ended with a two- or four-line refrain in *mozárabe*, a dialect of Hispano-Romance, the creolized form of Vulgar Latin that had become the vernacular throughout the Iberian Peninsula, and the source language from which Spanish (Castilian), Portuguese, Catalan, *gallego*, and all of the modern languages of the Peninsula—with the exception of Basque—evolved. The conquering "Black Muslims" adopted this vernacular, thereby creating *mozárabe*. Since in 711 A.D. Hispano-Romance was far from being a written language, the Moors used the only vehicle for writing that they knew, the Arabic language. Thus *mozárabe*, written in Arabic characters, actually became the first written version of Hispano-Romance. *Mozárabe* was the language of the short poems or refrains, which came to be known as *jarchas*. They were of a populist stamp in their form and content and apparently served as the base for the longer compositions which were of a markedly *culto* [self-consciously artistic] nature and were written in either Hebrew or Arabic.

It needs to be reasserted that, as our discussion has indicated so far, the speakers and writers of Hebrew and Arabic in the Iberian Peninsula at that time need not necessarily have been Europeans. Indeed, the majority of the speakers and writers of Hebrew and Arabic who live in the Mediterranean world of our time are non-Caucasoid peoples. There is no reason to suppose that things were any different in the 11th century, nor are there compelling historical data that support the assumption that the poets in question were other than black and brown folk. According to the renowned Hispanist Angel del Río, the earliest *jarchas* have been dated to 1040 A.D., a full century before the *Cantar de Mio Cid* [The Poem of the Cid] took definitive shape. This latter, the earliest written work in *castellano* [Castilian Spanish], the most important of the surviving dialects of Hispano-Romance, was the cycle of heroic verses celebrating the life and works of El Cid, whose pseudonym is a corruption of the Arabic *Seyyid* a word that means "master" (Lane-Poole 191).

Scholars generally opine that the *jarcha* was simply one of those popular refrains culled from the repertoire referenced by Lane-Poole "quoted by memory from some famous poet," and used by the individual Arabic or Hebrew poet to give a stamp of authenticity to their creations. The *jarchas* thus perform the function assigned to proverbs in Igbo culture, becoming the palm oil—or perhaps more correctly the olive oil—with which words—the creations of individual poets—were eaten. In the face of all these data, mainstream Hispanists, as is the custom in the white supremacist academy, have managed to eschew the most compelling conclusions by creating a series of *incognitas* [unresolved issues]. Scholars make a major issue of whether or not the *jarchas* were in fact refrains from a preexisting cycle of popular poems or were created by the Arabic and Hebrew creative artists with a view to giving a rustic touch, an air of "rootsyness," to their individual works. And even if the *jarchas* did spring from a preexisting popular tradition, was this Arabic or pre-Arabic?

Since it is quite common for academicians to offer this kind of calculated obfuscation as serious objective inquiry, it is no wonder that none of the Hispanists of the mainstream Western academy has, to my knowledge, sought to examine the African provenience of one of the most important literary types in Hispanic letters, the *pícaro*. In an earlier article, "The Trickster *Pícaro* in Three Contemporary Afro-Hispanic Novels," we established the connection that seems to be abundantly clear. The archetypal *pícaro* made his first appearance in Hispanic letters in the enormously popular *La vida de Lazarillo de Tormes y de sus fortunas y adversidades* in 1554. This was a time when the Moors were still physically present in Spain—it was not until 1570 that the final solution of deportation/expulsion back to Africa was set in place, to be completed in 1610. European scholars quite typically look to Europe for the source of the picaresque tradition. R. O. Jones, for example, in his introduction to a popular edition of the *Lazarillo* claims, absolutely begging the question, that it "reflects a growing interest in the ways of rogues and beggars that was responsible for a copious literature in sixteenth-century Europe" (xvii). He also points to what he calls simply a "folk tradition" in Spain itself as a possible source, making no attempt, naturally, to explore the African or at least the Islamic elements of the "folk tradition."

The article referred to in the previous paragraph argued for an integral connection between the Trickster figure envisioned by Gates and the picaresque protagonists of contemporary fiction written in Spanish by African-ancestored authors, focusing in particular on three such, who were posited as adequately representative. They were Adalberto Ortiz, from Ecuador, whose novel, *Juyungo* (1943), initiated the cycle of contemporary Hispanophone Africana fiction; the Colombian Arnoldo Palacios, whose novel, *Las estrellas son negras*, appeared in 1949; and Ramón Díaz Sánchez, a Venezuelan, author of *Cumboto* (1950). Furthermore, it offered for serious consideration the suggestion that since Africans were a significant cultural force in Europe and especially in Spain prior to the popularity of the picaresque tradition, and since the *pícaro* figure is clearly a Trickster, it would be fruitful for scholars to investigate the connection between the two.

Gates has argued that the characteristic cultural practice of African Americans labelled "signifying" is in fact a fundamental literary activity and that it is derived from Yoruba mythology. These views, which were explored earlier in this chapter, can be taken many steps further, for signifying serves as an important means by which an oppressed people seek a modicum of empowerment. All African-ancestored people in the Americas were faced with essentially the same kind of systematic, disenfranchising brutality visited upon them by Europeans. It is reasonable to expect that their responses would be similar. This expectation is further strengthened by the fact that in the case of one group, i.e. the African North Americans, a scholar has demonstrated that this response is an integral part of a cultural tradition that predates the African presence in the New World. In fact, if Gates had probed a little further he would have discovered, as we have been seeking to demonstrate, that this cultural tradition predates and is the source of Western civilization.

After becoming familiar with Gates's analysis of *Mumbo Jumbo*, we, in the article referred to, engaged in a deeper reading of the corpus of contemporary fiction written by Latin Americans of African ancestry . The discovery was made that the literary act for oppressed Africans from Latin American is fundamentally an act of what has been called *cimarronaje*, that is, an act of making oneself into a *cimarrón* [maroon] or self-liberated slave. This is true for all oppressed people, as Fanon adequately demonstrates, for literature is creativity, and freedom is a necessary condition for its realization—a point which will be elaborated upon in the final section of this current chapter. Indeed, all aspects of "signifying" are found in Hispanophone Africana culture. The literary act in particular, whether oral or scribal, has traditionally been one of the major ways this "signifying" is effected; and every act of *cimarronaje* is the act of a "signifyer" or Trickster. Specifically, then, the protagonists of three representative Hispanophone Africana novels are clearly conceived of as Tricksters engaged in *cimarronaje*. They may also be viewed simply as *pícaros* in the tradition of Euro-Hispanic literature. In light of our preceding discussion such a view would clearly be unnecessarily limiting.

Ascención Lastre, the protagonists of *Juyungo*, is in many respects a classic *pícaro*. He enters upon the scene as a young child cast adrift in a sea of adversity and has to learn to swim immediately lest he drown. Like the Lazarillo, at an early age he leaves what little shelter his "home" provides. Tutored both by his own "smarts" and by a series of contacts with others who served as his "masters" in a more or less formal way, he manages to negotiate the perils of existence as a black man in a white man's world. The author clearly adopts the picaresque paradigm in the development of Ascención's character:

> Dos, tres años serían los que anduvo en la canoa de Cástulo Canchingre. No le pagaba nada, pero le compraba ropa y le daba comida: de Limones a Tumaco, de Tumaco a Limones, contrabandeando aguardiente para los colombianos y trayendo telas y buenos pesos, más valiosos que el sucre ecuatoriano. (24)
>
> [It was about two, three years that he spent travelling around in Cástulo Canchingre's canoe. He didn't pay him a thing, but he bought him clothes and fed him; from Limones to Tumaco, from Tumaco to Limones, smuggling liquor into Colombia and returning with material and good *pesos*, worth more than the Ecuadorian *sucre*.]

Ascensión will never cease to be an *andariego* [wanderer] living by his wits and learning constantly from "masters." His most influential teacher is a mulatto intellectual à la Adalberto Ortiz, Nelson Díaz, who formally imparts to him the formula for accommodation to Eurocentrism and white superiority: "Ten siempre presente estas palabras, amigo mío: más que la raza, la clase" (91) [Always remember these words, my friend: it's not race, but class]. Just as the Lazarillo attains the peak of his good fortune through his marriage of convenience to the kept woman of a high official, Ascención attains his highest degree of peace and prosperity through an acceptance of the prevailing order in society, and, indeed, he manifests this acceptance through marriage to a white woman whom he himself acknowledges to be quite homely.

Ironically, and it is an irony that may even have escaped the implied author, this accommodation is literally fatally flawed, for it does not even assure the physical survival that the *pícaro* seeks. However, the protagonist is essentially a Trickster whose physical survival depends on his skill at his tricks. Lulled into a false consciousness by a mulatto who was barely black—the text describes him as "muy blanco por fuera, a pesar de que su abuela era una mulata oscura" (88) [very white in appearance, even though his grandmother was a dark-skinned mulatto woman]— his Trickster instinct fails him and he immolates himself fruitlessly on the altar of his new creed of nationalism and class before race. He fails in his *picardía*, but it had served as the mainstay of his character.

Irra, the young male protagonist of *Las estrellas son negras*, is also in many senses a *pícaro*. He is forced to confront desperate circumstances of poverty, hunger, and, above all, a pervasive racism. His response to life is clearly framed in terms that are close to the traditional picaresque paradigm:

> El estómago le ardía. Sintió más hambre aún . . . No había comido nada, cierto. . . . ¿Por qué no se moría? Era preferible morir. Al menos, la muerte ofrecía oportunidad ineludible de comer barro y gusanos bajo la tumba. Continuaba caminando con la cabeza gacha. Y se sentía en medio de la tempestad. Su cuerpo bamboleaba, frágil pelota en medio del océano tronante. ¿Por qué diablos no resolverse . . . y matarlo esa misma tarde? . . . ¿Era Irra un pusilánime? Entonces creyó que la falla residía justamente en su persona, en la estructura de su alma . . . La vida entera de Irra pasó velozmente por su

> cerebro. . . . No vio nada extraordinario en su existencia . . . (80-81)
>
> [His stomach was on fire. He felt even hungrier . . . He hadn't eaten a thing, to be sure. . . . Why wasn't he dying? It would be better to die. At least, death provided an inescapable opportunity to eat mud and worms down there in the tomb. He kept on walking with his head bowed. He felt he was in the eye of a storm. His body bobbed along, a fragile ball in the middle of a roaring ocean. Why the hell couldn't he take a determination . . . and kill him this very evening? . . . Was Irra pusillanimous? Then he thought that the fault lay precisely with his person, with the structure of his soul . . . Irra's entire life flashed through his mind. . . . He saw nothing special about his existence . . .]

In this rambling soliloquy, a young man—suffering the pangs of a hunger that is both physical and spiritual—tries to make a resolution regarding the direction of his life. He realizes that a determined even outrageous act of *picardía* is the only solution. Such an act would be a form of local, "down-scale" regicide, the murder of the *Intendente*, a rich man and a symbol par excellence of the racist oppressive power structure. It would transform him "de muchacho hambriento, tímido, desnutrido, sin voluntad, en un hombre indómito, hombre decidido a ejecutar algo grande" (94) [from a hungry, shy, undernourished, listless boy, into an indomitable man, a man determined to carry out a great feat]. He understands that whereas he shares some of the basic vital circumstances of the *pícaro*—the hunger, the rootlessness—he lacks the vital energy, the driving will to succeed. He understands that his lackluster *picardía* must be informed by a bold *cimarronaje*. It is interesting to note, too, how in this novel hunger is an ubiquitous force haunting with the same intensity this young African-ancestored Colombian of the twentieth century as it did the young Lazarillo of sixteenth century Spain.

Irra is an existentialist *pícaro*, and the absurdity of his situation ultimately overwhelms him. He does not execute the act of violence that Fanon terms a "cleansing force" (74) and he stumbles through a series of incoherently strung together and ambiguously resolved experiences, until he finds a kind of liberation, through what Lemuel A. Johnson describes as "an epiphany whose attendant certainties are at once lyrically powerful and yet fragile, even precarious, especially when set against the larger cracks and fissures of the gigantic body within which Palacios locates his Chocó" (9). He simply walks out into the waters of the river, and the novel ends with the following: "El agua le supo terrosa. Se lavó las piernas, los brazos. Y ensanchando el pecho respiró libre. ¡Libre!" (180) [The water tasted muddy to him. He washed his legs, his arms. And expanding his chest he took a breath of freedom. Freedom!]. The liberation he achieves is indeed "precarious," to say the least, for it is either death by drowning or a life of complete abandonment to illusion. Irra's final solution, however, structurally parallels that of the Lazarillo: it is an accommodation to the prevailing and ineluctable adversity.

Picardía is merely a perennial possibility for Natividad, *Cumboto*'s African-ancestored anti-protagonist. Consequently, he never amounts to anything more than a mere shadow of the real protagonist, Frederico, the white man, his master. Indeed, Natividad consciously rejects the call to liberation through *cimarronaje* and *picardía*. Consciously or unconsciously, the implied author sets up the basic paradigm that we have outlined; for example, very early in the novel, in the second chapter of the first of four parts, when the vicissitudes of his servile existence cast the young Natividad unexpectedly from the protection of the "casa grande," and he is taken under the wing of the old and seasoned Cervelión. This wise man immediately confronts his disoriented young "brother" with the following declaration:

> —Unc . . . , unc, mijito . . . Me parece que voy a tené que enseñáte mucha cosa a ti. Oyeme bien: lo negro tenemo que conocé mir maña pa defendeno. Aquí me tienej a mí: no sé leé pero me escriben. Tú estáj metío entre lo blanco, pero ere negro por lo cuatro costao y ello no van a enseñáte nada de lo que saben; así é que tienej que comé avipa si quierej viví como un hombre. (19)

> ["Uhm . . . , uhm, sonny boy . . . It look like I go have to teach you a lot of thing. Hear me well: we Negro people have to know a whole lot of trick to defend we self. Look at me, here; I don't know how to read but people does write things for me. You up there living right up under all them white people, but you black, black, black and they ain't go teach you a thing what they know; so you have to be sharp as a tack if you want to live like a man."]

It should be noted that "comé avispa" is the equivalent to Maloney's "juega vivo." Cervelión's declaration became a point of orientation for Natividad, but one that he would reject, over and over again, throughout the course of the novel. He says quite clearly, speaking of his relationship with the rest of the African-ancestored population on the plantation:

> Por poco observador que yo fuese, no podía dejar de notar la reserva, más aún, la hostilidad con que fui recibido. . . . todos aquellos hombres, todas aquellas mujeres, todos aquellos chiquillos—negros, mulatos y zambos—, me habían visto en pos de don Guillermo el *Musiú*, recorriendo el campo sombrío, como un perdiguero que orientase a su amo hacia el cobro de la presa herida. Yo era el perdiguero de don Guillermo; ellos eran los gatos, rebeldes y sigilosos. (67)

> [As unobservant as I was, I still couldn't miss noticing the reserve or rather the hostility with which I was greeted. . . . all of those men, all of those women, all of those little children—Negros, mulattoes and *zambos*—had seen me running around behind don Guillermo the *M'seur*, all through the shady countryside, like a bird dog helping his master locate the wounded prey. I was don Guillermo's bird dog; they were the cats, sneaky rebels.]

The antihero first-person narrator is even more trenchantly incisive in his self-analysis: "Más de una vez había pensado en huir, emanciparme y forjarme mi propia vida. Pero no lo hice" [Many a time I thought about running away, freeing myself and forging my own life. But I didn't do it]. He goes on to explain at the very end of the same paragraph: "pero la idea de partir sin un rumbo, sin una brújula que orientase mis pasos, me aterraba. ¡Me sentía tan débil e incapaz!" (89) [but the idea of setting off in no particular direction, without a compass to guide my steps terrified me. I felt so weak and ineffective!]. He will be forever, as he himself acknowledges, "una sombra" [a shadow] heavy with the menace of the complete annihilation foretold in the immortal closing line of the unforgettable sonnet by Luis de Góngora.[6]

If only as an unrealized possibility the Trickster/*pícaro* paradigm is intuited by Díaz Sánchez as it was by Ortiz and Palacios in their respective works. Perhaps the clearest use of this paradigm is to be found in Manuel Zapata Olivella's magnum opus,

Changó, el gran putas, that first appeared in 1983. The very title of the works proclaims the author's adherence to the conception—this novel will be analyzed in the following chapter.[7]

The structural similarities between the quintessential *pícaro* and the protagonists of these representative contemporary works by Spanish speaking authors of African origin can all, of course, be explained through the normal processes of intertextuality within any given literary tradition. The fascinating coincidences with the African North American literary and popular cultural tradition also result from intertextual processes. The linking texts, however, are those of the popular oral repertoire of African-ancestored people from all corners of North, Central and South America. The classical African cultural tradition, which first flowered in Kemet, is also a very probable basis for the original intra-Hispanic intertextuality, for it has been demonstrated that this tradition exercised a formative influence on Hispanic letters. Furthermore, and this is merely a fascinating detail, part of the cumulative weight of circumstantial evidence, Africa was physically present in the universe of the original *pícaro*. His newly widowed mother's first "friend" and the father of his half-brother was a "hombre moreno" (5) [black man]. Surely it must be of enormous significance that a black man would make this kind of presence on the very first page of this prototypical work in an epoch when the political tensions between *morenos*—literally "Moorish," that is blacks, and whites (Christians) had reached a most exacerbated peak.

Indeed, it is stunningly significant that the first person narrator, the young boy Lazarillo, tells on that very same first page of extremely stark narrative that his father had lost his life during the course of a military campaign "contra moros" (5) [against the Moors]. It is most instructive to recount the continuation of this thread of narrative. The first person narrator tells that as one thing led to another and "mi madre vino a darme un negrito muy bonito, el cual yo brincaba y ayudaba a calentar" (6) [my mother came to give me a cute little black baby boy, whom I would rock and help to keep warm]. However, this little brother since "vía a mi madre y a mí blancos, y a él no, huía dél con miedo para mi madre, y señalando con el dedo decía: '¡Madre, coco!'" (6) [he saw my mother and myself white, and not him (i.e. his father), would run from him in fear to my mother, and pointing with his finger he would say: 'Mama, look a booboo!'].

With viciously deadpan irony the narrative continues: "Respondió él riendo: '¡Hideputa!'" (6) [He replied laughing: 'Son of a whore']. The narrator had made it abundantly clear that his mother's relationship with the *moreno* was posited on the need for food and shelter. She is, then, operating strictly on the age-old principle rearticulated by The Mighty Sparrow in his "Monica": "no money, no love"; or by Guillén in his "Búcate plata" [Get some cash]: "pero amó con hambre, biejo, / ¡qué ba!" (1: 108) [but love on hungry belly, baby, / it don't work so!]. The densely layered irony attains the very pinnacle of searingly incisive commentary that nevertheless is brilliantly indirect as Lázaro observes:

> Yo, aunque bien mochacho, noté aquella palabra de mi hermanico, y dije entre mí:
>
> '¡Cuántos debe de haber en el mundo que huyen de otros porque no se veen a sí mesmos!' (6)
>
> [I, although a mere boy, took note of that word uttered by my little brother, and I said to myself:
>
> 'How many there must be in this world who run away from others for not seeing what they themselves look like!']

The sublimely clever author disarms her/his critics by confronting head-on the obvious disparity between the level of insight and the tender age of the narrator. She/he then "signifies on," "mamaguys" the Spanish society of the times in the most exquisite fashion, with consummate indirection. Spain of the midsixteenth century, externally at the zenith of its so-called "Golden Age," was, as Lane-Poole put it, merely a moon reflecting a borrowed light that would soon fade. It had killed the goose that laid the golden egg. It was like Lázaro's little brother, born of a black man, a *moreno*, whom it now scorned without realizing the self-annihilating stupidity of its actions. The *moreno*'s response is laughter in and through trickery, the trickery of reminding him with exquisite indirection that his mother is nothing but a whore, his whore.

It is significant that historians of Hispanic literature have declared themselves unable to identify the author of the prototypical picaresque novel. Those engaged in Afrocentric research have reason to suspect that the attribution of anonymity has frequently served Eurocentric scholars as a cover-up of African authorship. In any case, without any compelling indications of non-African authorship and with such strong supporting circumstantial evidence as we have presented in this chapter, we may reasonably, at this point, claim African authorship of the *Lazarillo*.

□ □ □

Africans in the Americas, subjected to the most brutal barbarism by a militarily superior band of thugs, have had, like the *pícaro* of Spanish letters, to respond with trickery. They have, indeed, made of the Trickster the revolutionary (*cimarrón*) par excellence. Gates has shown that as the Signifying Monkey of street culture in African North America, a Yoruba "god" central to Haitian culture has metamorphosed into a Trickster who is a peculiarly black American symbol of literariness. The literary act for the black American is, then, according to this set of ideas, the ultimate act of self-assertion, rejection of the essential racist paradigm. Conceived in these terms, it is an act of liberation. Fanon had made it quite clear that every truly artistic expression of an oppressed native is posited necessarily on the rejection of the colonial paradigm, which he views as essentially dichotomous, "Manichean" in his terms.[8] The ideas presented by Fanon and Gates are, then, mutually compatible.

Africans in the Americas have, then, maintained a fealty to theological principles that are as old as human civilization, principles that are themselves fundamentally African. It is this rootedness in history, this empowering affective and effective self-knowledge that has undergirded the most authentic, and hence the most aesthetically successful, expressions of culture in all of Afro-America. The critic who misses all this, who is unaware of this incredibly rich undergirding, is a significantly impoverished scholar, who can only produce effete pronouncements that rehash the largely irrelevant disquisitions of the Eurocentric academy. Conversely, the critic who is aware penetrates into the deepest recesses not only of the artistic product of African-ancestored writers, but, as was demonstrated in the preceding chapter, introduces incredible new possibilities for interpretation into the languid critical apparatus of the mainstream academy.

3

Here Comes the *Cimarrón*

In Chapter Two it was demonstrated that the *cimarrón* and the Trickster are the absolutely necessary matter and form of liberation for New World Africans, and, indeed, it could be argued, for all African peoples. The present chapter will focus on the roots of the *cimarrón* figure in the basic and peculiarly African philosophico-theological tradition. Kortright Davis, in a fairly recent study, showed conclusively that Christianity for the African in the Caribbean is a religion of liberation. The historical record attests to the fact that, in the New World, African liberation is grounded in traditional African spirituality, that is, traditional philosophy and theology. The two strands of analysis must be connected into a powerful conclusion: the Christian theology of liberation is a valid expression of the quintessentially African concept of *cimarronaje*. Not only are such historical *cimarrones* as Paul Bogle, José Antonio Aponte, Marcus Garvey, Jesus Menéndez, Malcolm X, or even the ahistorical—otherworldly—ones, like Shango and Legba grounded in African spirituality, but the bold assertion must be made that the liberation promised by Christianity is itself a true form of *cimarronaje*.

Davis, addressing the matter of "the underlying theme" of his book, indicates quite clearly in the preface that "It is an attempt to interpret contextually the meaning of human freedom in the light of a popular faith in the God of Jesus Christ, whose Gospel of liberation and whose life of historical confrontation have constantly inspired and strengthened such faith" (x). A professor of religion, an ordained Episcopalian priest, and a pastor, Davis had his book published by the press of The Catholic Foreign Mission Society of America (Maryknoll). His views are, then, representative of a valid brand of Christian orthodoxy. On the second page of his first chapter, Davis finds it necessary to reiterate his statement of intent: "It is therefore a fundamental theme of this book that the major force which Caribbean people have to call their own, religion, must become the primary instrument for their active engagement in the reconstruction and historical emancipation of their society. A new force of emancipation must emerge out of the realities of their sociocultural and historical context" (2).

Over and over again, with almost obsessive insistence, Davis will return to what he deems to be his "fundamental theme." Speaking specifically of freedom, he declares that "Freedom . . . is not merely the nature of God; it is also the will of God." He follows this with his formulaic assertion: "It is the fundamental theme of this book that the only freedom deep enough to offer and inspire emancipation, and authentic enough to be concretely functional, is essentially that which actively acknowledges its origins in the sovereign free God" (8). This freedom can be achieved through a sui generis Caribbean Christian ascesis, for "There is sufficient ground for a theology of liberation that is already on the way in the Caribbean. Much of what the people have been engaged in has had some emancipatory dimensions" (10).

Davis privileges the term "emancipation," which he declares "is the Caribbean word for liberation, not only because it denotes the major Caribbean event but also because it evokes a sense of accountability to the Caribbean forebears in slavery and to the Caribbean descendants in freedom" (71). Interestingly, it is the term "emancipate" that Bob Marley opted for in one of his signature lines, "emancipate yourself from mental slavery." And the term is obviously rooted in the peculiar experience of the so-called British West Indies. However, Davis leaves no room for doubt about his Pan-Caribbean focus and expressly indicts the fragmentation that has frustrated fruitful Caribbean scholarship and the fullness of Caribbean cultural life. He calls for precisely the kind of scholarship that a book like *Nicolás Guillén, Popular Poet of the Caribbean* has achieved. He asserts specifically that the cultural alienation which afflicts all Caribbean people demands a therapy of a deep respect for the sui generis Caribbean culture, the music, the food, the dance, and, clearly, the intellectual styles, the theological and philosophical proclivities. Furthermore, Caribbean culture is African and consequently it is inherently theological.

Just as Davis privileges "emancipation," Selwyn R. Cudjoe privileges "resistance." One of his best works is precisely *Resistance and Caribbean Literature*. Another Caribbean scholar, Patrick Taylor, has opted for the term "liberation" as in his *The Narrative of Liberation*. All of these terms bespeak the central engine of Caribbean cultural activity, namely, *cimarronaje*. It is the master Caribbean theoretician, Frantz Fanon, who has established the necessary emancipatory basis for authentic Caribbean culture, as, indeed, for all authentic postcolonial cultures. Davis's unique contribution is the grounding of these central lines of analysis in an unimpeachably Christian theological matrix without doing the slightest disservice to what he calls "The African Soul in Caribbean Religion" (50-67).

Addressing the vexing question of pervasive "dependency," Davis employs the language of correct Christian theology to describe the specifically Caribbean Christology that he has encountered. He sees it as "an active, concrete, and existential Christology. Christ is the mediatorial presence of God the Emancipator." He continues:

> The consistency of Christ in his faithfulness to God, as well as his faithfulness to Caribbean people, is in no doubt at all; and the Christological motivation to be self-determinative, in the light of the will and favor of God, is far more powerful than the fear of repercussions and consequences that might induce the people to compromise their high principles of independence. There must be some built-in religious and political guarantee which lets the world know

> that the Caribbean people are no longer for sale and that their dues have already been paid, not only by their ancestors in slavery but also by their brother Jesus Christ. (82)

Clearly, Christ is presented as the liberator, *cimarrón*, par excellence. Davis is absolutely consistent with orthodox Christian theology, and, as was shown in the preceding chapters, this is entirely consistent with classical African spirituality, which has its roots in Kemet. There is a particularly poignant linkage established in the last sentence of the above quote, namely, "ancestors in slavery" and "brother Jesus Christ." It was pointed out in our first chapter that Christian saints are essentially ancestors, that they, the living dead and the living, are held together in a mystical bond, a mystical organism which is termed in Christian theological parlance The Mystical Body of Christ. Jesus the Christ is the brother, the unifier, the savior of all mankind, and it is only through this Brother that the ancestors and the living interact with each other and with the Almighty. These theological postulates of classical Christianity are "old hat" for "unlettered" grassroots Caribbean people because they spring pure from the African cultural matrix.

Davis comes to the question of pervasive imitation, the "Mimic Men" syndrome in V.S. Naipaul's terms or the *imitamicos* [follow-fashion monkey] of Nicolás Guillén's "West Indies Ltd." This is one of the region's defining demons, and the following approach is presented for its exorcism:

> What is the antidote for such social, religious, and theological imitation, which eats away at the very soul of Caribbean spirituality? The answer lies in the direction of imagination and boldness; of accepting Caribbean realities as endowments of divine creativity, not the results of divine mistakes. . . . This move toward indigeneity would not be new to Caribbean spirituality. . . . The process, then, is one of building an awareness of the Caribbean selfhood, the Caribbean value system, and the Caribbean structure of faith and religious expression, which answers to no external authority for legitimacy or salvific assurance. (85).

This line of thinking echoes the evolving analysis of "West Indian-ness" that we ourselves have proffered. The very term "selfhood" is of great significance in our analysis of a peculiarly Caribbean literary expression undertaken in *Central American Writers of West Indian Origin: A New Hispanic Literature* (1984). The quest for Caribbean selfhood was seen to be especially ardent in the case of the literary activity of the Panamanian writer Cubena (Carlos Guillermo Wilson). The opening chapter of our 1990 study of Nicolás Guillén presented the case for the existence of a peculiarly Caribbean literary theory.

Since for Caribbean people, as for any African or neo-African people, spirituality is inseparable from culture, this indigeneity—what we termed specifically "West Indianness"—in the realm of theology is of the utmost importance. On this question Davis claims that "It is through the grace of God that Caribbean people are able to come to a fresh awareness of who they are called to be, and to renounce all forms of religious imitation as degrading forms of flattery and aspects of spiritual abomination. With Saul of Tarsus, Caribbean people can fully affirm that by the grace of God they are who they are, and that that grace, which was fully bestowed, 'was not bestowed in vain'" (85). The declaration is, then, valid and contributes to the growing body of discursive and creative literature that effects Caribbean liberation, literature that constitutes *cimarronaje*.

Just as *Nicolás Guillén, Popular Poet of the Caribbean* presented itself as an act of literary criticism undergirded by a Caribbean literary theory, Davis attempts a "Praxis for Theological Emancipation" (88-104). Its general parameters are analogous to those of the Caribbean literary theory. Davis poses the question: "Is there a need for an indigenous Caribbean theological methodology; or does such a methodology already exist, needing only to be recognized, affirmed, and proclaimed without apology?" (88). His answer is that "An appropriate theological methodology does not necessarily require the total abandonment of that which is currently employed, but it does require a radical assessment of the needs of the Caribbean constituency which is attempting to interpret the meaning of the Gospel of emancipation in the Caribbean context" (89).

He is proposing fundamentally a Caribbean contextual theology, using those methodologies that have worked for

Eurocentric theological explorations, but cleansed of cultural bias. It is interesting to compare this strategy to the one employed in our 1990 book. Very early in the opening chapter it was made quite clear that Caribbean literature has to be viewed somewhat like Jes Grew of Ishmael Reed's *Mumbo Jumbo* in that it has yet to find its text. Since, it was argued, this is a scribal literature and indisputably a component of world literature, its text, that is, its theory, already exists. To speak of inventing the text as Alejo Carpentier might have put it was to speak loosely.[1] Reed's metaphor was seen as much more in touch with the basic sense of the process. The task of the committed Caribbean critic, it was affirmed, was not to reinvent the wheel, but rather to decide for her/himself what will be the most appropriate way of using the wheel. The key insights of Fanon, among others, are part of the constituent elements of the indigenous literary theory, the "text" that must now be found. In the chapter "Conclusion: Towards a Pan-Caribbean Literature" of our book on Central American writers of West Indian origin, there is a summary of the current state of West Indian literary theory. It is still true that whereas the idea of a Pan-Caribbean culture, identity, and literary theory continues to gain acceptance as a scholarly premise, the consequent rigorous theoretical elaborations have been largely absent.

In seeking to establish an appropriate Caribbean literary hermeneutics, we indicated that there existed a thriving and long-standing popular oral poetry in the Caribbean and that this is constantly being subjected to review and criticism in the most basic, if apparently informal, fashion. The Trinidadian kaiso, the Jamaican reggae, the *plena*, the *bomba* from Puerto Rico, the many Cuban forms, the *son*, the *guaguanco*, the *rumba*, etc., are all examples of this popular poetry that is constantly subjected to the "appreciating principle" of popular taste, that is, to the "implied Caribbean reader/listener." There is, then, it was argued, demonstrably in place a critical apparatus, a Caribbean literary hermeneutics. It assesses all of the literary art that comes before the public; it is the principle that accounts for the popularity of any artistic product.

Subsequent to completing the final version of our manuscript, we found that our theorizing on this matter was confirmed by Henry Louis Gates's further elaboration on the role of the Signifying Monkey as articulated in *The Signifying Monkey: A Theory of African-American Literary Criticism*, published in 1988. Beyond any doubt, Gates posits the existence of a valid African American literary theory, however, the biases of his training, the toxicity of inveterate, hegemonic, white supremacist ideology have seeped into the deep structure of this highly regarded (and apparently similarly recompensed) "authentic" "ethnic" scholar. In his preface he speaks of Roger D. Abrahams, Claudia Mitchell-Kernan, Geneva Smitherman, John Szwed and Bruce Jackson encouraging what Gates with unconscious disingenuousness characterizes as his attempts to "*lift* the discourse of Signifyin(g) from the vernacular to the discourse of literary criticism" (xi, my emphasis). The air of superiority, the trace of the patronizing big-white-brother approach, is confirmed as his exposition proceeds. In the very next paragraph he pays homage to the homespun but valid literary theorizing, the "talk about talking," that black people engage in "in ritual settings such as barbershops and pool halls, street corners and family reunions" (xi). This is precisely the kind of activity that we identified as constituting an authentic Caribbean literary hermeneutics.

However, unlike Gates, we did not see this as merely valid on the "folksy" level and needing the strong guiding hand of a properly trained (that is, versed in a hegemonic Eurocentric hermeneutics) scholar to "lift" up the discourse, to clean up the language, to give class and form to the rough, uncut, potency of barbaric natural forces, albeit emanating from the intellectual realm. The spirit of Domingo F. Sarmiento, as exposed in Chapter One of the present book, is not far from Gates's disquisitions. And Gates ends the paragraph referenced above with the following lines: "Very few black people are not conscious, at some level, of peculiarly black texts of being. These are *our* texts, to be delighted in, enjoyed, contemplated, explicated, and willed through repetition to our daughters and to our sons. I acknowledge my father's capacities, not only to pay him homage but because I learned to read the tradition by thinking intensely about one of its most salient aspects. This is my father's book, even if cast in a language he does not use" (xii). The question that immediately arises is why does Gates think it necessary to "cast" this important book, his "father's book . . . in a language he does not use." The contradiction appears to escape Gates. We, indeed, on the other hand, sought to cast our book in precisely the language that our own father—a Trinidadian man—uses.

We affirmed in our book on Guillén that it is not possible to "demonstrate," in the proper sense of the term, the existence of a Pan-Caribbean identity and culture. The question had to be approached with the spirit of Aimé Césaire's defiant if somewhat immature declaration in the *Cahier*: "Take me as I am. I don't adapt to you" (86). Our approach to Guillén was exactly analogous to the popular approach to the kaiso. For, according to the claim made by the most authoritative voice to emerge so far on the Trinidad and Tobago kaiso, the ultimate determiner of the artistic merits of the genre, is the vox populi. This assertion is made by Raymond Quevedo (1892-1962), one of the leading exponents of the art form, whose nom de guerre was appropriately Atilla the Hun. The claim is made in a book entitled *Atilla's Kaiso: A Short History of Trinidad Calypso*, which was completed shortly after 1951 but did not appear in print until 1983, consequent on the valiant scholarly labors of Errol Hill: "The judges who decided on your excellence or otherwise was [sic] the general public, the sternest and most merciless adjudicators as they have always been since history began" (84). This appreciating principle or indigenous hermeneutics had been invoked indirectly at least in a work such as Rito Llerena Villalobos's on the *vallenato*, which was referenced in Chapter Two of the current book.

□ □ □

The Ancient African Connections

The thrust towards liberation is of its very nature an evolving process, always admitting of improvement, refinements, adjustments. As such Davis's theorizing still needs the firm grounding that comes from a deep knowledge of the classical African civilization which flourished in Kemet, of the amazing connections. The African soul that he clearly perceives at the core of Caribbean spirituality and culture is one that belongs to the folksy realm: "In addition, theological educators cannot afford to ignore Caribbean folk wisdom and cultural history." The "indigenous religious activity" is for him the province of the "underclasses of Caribbean societies" (90). It undoubtedly is their source of "spiritual and cultural power." But, along the lines of Gates's theorizing, which concurred in some respects with the fundamentals of the Sarmiento approach (as was delineated in the last chapter), this power is simply raw potential that can only be fully realized in and through the intellectual frameworks of Western civilization. And so-called "Western" civilization is conceived of as quintessentially Eurocentric, quite distinct from African civilization. Indeed, Davis claims explicitly that in the cases of these indigenous African Caribbean elements, the very soul of Caribbean spirituality and culture, the African "religious and cultural antecedents have not disappeared, even if the outward forms of religious observances have been overtaken by Western traditions" (90).

Certainly, Davis and Gates, along with perhaps the vast majority of African-ancestored intellectuals currently engaged in significant scholarship focused on their reality, have not fully appreciated the import of such works as Yosef ben-Jochannan's *African Origins of the Major "Western Religions,"* or Martin Bernal's two volumes (so far) of *Black Athena: The Afroasiatic Roots of Classical Civilization*, or Cheikh Anta Diop's *The African Origin of Civilization: Myth or Reality*, or Charles S. Finch's *Echoes of the Old Darkland*, or George G. M. James's

Stolen Legacy, or Ivan Van Sertima's many volumes, *Egypt Revisited*, for example. All of these works, and many others, in sum make the compelling argument that so-called "Western civilization" is but a branch of the tree of human culture that is firmly rooted in classical Africa. As such "Western civilization" is neither an improvement on nor a model for those cultures that have evolved in fuller fealty to and closer contact with the source of all human civilization.

Bernal's articulation of the argument is perhaps the least unpalatable to the current academy, for he is the most accommodating of these new scholars. He, however, is the scholar who has cogently described the genesis of the white supremacist perspective on "Western civilization." He unmasks a process which he labels "The Fabrication of Ancient Greece" and which he dates 1785-1985. It is clearly of great significance that the fabrication occurred precisely at the time of the so-called Enlightenment. Bernal makes his point assertively on the first page of his introduction to the first volume:

> These volumes are concerned with two models of Greek History: one viewing Greece as essentially European or Aryan, and the other seeing it as Levantine, on the periphery of the Egyptian and Semitic cultural area. I call them the 'Aryan' and the 'Ancient' models. The 'Ancient Model' was the conventional view among Greeks in the Classical and Hellenistic ages. According to it, Greek culture had arisen as the result of colonization, around 1500 BC, by Egyptians and Phoenicians who had civilized the native inhabitants. Furthermore, Greeks had continued to borrow heavily from Near Eastern cultures.
>
> Most people are surprised to learn that the Aryan Model, which most of us have been brought up to believe, developed only during the first half of the 19th century. . . . According to the Aryan Model, there had been an invasion from the north - unreported in ancient tradition - which had overwhelmed the local 'Aegean' or 'Pre-Hellenic' culture. Greek civilization is seen as the result of the mixture of the Indo-European-speaking Hellenes and their indigenous subjects. It is from the construction of this Aryan Model that I call this volume *The Fabrication of Ancient Greece 1785-1985*. (1-2)

The representatives of the ideology that currently dominates the Western academy have branded the thinkers who dare to challenge their racist assumptions "fantasy historians." It is particularly apt that Bernal would call attention to the fundamentally ideological—as distinct from scientific or objective—nature of Western scholarship on the basic question of the origin of civilization. Ancient Greece, as presented by the Western academy, is a pernicious fabrication construed by conspiracy for the viciously immoral purpose of justifying the unjustifiable, namely, slavery, the slave trade, and the consequent dehumanization, demonization of the majority of mankind.

Scholars like James and ben-Jochannan are considerably less sanguine than Bernal in exposing the academy's cruel hoax. It is Diop, as was pointed out in Chapter One, who achieves the most forceful, rational, and holistic articulation of the challenging theory. There is no need, then, to construct a sui generis Caribbean theology from the raw material of a folksy spirituality preserved in oral tradition, in the "songs, myths, dance, movements, dietary habits, domestic customs, music and even creole technology" of the "underclasses" (90). Experts have only to look and they will find the countless texts of every imaginable aspect of a sui generis Caribbean hermeneutics. They have to understand the importance of the amazing connection to classical African civilization. Lancine Keita claimed with all the care and correction of a budding young scholar in his 1977 article, "African Philosophical Systems: A Rational Reconstruction," that there is a well-defined and easily accessible body of African philosophical writings. "But the bulk of what may be considered a genuine African classical thought is to be found in a set of writings known as the *Hermitica*. There has been some controversy as to the extent of the Egyptian element in the *Hermitica*, but any unbiased study of its contents leaves little doubt that it represents the core of ancient Egypt's philosophical theories, if only because the writings focus exclusively on the religious and philosophical beliefs of the Egyptians" (173). In the two decades that have elapsed since Keita undertook his research for the above referenced article, scholarship has advanced almost by leaps and bounds. Diop, Bernal, James, Finch, Van Sertima, as well as Théophile Obenga, Asa Hilliard, and a whole host of scholars have clearly alerted the academy to the existence of a well-defined, easily accessible, and quite considerable body of African philosophico-theological literature. It is to this corpus that Davis should have turned to undergird a Caribbean theology.

□ □ □

The African-in-the-Americas Connection

Davis prescribed that "Caribbean theological formations . . . seek Christian unity at all levels of the church, as well as Caribbean unity at other levels" (92). The question of Caribbean unity leads naturally into the discussion of the intrinsic and significant interrelatedness between emancipation and *cimarronaje*. The term "emancipation" is privileged over "liberation" because it connotes "that spirituality of freedom" pursued by Caribbean people, and because it "links us existentially with the struggle of our slave ancestors, since we are the inheritors of that struggle" (102-03). Since the Caribbean was the major American port of call for the nefarious triangular trade, it is largely true that these "slave ancestors" were the same for all African peoples in the Americas. Furthermore, it is a given that the common ancestors could only have been "slave ancestors." Even accepting the compelling arguments presented by Van Sertima's *They Came Before Columbus*, those Africans who brought the gift of cultural renewal to the Western Hemisphere starting from the 8th century B.C. could not be posited as common ancestors of the contemporary New World African population. Those bringers of light and leadership would have to be claimed by their spiritual progeny, the Olmecs, the Aztecs, the Incas, the Mayas, etc.

The term "emancipation," then, is synonymous with "*cimarronaje*," and "slave" must be paired with "maroon." Davis is definitely on the right track as he understands fully the importance of the fundamental connectedness of Africans through the ancestors. However, the lenses of his analysis still need some adjusting. He has not attained the exact focus on what he terms so powerfully "The Black Story"; he has not seen clearly that Africa is the cradle not only of the human species, but of human civilization. Davis claims that "The Black Story historically begins in Europe and passes through Africa to the Caribbean and the Americas, where it establishes its ontological rootage" (118). This, however, is only a piece of the picture. A more complete understanding of the drama of contemporary racism can only be attained with a full grasp of the insightful research and writings of such thinkers of our epoch as Diop, Hilliard, James, or Bernal; and those of yesteryear, such as Gerald Massey or Chassebeuf de Volney, whose much cited passage on African Ethiopia was referenced in the opening pages of Chapter One.

The limited parameters Davis has staked out for his sui generis Caribbean theology and biblical hermeneutics still, however, exude a profound respect for the Black Experience and lead to the following affirmation:

> The Black Story is thus a most powerful framework through which Caribbeans and Americans, especially those of African descent, can move forward in an intercultural theological process in the struggle for Christian solidarity and the search for more concrete expressions of human freedom. We can contribute to each other's freedom by the collective engagement in the common discovery of our rich heritage. Most of the tensions that have historically tended to exist between Afro-Caribbeans and African-Americans have resulted from a lack of knowledge about each other—from our reluctance to understand each other's historical and cultural struggles and from our insensitivity in communicating with each other. (126)

A common experience of the working of Christian liberation in a common context of slavery and oppression is posited as the vehicle of unity and fuller insight. Davis's position recalls that of the young Léopold Sédar Senghor, Léon Gontran Damas, and Césaire when they launched their Negritude movement in the Paris of the 1930s. They were "nègres" [niggers] (as distinct from "noirs"[blacks]) and proud to be that. They cheered their "niggerness" in Césaire's poignant voice through the powerful pages of his *Cahier*:

> my Negritude is not a stone, its deafness
> thrown against the clamour of the day
> my Negritude is not a speck of dead water

on the dead eye of earth
  my Negritude is neither a tower nor a cathedral

. . . .

Eia for those who invented nothing
for those who have never discovered
for those who have never conquered

  but, struck, deliver themselves to the essence of all things, (116)

I accept... I accept... totally, without reserve...

  my race which no ablution of hyssop or mixed lilies could purify
  my race eaten by macula
  my race ripe grape for drunken feet
  my queen of spittle and lepers
  my queen of whips and scrofula
  my queen of squasms and chloasms. (128)

Davis urges the Caribbean native to accept himself as he is: "Many of them cannot read, but they are more literate in the Word of God than many an erudite scholar and theologian." In fact, couching his argument with what smacks of sour grapes he declares that "Oral literature is older, more valuable, and more durable than the written species. Furthermore, human history has repeatedly demonstrated that, where the letter kills, the spirit gives life" (123). The road taken is ultimately not as important as the destination, so even this low road leads to Caribbean unity, an African American consciousness, and, indeed, to an incipient Pan-Africanism.

□ □ □

The Caribbean Carnival Connection

One of the axes of Caribbean unity and an enlightened Afro-centricity is precisely carnival. Its incredible hermeneutical wealth can be appreciated through the approach advocated by Davis and realized in our earlier book on Nicolás Guillén. Therein it was argued that, in the first instance, for Caribbean people, as for all people who have been subjected to colonization, the quest for liberation, self-determination, self-affirmation is a force that drives the culture in a fundamental way. Further to this the historical record clearly indicates that in the Caribbean, as in the rest of Afro-America, the literary genius of the masses has found expression principally through oral forms, the Cuban *son* and the Trinidad and Tobago kaiso being two of the many significant forms of Caribbean oral poetry. Pre-Castro Cuba and contemporary Trinidad and Tobago have most of the attributes of the classic "neocolony," and thus *son* and kaiso are the two most interesting indicators of the compelling unity that exists in the rich diversity of contemporary Caribbean society.

For Atilla, in his book referenced earlier on, the kaiso is basically the "work song" of the masked participants who come out onto the streets in organized bands at carnival time. As has been reported for the *congo* groups of Colombia and Panama, these masked players are bent on affirming their root culture, to the point of somewhat belligerent defiance of the prevailing societal norms imposed by the colonial or neocolonial authorities. The kaiso, and all of the artistic forms of its type, employs the call-response format. The accompanying music is characteristically intensely rhythmic, the instruments principally percussive and developed by the local population using aesthetic and technological principles handed down from generation to generation. In this respect the kaiso and all of the many oral literary forms in the Americas that evolved around the carnival celebrations perfectly parallel the "go-go" musical expressions developed by inner city

African North Americans during the 1970s. The kaiso, the "go-go," and all similar forms are manifestations of what Fanon labels a "fighting literature." Errol Hill's *The Trinidad Carnival: Mandate for a National Theatre* proclaims the obvious, and, since there can be no carnival without kaiso, this latter has to be considered also a prime example of "a national literature." Many would argue that Trinidad and Tobago could not be considered a land of revolutions, as say Cuba or Colombia, in spite of the relatively minor political upheavals of 1970 and 1990. Until 1979 Grenada, a land of a remarkably similar culture to that of Trinidad and Tobago, would not have been considered a potentially revolutionary nation. But, any society that has suffered the barbarism of colonization is potentially revolutionary. This is the sense of Fanon's theorizing, and it would not be far-fetched to attribute to the kaiso the third Fanonian quality, namely, that of being "a revolutionary literature" (179).

Nicolás Guillén is the most representative poet of revolutionary Cuba. He was named its *Poeta Nacional* [National Poet]. His work, as our 1990 book demonstrated, has to be deemed a fully legitimate manifestation of "a fighting literature, a revolutionary literature, and a national literature" in the Fanonian sense. Certain scholars, the most representative of whom is Vera M. Kutzinski, have sought to understand and appreciate Guillén entirely within the confines of a militantly Eurocentric perspective. Their efforts, as we indicated before, have borne little fruit. Thus even though with her essay "The Carnivalization of Poetry: Nicolás Guillén's Chronicles" she appears to have grasped the importance of carnival, the carnival she and scholars of her ilk envisage is one bereft of its African roots.

For the past two decades our scholarship has used the label "West Indianness" for the common connecting element in all authentic Caribbean literature. This element derives from the common African cultural heritage and is basically a quest for self-affirmation and liberation, the "resistance" that Cudjoe speaks about with such eloquence. The centrality of the *son* to Guillén's art was an important point of focus. Furthermore, following the masterful intellectual lead of the eminent Zulu poet, Mazisi

Kunene—who during the early 70s was the unofficial but real mentor of many of the African-ancestored graduate students at the University of California, Los Angeles—much attention has been given to the close ties between the *son* and the kaiso as well as the *beguin*, the merengue, the reggae, etc. In fact, our writings over the past two decades have outlined the clear relationship between kaiso, *son*, and carnival. The analyses penned by Kutzinski and company are, then, ultimately derivative and serve, in fact—irony of ironies—to corroborate the validity of this fundamentally Afrocentric approach to Guillén and, indeed, to all Caribbean cultural expressions.

The *son* and the kaiso, it can be asserted, play profoundly the same but accidentally different roles in the process of *cimarronaje* that constitutes the bedrock of Caribbean culture. Atilla's chapter "State Interference" speaks eloquently to the fighting history of kaiso and carnival. During the days of slavery, Africans could be openly prohibited from developing their cultural expressions, even those that on the surface resembled the European carnival festivities. However, upon emancipation "free coloureds and the ex-slaves could no more be restricted or debarred from freely taking part in these celebrations." But "interference assumed a new form," principally the subjecting of the institution "to the venomous fire of press, pulpit and state" (55). The most intense manifestation of the confrontation between African masses, adhering doggedly to their cultural traditions, and the colonial government were the much discussed canboulay riots of 1881 that ensued when the colonial police forces moved in to interrupt the central street dancing activity. This event is considered a watershed in the history of the cultural development in Trinidad and Tobago. It contains a message that is frequently lost. The "cannes brulées" [burnt cane] harvest celebrations were an occasion for a carnival type activity, but this activity was clearly not restricted to nor essentially derived from the European pre-Lenten revelries.

A careful analysis of these important historical data would support the thesis of the merely superficial, accidental—typically syncretic—relationship between the European, largely Latin, carnival and the festival that has developed among Africans in the

Americas. In fact, the canboulay riots of 1881 took place not during the pre-Lenten period but rather in August, another period of "cannes brulées" or sugarcane-harvest activities. Furthermore, it is clear that what the African masses celebrated at this August canboulay was, indeed, the anniversary of their emancipation. Anyone who grew up in Trinidad and Tobago in the 50s can vividly recall the tension that surrounded the August carnival celebrations. They were merely tolerated by the authorities, but were considered a "God-given" right by the people of Trinidad and Tobago. The act of taking to the streets in processional dance was and continues to be seen instinctively by all Trinidadians and Tobagonians—and certainly by many other, if not all, African-ancestored peoples—as a natural expression. It is the most appropriate way of effecting any celebration, from that of a victory in a soccer match between two archrival secondary schools to that of manifesting the joyful Christmas spirit. True to the Fanonian model of the Manichean colonial situation, these manifestations are seen as inherently "pagan," "barbaric," "uncivilized," "evil," "sinful," "uncouth," etc. etc. They are suppressed with all possible brutality by the colonial masters and their local agents.

The full significance of the profound self-affirmation that carnival represents can only be appreciated through a review of its deepest roots, which go back to the very dawn of human history, literally, from time immemorial. Indeed, Atilla's review of the history of the form points ineluctably to its African origin. The original kaiso singers, the chantwells or lead singers of the carnival bands, functioned in exactly the same way as the lead singers, also called chantwells, of the work gangs. One of the most characteristic of the carnival band songs was the kalenda, a particularly vigorous, almost aggressive, chant in the usual call-response mode that was associated with the stickfighting bands. The following is a sample that has been cited by Atilla:

Ja Ja Romey Eh
Ja Ja Romey Shango

Ja Ja Romey Eh Mete Beni
Ja Ja Romey Shango. (6)

With the reference to Shango it can be assumed that the language of the piece is Yoruba. The overtly theological theme expressed in an African language recalls those few samples of popular oral literature extant from slavery days in Cuba that have been anthologized in Rosa E. Valdés-Cruz's useful collection, *La poesía negoride en America* (83-85) [Negrista Poetry in the Americas]. However, as a sample it is extremely rare, for French Creole, a new African language, is, according to the overwhelming weight of the evidence, the original language of the kaiso.

As was argued in Chapter One, it may be reasonably asserted that all of the essential features of carnival are more profoundly rooted in Kemet than was commonly believed heretofore. The German anthropologist Alexander Orloff in a long essay, "Time outside of Time: The Mythological Origin of Carnival," has presented an interpretation of carnival that parallels the preceding approach in some ways. This interpretation was brought to our attention in a manner that should be recorded, for it attests to the growing sense among Caribbean peoples, academic and nonacademic alike, of the central importance of carnival. It was proffered by a Trinidadian friend, a highly educated professional, but not a trained anthropologist, someone who participates in carnival in the most intense fashion—returning yearly, taking leave of his professional life in Washington, D.C., to Trinidad for the celebration. Orloff's scholarship is fatally flawed by the compartmentalization, the tunnel vision of white supremacist thinking. This ideological persuasion leads him to miss the big picture. He is content to posit the vaguely identified "common human essence" as the source of certain profoundly similar elements in all carnivalesque celebrations throughout the world. His ideological commitment proscribes his investigating any lines of influence lest these lead back to Africa. In this respect Orloff is representative of all Eurocentric scholars, even the ones of good will, and even the ones who are African-ancestored.

The Trinidadian novelist, Earl Lovelace, has exquisitely tapped the artistic potential of the essential "warriorhood" (a word that he himself uses) of the carnival tradition. His novels, *The Dragon Can't Dance* (1979) and *The Wine of Astonishment* (1982), exude the sense of the centrality of kaiso and carnival to Caribbean culture, this culture being one of resistance, essentially a *cimarronaje*. The *Dragon* chronicles the tragic loss of virility in an entire community of once authentic Caribbean folk. The central symbol is the dragon's (Aldrick's) metamorphosis from folk hero from the "Hill," rooted in the virile, vibrant carnival tradition of the masses, to anachronism, a misfit in the new post-"independence" society.

> Up on the Hill Carnival Monday morning breaks upon the backs of these thin shacks . . . sweeping yards in a ritual, heralding the masqueraders' coming, that goes back centuries for its beginnings, back across the Middle Passage. . . .
>
> . . . Once upon a time the entire Carnival was expressions of rebellion. Once there were stickfighters who assembled each year to keep alive in battles between themselves the practice of warriorhood born in them; and there were devils, black men who blackened themselves further with black grease to make of their very blackness a menace, a threat. . . .
>
> . . . Aldrick felt a tallness and a pride, felt his hair rise on his head, felt: 'No, this ain't no joke. This is warriors going to battle. This is the guts of the people, their blood; this is the self of the people that they screaming out they possess, that they scrimp and save and whore and work and thief to drag out of the hard rockstone and dirt to show the world they is people.'. . . [They are a] people before whom and on whose behalf he could dance the dragon. . . .
>
> For two full days Aldrick was a dragon in Port of Spain, moving through the loud, hot streets, dancing the bad-devil dance, dancing the stickman dance. . . . He was Manzanilla, Calvary Hill, Congo, Dahomey, Ghana. He was Africa, the ancestral Masker, affirming the power of the warrior, prancing and bowing, breathing out fire. (120-23)

Lovelace's artful poetic prose needs no commentary. The full sense and power of his vision is made manifest, as the novel enters its concluding phase, through the words of the bright young lawyer who works on behalf of Aldrick and eight brother defendants accused of heading a rebellion:

> 'The authorities trusted these men to fail. . . . They trusted that they would be unable to make of their frustration anything better than a dragon dance, a threatening gesture. . . .
>
> 'The action undertaken by these men was an attempt to not even seize power, as we have seen, but to affirm a personhood for themselves, and beyond themselves, to proclaim a personhood for people deprived and

> illegitimized as they: the people of the Hill, of the slums and shanty towns. (183)

In jail Aldrick and company see clearly that "their efforts at rebellion was just a dragon dance." Fisheye, one of the group of nine codefendants that included Aldrick, comments: "'We really play a mas', eh, Aldrick? You couldn't play a better dragon'" (186).

The later novel, *The Wine of Astonishment*, ends on a note of optimism that really glosses over a deeper systemic sense of tragedy. The warrior figure par excellence, the badjohn (thug) Bolo, suffers from the same obsolescence as do Aldrick and the other eight of the earlier novel. In fact, Bolo's obsolescence is literally terminal—he is killed. The authentic Afro-Christian Spiritual Baptist group loses its vitality after years of brutal persecution by the colonial authorities and their local agents. Dancing is an important, indeed, central metaphor and symbol in this novel as well, for it is the activity by which the Spiritual Baptists make manifest the fullness of their religious life, reflected in possession by the Spirit. As the first-person narrator, the wife of the religious leader, makes her way home after a failed attempt to call down the Spirit, she muses:

> Then, as we turn the corner where Miss Hilda living . . . in the next yard there, with bamboo for posts and coconut branches for a roof, is a steelband tent . . . and playing these pans is some young fellows, bare-back and with tear-up clothes . . . I listening to the music; for the music that those boys playing on the steelband have in it the same Spirit that we miss in our church: the same Spirit; and listening to them, my heart swell and it is like resurrection morning. I watch Bee, Bee watch me. I don't say nothing to him and he don't say nothing to me, the both of us bow, nod, as if, yes, God is great, and like if we passing in front of something holy. (146)

The novel ends with the final words of the quote above. The thoughtful reader of Lovelace will, however, be devastated by the realization that the "bare-back" boys referred to will grow into Aldricks and presumably Bolos.[2]

It was further argued in the chapter, "The Poet," of our book on Guillén that not just in structure and language, but as well in terms of the very function, poetry is for Guillén exactly what it is for the culture of the region. Keenly aware of the significance of his art, the poet declared in a 1930 interview: "Mis *poemas sones* me sirven además para reivindicar lo único que nos va quedando que sea verdaderamente nuestro" (Augier 91) [My *son* poems serve me as a means of giving due recognition to the only remaining aspect of our culture that is truly ours]. He is the *sonero*—creator of songs—par excellence, his most important book being *El son entero* [The Complete *son*]. The term "kaisonian" would be rendered in Spanish "*kaisero.*" Thus the title is exactly analogous to one such as *The Complete Kaiso* for a Trinidadian poet, or *The Complete Reggae* for a Jamaican. Kutzinski ascribes central importance to the poem "Sensemayá," (de)constructing a convoluted interpretation (Kutzinski 136-45) flowing from the fact that the work is based on a carnival song and dance used during the *Día de Reyes* [Feast of the Epiphany] festival. It is of great significance that this Cuban carnival took place on January 6. It was one of the occasions on which the barbaric slave owners permitted their captives to perform the rituals of their native African cultures/religions. The fact that these rituals resembled the Latin style carnival points not only to their common classical African source but to the relative, contextual, nature of their function. In other words, whether or not the period of permitted festivity corresponded with the period of Latin carnival, Africans in the Caribbean—and, obviously, elsewhere in the New World as well—developed a carnivalesque style of celebration. It can be asserted with confidence, then, that this style was both native to them and considered to be of profound cultural/religious importance.

Atilla uncovered many important Pan-Caribbean features of the kaiso. Any such features must of necessity flow from the Pan-African essence of Caribbean culture and must be seen as markers of Pan-Americanism. This is not what Atilla argues, however. He sees them as a direct consequence of the actual contacts established by the African peoples who inhabited the various islands, through the inter-island shipping activity between the territories ruled by Britain. This shipping activity was driven by the self-interest of the

British colonial machine and not by any cultural imperative of the colonized masses. Thus the popular poetic traditions of islands like St. Vincent, Grenada, Jamaica, and Barbados influenced the kaiso. But he determines that the "musical affinity between the kaisos from French speaking territories with those of Trinidad . . . should lead to the clear conclusion that the distinctiveness of the Trinidad kaiso may be attributed, in large part, to the stimulus of French influence in our cultural heritage" (19). His argument is posited on the observation that kaisos from Jamaica and Barbados evince a certain "correctness of measurement," a certain "rather staid, prim and proper melodic structure." This is in marked contrast to those others which, he affirms, come from

> other territories [presumably the French-speaking ones along with Trinidad and] show a tendency to have acceleration and deceleration of tempo, a lively, vivacious melodic structure, a certain rhythmic unevenness including departure from the return to rhythm, breaking and remeshing the words with music, a rendering of the half beat which makes kaiso music of a certain type so difficult to score (no doubt connected with the drum accompaniment of a former period also used in kalenda and congo) and a nuance in presentation which are some of the identifiable characteristics found in the Trinidad kaiso. (19)

Atilla's flawed analysis is particularly instructive, for it errs precisely because he is unaware of the "amazing connections" that are the subject matter of this work. It is especially ironic that this man whose very person serves as one of those privileged connectors between Hispanophone and Anglophone Africana would miss the common Africana essence and focus on an accidental link that is the Francophone one. He found a differential staidness or prim and proper quality in the oral literature of Jamaica and Barbados that must be attributed (if they do in fact exist) to a deviation from the common African model. Such adulterations are not uncommon in the expressions of colonized natives slumped in the first, the Capitulation phase (see pp. 106-07). Atilla, whose real name was Raymond Quevedo, was the son of a Trinidadian mother and a Venezuelan father. One of his most famous contemporaries was Phillip Garcia, both of whose parents were Venezuelan. The four-string guitar that we Anglophone Trinidadians call a *cuatro*, is correctly identified by Atilla as a "South American instrument" (11). It is one of the basic instruments of the kaiso singer. The island of Trinidad nestles close to the Venezuelan shore, and Venezuela is contiguous to Colombia, along the Caribbean littoral.

A scholar sensitive to the amazing connections would immediately perceive the deep resonances of the geographic, the cultural, indeed, intimately biographical reality. The first chapter, "From Kaiso to *Son* and Beyond," of our 1990 book explores these resonances. Carpentier in his pivotal study *La música en Cuba* [Music in Cuba] highlighted the polyrhythmic drum poetry of the quintessentially Cuban form, the *son*. All of the characteristics indicated by Carpentier mirrored not only those identified by Atilla as common to the kaisos from Trinidad and Tobago and the French-speaking territories, but those described by Senghor (one of the three original founders of the Negritude movement) as defining characteristics of African rhythm, namely, vitality, syncopation, irregularity, unity in diversity. For Senghor these are the distinguishing features of North American "swing." It would be unrealistic to have expected Atilla to see the Cuban connection. The Colombian-Venezuelan link, however, should have been obvious to him. Llerena Villalobos's *Memoria cultural en el vallenato: Un modelo de textualidad en la canción folclórica colombiana* (1984) [Cultural Content in the *Vallenato*: A Model for Intertextuality in the Colombian Folk Song] is a fine example of Caribbean literary criticism. It focuses on the *vallenato*, a popular Colombian oral literary form, bearing a startling resemblance to the kaiso, that is the typical music of Colombia's northern costal (Caribbean) section, between Venezuela to the east and Panama to the west. Gabriel García Márquez was born here, and this is where he places his Macondo. This is his principal artistic source, for he proudly proclaims himself to be a Caribbean man.

Llerena provides a laboriously worked out and quite exhaustive listing of the features of the oral literary form itself as well as the sociocultural environment which nurtured it. These features include what he terms, in the unenlightened language of Eurocentric anthropology, a syncretic, animistic, fetishistic and superstitious religiosity. He also points to the custom of passing down carnival roles from generation to generation: "El señor Víctor Camarillo, de Valledupar, todos los años para la época del carnaval se disfraza de diablo; esta tradición la heredó de familiares que le antecedieron" (27) [Mr. Victor Camarillo, from Valledupar, every year plays devil for carnival; this tradition was handed down to him from family members who preceded him]. Lovelace's Aldrick Prospect is deeply conscious too of this primordial connectedness. He fully understands that the ritual of carnival "goes back centuries for its beginnings, back across the Middle Passage" (*The Dragon* 120). What Lovelace views insightfully as "warriorhood," Llerena sees as "enfrentamiento competitivo" (28) [competitive confrontation], a spirit that pervades the cultural environment of the land of the *vallenato*, that is, of Caribbean Colombia.

There is a feature of this Colombian culture unearthed by Llerena that we deemed in our book on Guillén to be "of stunning Pan-Caribbean relevance" (18). It is proclaimed in the verse:

> Es mi pueblo costumbrista
> gran gallero y cumbiambero
> trompeador, mamagallista
> que es la creencia de mis abuelos. (98)
>
> [My people believe in their customs
> their cock fighting and their cumbia.
> They are macho and great mamaguyers,
> and this is how it was with my grandparents.]

The "Trinidadian" term "mamaguy" comes from Colombia. This bit of information is a shocking surprise to most people from Trinidad and Tobago, even to the scholars. It would not be news to any researcher who is aware of the amazing connections. Indeed, our chapter, "The Smartman," of the book on Guillén makes the point that some kind of "mamaguying," "picong," *choteo*, "giving fatigue," "signifying," etc. is essential to the culture of most, if not all the communities of African-ancestored peoples that have developed in the Americas.

The accordion is the musical instrument of choice for the *vallenato*. Analogously, the music of Trinidad and Tobago carnival is steelband music. Carnival and its music have always been expressions of *cimarronaje*, emancipation, liberation, etc., and have always been proscribed legally, morally, and socially by the barbaric colonial machine. Llerena cites this revealing declaration by one of his informants:

> Además los creadores e intérpretes de vallenatos eran gentes del campo, poetas primitivos que apenas sí sabían leer y escribir y que ignoraban por completo las leyes de la música. Tocaban de oídas el acordéon, que nadie sabía cuándo ni por dónde les había llegado y las familias encopetadas de la región consideraban que los cantos vallenatos eran cosas de peones descalzos y si acaso muy buenas para entretener borrachos pero no para entrar con la pata en el suelo en casas decentes. (38)
>
> [Furthermore, the creators and interpreters of *vallenatos* were country folks, primitive poets who could hardly read nor write, and who were completely ignorant of the laws of music. They played by air the accordions which they had acquired from God knows where, and the better-off families of the region considered the *vallenato* songs to be the province of barefoot peasants, just good enough perhaps to entertain drunks but not ever under any circumstances to cross the threshold of a decent home.]

Lovelace's celebration of the "bare-back" boy "with tear-up clothes" that brings closure to *The Wine of Astonishment* was itself an act of defiance of the prevailing standards. Clearly these same Eurocentric standards prevail in Caribbean Colombian society.

They prevail too in Ecuador as Nelson Estupiñán Bass makes clear in his 1981 novel *Bajo el cielo nublado* [Under an Overcast Sky]. The "marimba, a wooden xylophone—a popular musical instrument of the African-ancestored population of his native province of Esmeraldas," is shown to suffer the same fate as the steelband and the accordion in their respective societies (Smart, *Guillén* 20). In *La jornada novelística de Nelson Estupiñán Bass: búsqueda de la perfección* [Nelson Estupiñán Bass's Novelistic

Craft: A Search for Perfection], Henry J. Richards argues that the personification of the marimba is an instance of Estupiñán's use of characteristically neo-African aesthetic features (127-29). Indeed, the Ecuadorian novelist achieved a particularly felicitous Afro-centric expression, harmoniously fusing form and content. Focusing on the sociopolitical relevance of the text, we affirmed that when the marimba speaks of itself—for in this experimental and very beautiful work certain inanimate objects and elements of nature are allowed to make their voices heard—it says: "Vine de Africa, en el equipaje espiritual del negro" (*Bajo el cielo nublado*15) [I came from Africa, part of the Black man's cultural baggage]. Furthermore, in the epilogue of the work when the normally voiceless elements are again given voice, the marimba tells of a campaign to banish "la marimba y toda la despreciable música africana" (*Bajo el cielo nublado* 227) [the marimba and all other forms of disgusting African music] from the province.

The preceding discussion served to show that the processes of colonization and white supremacy are the same throughout the world. The barbaric system is posited on the dehumanization of the African and the Asiatic. In the specific case of the African in the Americas there are many instances of the dehumanizing, de-legitimizing of authentic expressions of black culture by the hegemonic Eurocentric minority: from jazz to go-go, from carnival to Kumina, from *son* to kaiso and beyond.

□ □ □

Cimarronaje as Emancipation or Liberation

Emancipation, *cimarronaje*, liberation, and resistance undergird Caribbean culture, forge Caribbean unity and a legitimate Pan-Africanism in a way that is direct and apparent to the observer. For, as Davis points out, emancipatory spirituality has created a long line of Caribbean heroes, freedom fighters, *cimarrones*. Indeed, the resistance struggle in the Caribbean as in the rest of Afro-America is spiritually rooted and Davis rightly concludes:

> Fourth, we need to acknowledge each other's *heroes and heroines*. Apart from Malcolm X and Martin Luther King, Jr., very few Afro-American heroes are known to people in the Caribbean; and more portraits of John F. Kennedy adorn the homes of Caribbean families than of Martin Luther King, Jr. Fannie Lou Hamer, Mary McCleod Bethune, and other heroines are not heard about. From the Caribbean side, no heroes and heroines ever seem to appear on the horizon, especially since Caribbean heroes usually are cricket players, and cricket is neither played nor understood in the United States to any great extent. Political heroes in the Caribbean tend to be localized, so that their capacity to inspire large sectors of people across the seas is minimal. Clearly, we need to affirm the Black Story and its intercultural connections in a much more popular and demonstrable way. (128)

As the discussion in the next two chapters will make clear, Manuel Zapata Olivella and Quince Duncan have attended fully to every aspect of Davis's prescriptions. Our own discussion of Guillén's literary art includes an entire chapter on "The Hero." Therein Guillén is presented as one of the most effective agents for Caribbean cultural unity through *cimarronaje*. Since he was born in 1902, his life is exactly contemporaneous with that of the independent, or more precisely, postcolonial, Cuban nation. His native land came into being as a nation only with the defeat of Spain in 1898, in what has been called the Spanish-American war. The full potential of the new historical situation was only formalized through the Platt Amendment, by which the United States became the undisguised neocolonial power exercising open control over the very Constitution of the Republic established on May 20, 1902.[3] For all the talk and, indeed, the sentiment of nationhood and uniqueness, Cuba, which had been totally vanquished and brutally colonized with the arrival of Columbus, remained in this state of languor until 1959. Its history, then, exactly parallels that of the smaller English-speaking islands of the Caribbean, for many of them too emerged from colonial status in the sixth to seventh decade of the current century.

Guillén's life as man and artist was seen to fit neatly into the schema developed by Fanon in *The Wretched of the Earth*, and later refined by Amilcar Cabral into the full-blown Dialectical Theory of Identification.[4] According to that Theory there are three basic phases in the development of a native artist or intellectual, namely, Capitulation, Revitalization, and Radicalization. In the Capitulation phase the native is fully assimilated. Such was the young Guillén, a postmodernist Latin American poet, a faithful disciple of the Eurocentric Nicaraguan Rubén Darío, who is considered one of the founding fathers of modern Latin American literature. Guillén began to awaken from colonial slumber in 1922 when he abandoned his law studies. It was not until 1930, shortly after meeting the African North American Langston Hughes, a light-skinned Black like himself, that the Cuban moved properly into the Revitalization phase. As was the case with Trumper at the end of George Lamming's *In the Castle of My Skin*, the expression "my people" took on new meaning for Guillén. This second phase is merely transitory and is soon followed by the Radicalization or "the fighting phase." We deemed Guillén to have entered into Radicalization in 1934 with the writing of "West Indies Ltd."

However, it is the poem "Sabás," dedicated to Langston Hughes, that most powerfully expresses the spirit of the new phase. It begins:

> Yo vi a Sabás, el negro sin veneno,
> pedir su pan de puerta en puerta.
> ¿Por qué, Sabás, la mano abierta?
> (Este Sabás es un negro bueno.) (1: 140)
>
> [I saw Sabás, the innocuous Negro,
> begging his bread from door to door.
> Why, Sabás, the open hand?
> (This Sabás is a good Negro.)]

And builds up to a vigorous invitation to revolutionary action:

> Coge tu pan, pero no lo pidas;
> coge tu luz, coge tu esperanza cierta
> como a un caballo por las bridas.
> Plántate en medio de la puerta,

pero no con la mano abierta,
ni con tu cordura de loco:
. . . .

¡Caramba, Sabás, que no se diga!
. . . .
La muerte, a veces, es buena amiga,
y el no comer, cuando es preciso
para comer, el pan sumiso,
tiene belleza. El cielo abriga.
. . . .
¡Caramba, Sabás, no seas tan loco!
¡Sabás, no seas tan bruto,
ni tan bueno! (1: 141)

[Get up and get your bread, don't just beg for it;
get up and get your light, your true hope,
grab hold of the reins, man.
Plant yourself squarely in the door,
but not with an outstretched hand,
nor with your crazy good behavior:
. . . .

Dammit, Sabás, get yourself together!
. . . .
Death, at times, can be a good friend,
and hunger, if eating means having
to swallow the bread of submission,
can be beautiful. Heaven protects us.
. . . .
Dammit, Sabás, don't be so crazy!
Sabás, don't be so stupid,
don't be so good!]

We argue that by joining the Communist Party in 1937 Guillén moved his Radicalization into a "post-race-conscious stage" that had not been envisaged by the Theory. However, the poem dedicated to Jesús Menéndez, a real-life Cuban hero, is the poet's most enduring expression of the *cimarronaje* that drives his creativity. And this poem, the first version of which was completed in 1951, three years after the assassination of Jesús, did not take final form until 1958. It thus belongs definitively to the post-

Dialectical-Theory-of-Identification stage. Jesús is a modern Caribbean hero sprung from the sugarcane fields. Like Toussaint L'Ouverture and all the masters of resistance in the long list of *cimarrones*, the focus of his action is the plantation, "the sugar plantation and Negro slavery" that C.L.R. James (391) has identified as the central shaping elements of Caribbean—and indeed, if Zapata Olivella is right, all American—societies. Furthermore, Jesús's heroicity irradiates the entire sweep of what José Martí termed "Nuestra América" [Our America], from "la punta sur de nuestro mapa" [the southern point of our map] to the frozen north, including "Washington y Nueva York, donde bulle el festín de Baltasar" (1: 431) [Washington and New York, where the sounds of Baltasar's orgy spew forth]. Guillén fashions his hero's action on the model employed by Zapata Olivella and Duncan, for Jesús is poetically transformed into both Shango and the Christian Messiah, his divine namesake.

It could appear that Davis has misread the impact of true Caribbean heroes on the Pan-Caribbean society for he claims that "political heroes" have tended "to be localized" (128). Localized or not, these true heroes have a powerful impact, in Davis's terminology, "from below." His argument is as usual quite compelling:

> To be fully human is to be fully emancipated, and no one can properly grant such a condition from the outside. Thus, Caribbean history is replete with twentieth-century attempts to discover what emancipation from below entails concretely. The names of Marcus Garvey, Uriah Butler, Robert Bradshaw, Albert Marryshow, Norman Manley, Fidel Castro, Maurice Bishop, Walter Rodney, Errol Barrow, Grantley Adams, and Vere Cornwall Bird must find a place among others in the long list of Caribbean practitioners of emancipation. They have tried—each in his own way—to work out historically what it all means. Early in this century, for example, we find Marcus Garvey calling for a second emancipation, an emancipation of the mind. (132)

We had asserted in our 1990 book that since it is almost axiomatic that a people's literature would "exalt the peculiar values and the representative personalities of that culture, it is only to be expected that Caribbean popular literature abounds with celebrations of popular regional heroes" (Smart, *Guillén* 121). We demonstrated that the region's heroic figures have all been precisely *cimarrones*. We affirmed that the main character of Césaire's *Et Les chiens se taisaient* [And the Dogs Were Silent], "Le Rebelle," is essentially the same figure as Henri Christophe in his *La tragédie du roi Christophe* [The Tragedy of King Christophe]. Paul Bogle, who rose up to resist Jamaica's post-Emancipation plantation system is celebrated in Vic Reid's poetic and linguistically essential Caribbean novel, *New Day*. The marvelous life of Nanny the maroon is sung by the Jamaican Lorna Goodison in her second book of poetry, *I Am Becoming My Mother*. The Gerardo Maloney poem, "En 1920" [In 1920] (signed, Panamá 1980), majestically enthrones a twentieth century *cimarrón* who arose from the shackles of a most peculiar version of the plantation that was the Panama Canal:

> Preston Stoute
> Maestro barbadiense y dirigente de la gesta [5]
>
> [Preston Stoute
> Barbadian school teacher and leader of the feat.]

"Another contemporary West Indian Panamanian writer, Carlos Guillermo Wilson, has as his clear objective—patently so—the same exalting of the forgotten heroes, the recounting of passages [as Maloney 20 puts it] 'casi jamás contadas' [almost never recounted] of his nation's historical record. Thus his first novel, *Chombo*, functions as a roll call of the heroic masses who resisted the present-day Panamanian plantation system" (Smart, *Guillén* 123).

□ □ □

The essential emancipatory thrust of popular (grassroots) Caribbean literature is certainly recognized by Davis. He terms it "emancipation from below" and declares that "it was already on the way long before the other form was eventually decreed." He adds: "The persistence of the African soul in Caribbean religion is therefore a concrete testimony to the reality of emancipation from below" (136). My book demonstrated that Nicolás Guillén was an agent of this process not only as a creator of heroes but as a flesh-and-blood hero in his own right. We have shown, too, that many other poets from the entire Caribbean area share with Guillén the commitment to create Caribbean heroines and heroes. The list we have proffered is by no means exhaustive. In recent years there have arisen significant numbers of writers in Cuba, for example, whose dedication to liberation is even more intense. Our analysis serves, then, only to open the door on the amazing connections, understanding that the process of exploration will be a long one involving many scholars. In this regard the links between scribal and oral poets are incontrovertible. Guillén and the others can be considered scribal literary versions of a Celia Cruz, a Beny More, a Bob Marley, a Mighty Sparrow, a Black Stalin, among many others.

Emancipation, liberation, *cimarronaje*, resistance are central to authentic Caribbean culture. They are grounded in the African tradition which is fundamentally spiritual, integrated into the religious experience of the people. This religious experience can be either pre- or post-Christian. Furthermore, this religious experience is the core not only of Caribbean unity, but of the basic unity of all African peoples living in the Americas.

4

Changó the *Cimarrón*

Nicolás Guillén was shown in the preceding chapter to be eminently liberationist in his life and literature. Much of the necessary theoretical discussion of the concept of liberation in the Caribbean context was culled from Kortright Davis's work. More so than Guillén, more so than any of the Caribbean writers from any part of the region, two contemporary Hispanophone Africana writers from Latin America, Manuel Zapata Olivella, from Colombia, and Quince Duncan, from Costa Rica, merit consideration for being the most liberationist of the Hispanophone Caribbean writers best known (or more precisely, least ignored) by the mainstream North American academy. It is worthy of note that both of these authors have been overlooked by Davis, Selwyn Cudjoe, and even Patrick Taylor, another Anglophone Caribbean scholar who has framed his approach to the literature of his peers in precisely liberationist terms. His 1989 book is entitled *The Narrative of Liberation*. This current chapter of our book will focus on Zapata Olivella's sterling contribution, the following will discuss the singular merits of Quince Duncan. They will show how these contemporary Hispanophone Africana writers through their fiction have created an aesthetic and a view of the world that attest to the validity and relevance of the theories advanced in Chapter Three.

Zapata Olivella was born in the town of Lorica in the province of Córdoba on March 17, 1920 and has enjoyed a long and distinguished career as a writer. However, it was not until the publication of his 1983, *Changó, el gran putas* [Shango, the baddest SOB] (the significance of this title, and indeed the question of the appropriate English translation will be treated later on in this chapter), that he attained the fullness of liberation literature. Appropriate appreciation of this monumental work can only be achieved by situating it in the context of Zapata's total literary production. It must be stated from the outset that Zapata is legitimately a Caribbean writer. He was born in and is a cultural son of Colombia's Caribbean region, the region of the *vallenato*, the same region that gave physical and, above all, spiritual birth to Gabriel García Márquez. Zapata is a fully qualified physician and, to all intents and purposes, has sacrificed the practice of his profession to the pursuit of liberating knowledge and creativity. He is a full-time folklorist, essayist, novelist, and globetrotter. He describes himself as an *andariego* (a poetic designation for "vagabond"). His globetrotting does not preclude his rootedness as a Colombian and more precisely as a *bogotano* (resident of the capital, Bogotá). The scholar who has best captured the essence of Zapata's literary genius is Yvonne Captain Hidalgo, whose book, *The Culture of Fiction in the Works of Manuel Zapata Olivella*, was recently published.

The trajectory of Zapata's published writings bespeaks the singular importance of his 1983 novel. Richard L. Jackson was the first North American scholar to focus the attention of the academy on the works of writers like Zapata Olivella and the other significant African-ancestored contributors to the corpus of contemporary Latin American literature. Of the Afro-Hispanists who can be considered Jackson's intellectual progeny, it was Marvin A. Lewis who for many years headed the list of experts on Zapata. Lewis, in his 1987 book, *Treading the Ebony Path: Ideology and Violence in Contemporary Afro-Colombian Prose Fiction*, conveniently sums up the Colombian's contribution as follows: "In addition to a volume of short stories, his publications include seven novels:

The Drenched Earth (1947), *10th Street* (1960), *Behind the Mask* (1963), *Chambacú, a Black Ghetto* (1963), *In Chimá a Saint is Born* (1964), *Changó, the Great SOB* (1983) and *El fusilamiento del Diablo* (The Execution of the Devil, 1986)" (85).

Almost twenty years elapsed between the appearance of *Changó* and that of the immediately preceding work. There is also a considerable—albeit not quite as extensive—gap between the first and second novels. This latter phenomenon, however, is not unusual in the earlier years of a writer's development as she or he seeks to find and refine her or his true voice. The years between 1964 and 1983 represented for Zapata a period of excruciatingly painstaking preparation for the producing of his most profound expression, the summation of his creativity, the veritable raison d'etre of his artistic existence. This is his magnum opus of "liberation literature," an example of what Frantz Fanon in *The Wretched of the Earth*, called "a fighting literature, a revolutionary literature, and a national literature" (179). The novel in question, like every cultural expression emanating from an oppressed group—African or otherwise—is self-consciously liberationist; it speaks about liberation. More importantly, built on demonstrably African aesthetic principles, it affirms the existence and validity of a peculiar and systematic African culture; it acts out the liberation about which it speaks.

Zapata's creative intention is quite clear: his novel is meant to construct an African mythological framework that will explicate not merely his fictional universe but, more pertinently, the real world. The novel is made up of five parts, the first of which is "Los Orígenes" [Origins], and the opening section of this part, entitled "La Tierra de los Ancestros" [Land of the Ancestors], is basically a long epic poem declaimed by Ngafúa, a mythical ancestor. The Cuban-born intellectual Alejo Carpentier, in his prologue to the original 1949 edition of the pivotal novel *El reino de este mundo* [The Kingdom of This World], insightfully proclaimed that "la historia de América toda" [the history of all the Americas] was nothing but "una crónica de lo real-maravilloso" (17) [a chronicling of marvelous reality]. This premise is one of the central elements of what became known as magical realism, which itself became the rage, the aesthetic approach of choice in Latin American letters.

As is the case with all of the approaches and premises that have been accepted uncritically by the mainstream, it is important to view the magical realism theory through the prism of a balanced, Afrocentric or multicultural perspective. To his credit Carpentier himself led the way in this kind of self-correction, judging his first Afro-Cuban novel, *Écue-Yamba-Ó* published in 1933, to have missed the mark in terms of authenticity. In his October 1975 prologue to the 1977 Havana reedition of the work, he speaks candidly of that work's shortcomings:

> *Écue-Yamba-Ó*, libro que se resiente de todas las angustias, desconciertos, perplejidades y titubeos que implica el proceso de un aprendizaje. . . . La época [vanguardista], las tendencias afirmadas en manifiestos estrepitosos, la fiebre renovadora . . . nos imponían sus deformaciones, su ecología verbal, sus locas proliferaciones de metáforas, de símiles mecánicos, su lenguaje puesto al ritmo de la estética futurista. . . .
>
> . . . Y debo decir que durante años, muchos años, me opuse a la reimpresión de esta novela que vio la luz en Madrid, en 1933. . . . Y digo que me opuse a su reimpresión, porque después de mi ciclo americano que se inicia con *El reino de este mundo*, veía *Écue-Yamba-Ó* como cosa novata, pintoresca, sin profundidad—escalas y arpegios de estudiante. . . . Creí conocer a mis personajes, pero con el tiempo vi que, observándolos superficialmente, desde fuera, se me habían escurrido en alma profunda, en dolor amordazado, en recónditas pulsiones de rebeldía: en creencias y prácticas ancestrales que significaban, en realidad, una resistencia contra el poder disolvente de factores externos... (10-12)

> [*Écue-Yamba-Ó*, a book that suffers from all the anguish, unease, perplexity and faux pas that are a necessary part of the learning process. . . . The [vanguard] historical moment, the tendencies that found expression in noise, the fervor for renewal . . . imposed its deformities, its verbal ecology, its crazy proliferation of metaphors, of stock similes, its language calibrated to the rhythm of the futurist aesthetic . . . .
>
> . . . And I must say that for years, many years, I opposed the republication of this novel that first saw the light of day in Madrid, in 1933. . . . And I'll say that I opposed its republication because after my American cycle that opened with *El reino de este mundo* (The kingdom of this world), *Écue-Yamba-Ó* appeared sophomoric, folksy, superficial—a student exercise with scales and chords. . . . I thought I knew my characters, but with the passage of time I realized that, I had merely seen them superficially, from the outside, and they had slipped away from me with their deep souls, their muffled pain, the

> recondite pulsation of their rebellion: with their ancestral beliefs and practices which were for them, in point of fact, a symbol of resistance to the disintegrating force of external factors...]

Having repudiated the work on the basis of his insightful self-criticism, Carpentier found himself obliged to overrule his aesthetic scruples when in 1968 the Xanandú Press of Buenos Aires issued a pirate edition of the work.

The most compelling element of Carpentier's self-criticism is what he trenchantly terms his superficial and from-the-outside perspective. With what the exegetes of so-called "classical" drama call dramatic irony, Carpentier contrasts the assumed authenticity of his 1949 novel, *El reino de este mundo*, which he sees as the work that initiates his *ciclo americano* [American cycle], with the neophyte status, the exoticism, and lack of depth in the earlier (1933) novel. The irony can only be perceived by those whose critical perspectives have been informed by the work of Cheikh Anta Diop, George G. M. James, Asa Hilliard, Ivan Van Sertima, Molefi Asante, and all of the other stalwarts of Afrocentric scholarship. Carpentier, the politically liberal, Cuban-born son of a Russian mother and a Swiss father, was just as European and Eurocentric in 1949 as he was in 1933, and as he continued to be in October 1975 when he wrote the lines cited above. The Carpentier who in 1949 presumes to speak on behalf of negritude and to present an authentic vision of the Haitian Revolution is not any closer to a convincing identification with Africans living in the Americas than he was in 1933 when he presumed to speak on behalf of *negrismo* and to present a putatively "authentic" vision of the worldview of African Cubans.

Clearly, then, the only "authentic" approach to any aspect of African culture and civilization is one that is grounded is an Afrocentricity. Any other approach is necessarily exogenous. It may be insightful and very useful, but it can never be as valid as the Afrocentric one. Having missed this point, Carpentier self-destructs as an analyst of African American culture and civilization. His theory of magical realism is fundamentally oxymoronic, defying the principle of non-contradiction. Furthermore, his theory is an old one. It is the warmed-over romanticism in the tradition of Chateaubriand and all the hoopla about the noble savage. It is a less poetically valid affirmation of the immortal repeated refrain from Charles Baudelaire's pivotal poem, "L'invitation au voyage" [Invitation to Voyage]:

> Là, tout n'est qu'ordre et beauté,
> Luxe, calme et volupté. (*Les fleurs du mal* 66)
>
> [Over there, all is order and beauty,
> a lush, voluptuous calm.]

The "Là" is the exotic magical space, what Henry Louis Gates signals as the "là-bas" for the African American tradition as represented in Ishmael Reed's *Mumbo Jumbo*. For Carpentier, Baudelaire, Chateaubriand, and any one of millions of European travellers and tourists, this exuberant "Là" or "là-bas" is what millions of other people, who are just as real and among whom the current author numbers himself, recognize as the familiar, routine, everyday reality.

In his prologue to *El reino de este mundo*, Carpentier signals the contrast between "la maravillosa realidad recién visitada a la agotante pretensión de suscitar lo maravilloso que caracterizó ciertas literaturas europeas de estos últimos treinta años" (7-8) [the marvelous reality I recently visited with the jaded efforts to evoke the marvelous that have characterized certain European literatures in the past thirty years]. For the European creators of fantastic literature, the marvelous resided merely in the imagination, frequently an effete one at that. For Haitians and all other Americans (in the Latin American tradition this term refers first and foremost to Latin Americans), reality itself is marvelous. At its very core Carpentier's theorizing deconstructs itself, floundering in the vortex of self-contradiction, succumbing to absurdity. He cannot see that for something to be marvelous it must necessarily be unreal. A phenomenon can only be deemed marvelous when viewed from an outsider's perspective.

Carpentier situates himself squarely and, indeed, disrespectfully so, outside of the phenomena that constitute American reality. It was in the course of a *visit* to Haiti that he *discovered* the marvelous nature of American reality, as he himself reports: "al hallarme en contacto cotidiano con algo que podríamos llamar lo *real maravilloso*" (12-13) [on finding myself in contact on a day-to-day basis with what we could call a *marvelous reality*]. He continues with deconstructively revealing candor:

> Pisaba yo una tierra donde millares de hombres ansiosos de libertad creyeron en los poderes licantrópicos de Mackandal, a punto de que esa fe colectiva produjera un milagro el día de su ejecución. . . . Había estado en la Ciudadela La Ferriére, obra sin antecedentes arquitectónicos, únicamente anunciada por las *Prisiones Imaginarias* del Piranese. Había respirado la atmósfera creada por Henri Christophe, monarca de increíbles empeños, mucho más sorprendente que todos los reyes crueles inventados por los surrealistas, muy afectos a tiranías imaginarias, aunque no padecidas. A cada paso hallaba lo *real maravilloso*. Pero pensaba, además, que esa presencia y vigencia de lo real maravilloso no era privilegio único de Haití, sino patrimonio de la América entera, donde todavía no se ha terminado de establecer, por ejemplo, un recuento de cosmogonías. (13)

> [I had set foot on a land where thousands of men yearning for freedom put their faith in Mackandal's lycanthropy, so much so that their collective faith could produce a miracle on the day he was executed. . . . I had been to the La Ferrière Citadelle, an architectural monument without precedent, except only for Piranesi's *Prisons of the Imagination*. I had breathed in the ambience created by Henri Christophe, a monarch of incredible projects, much more surprising than all of the cruel kings invented by the surrealists, who had quite a penchant for tyrannies created by the imagination but that never actually existed. At every step I encountered a marvelous reality. But I figured, furthermore, that it was not Haiti alone that was privileged with the presence and actuality of a marvelous reality, it was, indeed, the patrimony of all America, where, for example, a full accounting is yet to be made of the various cosmogonies.]

It is a "faith," a collective pathology, that makes this fantasy real for the natives. Surely this is simply a 1949 version of the noble savage theory. Mackandal and Bouckman, leaders of the only authentic revolution in the Americas, a revolution through which de facto and not just in theory the grassroots, the brutally oppressed, seized power, are reduced to the status of literary boogey men. Out of a colossal and indictable ignorance of the basic data of history, the manifestation of African architectural genius—a genius that inspired architectural wonders from the beginning of time and in many regions of the world within and beyond the geographical limits of the continent of Africa—is reduced to a product of the effete European literary imagination, "las *Prisiones Imaginarias* del Piranese."

The most glaring of Carpentier's series of insults cited above is his sweeping judgment of Henri Christophe. No Eurocentric commentator, terminally blinded by the bias of white supremacy, can even begin to appreciate the contribution of a Henri Christophe. Carpentier's contact with the reality of Haiti and the Haitian Revolution occurred more than a decade after C.L.R. James had written his insightful study of that phenomenon, *The Black Jacobins*. Carpentier's novel, published in 1949, appeared five years after the publication of Eric Williams's watershed analysis of slavery in the Caribbean, *Capitalism and Slavery*. Carpentier's ignorance is, then, culpable, and it fits into the pattern of vapid commentary that passes for intellectual inquiry in this document of white supremacist diatribe that is his introduction to *El reino de este mundo*. Christophe is reduced to the level of European literary reality, he is nothing more than "A figment of the [literary] imagination, a banana of the mind" (297) as Derek Walcott put it in his inimitable *Dream on Monkey Mountain*.[1] Christophe is the monarch of *incredible*, that is, unbelievable to those grounded in "real" reality, undertakings. He is "much more surprising than all of the cruel kings invented by the surrealists." The phenomena of Haiti are only accessible to Carpentier's Eurocentrically effete mind in terms that fundamentally distort them, that fundamentally negate their existence in the world out there. And Carpentier reiterates at this point his basic belief that marvelous reality is the "patrimony" of all of America (that is, specifically Latin America).

At the end of his introductory essay to *El reino de este mundo*, Carpentier spells out with clarity the cardinal principle of his theory. He declares that todo resulta maravilloso en una historia imposible de situar en Europa, y que es tan real, sin embargo, como cualquier suceso ejemplar de los consignados, para pedagógica edificación, en los manuales escolares. ¿Pero qué es la historia de América toda sino una crónica de lo real-maravilloso? (16-17)

[everything turns out to be marvelous in this historical account that one would be hard put to place in Europe, and yet one that is as real as any of those exemplary occurrences consigned, in the interest of pedagogical edification, to the school manuals. But what else is the history of all America but a chronicling of a marvelous reality?]

Carpentier, then, in 1949 was suffering from the same addiction to exoticism as he had self-diagnosed in 1933. In this earlier period he was under the direct influence of a school of writers who, with revealing arrogance, considered themselves Afro-Antillean or Afro-Cuban. Carpentier, indeed, was a prominent member of this coterie of white male poets who, following the rage of the Roaring Twenties, became fascinated with things black. The movement was initiated by the ostensibly white Puerto Rican Luis Palés Matos, who in 1926 (within a year of the publication of Alain Locke's watershed collection, *New Negro Voices,* which launched the so-called Harlem Renaissance) penned the first of the poems that focused on the exotic and erotic aspects of Caribbean "Negro" life and culture. Palés Matos' poem is entitled "Pueblo negro," and its opening lines portray with searing clarity the author's view of black people. They read:

Esta noche me obsede la remota
visión de un pueblo negro...
—Mussumba, Tumbuctú, Farafangana—.
Es un pueblo de sueño,
tumbado allá en mis brumas interiores
a la sombra de claros cocoteros. (150)

[Tonight I'm haunted by
the vision of a far-off Negro village...
—Mussumba, Timbuktu, Farafangana—.
A village from my dreams,
sprawled there in the inner mists
under the shade of bright coconut trees.]

Puerto Rico was at that time still reporting its population figures by race, and it was officially, according to Isabelo Zenón Cruz in *Narciso descubre su trasero*, a nation with a 23% black population (1: 136). In Latin America race is generally determined by phenotype alone, so that the 23% would translate into a significantly higher percentage by mainland (United States) criteria. In other words, there was absolutely no shortage of flesh-and-blood, real-life, sweaty black folks in Palés Matos' environment. Clearly, in his poetic world he opts to ignore them in favor of the much more acceptable "far-off," "dream" people located "far-off there in [his] inner mists / under the shade of bright coconut trees."

At the center of this world, a "là" or "là-bas," where all is "luxe, calme et volupté," is, of course, the element that triggers the poet's obsession (Tonight I'm haunted by/the vision of a far-off Negro village):

> Es la negra que canta
> su sobria vida de animal doméstico;
> la negra de las zonas soleadas
> que huele a tierra, a salvajina, a sexo.
> Es la negra que canta,
> y su canto sensual se va extendiendo,
> como una clara atmósfera de dicha
> bajo la sombra de los cocoteros. (151)
>
> [It is the black woman singing
> her dull life of a domesticated animal;
> the black woman of the sun-drenched lands
> redolent of earth, wild meat, and sex.
> It is the black woman singing,
> and her sensual song reaches out
> like the bright air of happiness
> under the shade of the coconut trees.]

"Cherchez la femme" encapsulates the wisdom culled from the experience of an entire people, one reputedly especially versed in this aspect of the human condition. The search, then, stops at this stanza.

This is precisely the kind of "femme" that pops up in all of the so-called Afro-Antillean poetry: she is the "domesticated animal" who is "redolent of earth, wild meat, and sex." It must be pointed out that this female poetic persona is not limited to the creative universe of white male implied authors; it turns up in the literature of the Harlem Renaissance, in Claude McKay's *Home to Harlem*, for example. Fuelled by images of this kind, Afro-Antillean poetry became the rage among the Caribbean literati, generally an exclusive white male club.

In the years immediately succeeding the appearance of Palés Matos's poem, white-skinned Cubans caught the contagion of their Puerto Rican counterpart and went into an almost frenzied state of creativity, producing exotic, erotic verses in which the black female persona of generously proportioned hips and *nalgas* [buttocks], positively exuding earthy, sultry sensuality, literally held sway. In fact, as early as 1928, the white-skinned Cuban, Ramón Guirao, published an anthology of "Afro-Cuban" poetry of this stripe. But it is his 1939 *Orbita de la poesía afrocubana* [The Afro-Cuban Poetic World] that best conserves for us the flavor of this poetry. Its chief exponents were, along with Carpentier, José Z. Tallet, Emilio Ballagas, and, of course, Guirao himself. Tallet's *negra* Tomasa of the poem "La rumba" is representative. He puts her through her paces in a steamy nightclub style dancing scene with the *negro* José Encarnación. Tallet has them execute the following step:

> Ella mueve una nalga, ella mueve la otra,
> él se estira, se encoge, dispara la grupa. (Valdés-Cruz 94)
>
> [She moves one buttock, she moves the other,
> He stretches, pulls back, shoots out his flank.]

Tallet's poem, which is a realistic description of the rumba dance—derived from the liturgical representation of the contact, confrontation between Shango and one of his wives, Oshun (Jahn 82)—climaxes literally with the erotic coupling of the male and female:

> Al suelo se viene la niña Tomasa,
> al suelo se viene José Encarnación;

allí se revuelcan con mil contorsiones,
se les sube el santo, se rompió el bongó,
se acabó la rumba, ¡con-con-co-mabó!
¡Pa-ca, pa-ca, pa-ca, pa-ca!
¡Pam! ¡Pam! ¡Pam! (Valdes-Cruz 96)

[Niña Tomasa falls down to the ground,
José Encarnación falls down too;
they twist and turn in a thousand contortions,
they catch the power, the bongo broke loose,
the rhumba is over, con-con-co-mabó!
¡Pa-ca, pa-ca, pa-ca, pa-ca!
Pam! Pam! Pam!]

Tallet's poem is probably the most lurid of those of the school that are still published in anthologies. Its most representative feature is perhaps the so-called *jitanjáfora* (a purely rhythmic nonsense word designed to inject an African flavor into the language) which the poet, in this case, uses to provide some closure for his work. Here, however, the device rings through as trite, an almost silly cliché stuck in in lieu of an ending.

The only African-ancestored Cubans whose works are published in anthologies of so-called "Afro-Antillean" poetry are, of course, Guillén, along with Regino Pedroso and Marcelino Arozarena. Understandably, these writers—as well as the general African-ancestored public—were somewhat uncomfortable with the phenomenon, although they did not escape the contagion. Indeed, Arozarena's best known poems bear as titles the names of two black women of the stripe of Tallet's Tomasa: "Caridá" and "Amalia." In fact, "Amalia" is an even more boldly erotic piece than Tallet's "La rumba." However, its sexual references are veiled in a symbolic slang language generally unaccessible to the non-Cuban, and indeed non-specialist, reader. It is fully grounded in the real reality, and, for this reason precisely, it is not normally included in anthologies.

The jazz age has to be seen in the terms of the analysis set up in the preceding discussion. It was not just in the United States that effete white aesthetes turned to the reputedly more vibrant "primitive" Negro aesthetic tradition for inspiration. Pablo Picasso is the most significant of these white males who turned to Africa for resuscitation. His cubism is nothing short of a plagiarism of aesthetic principles employed by West African plastic arts from time immemorial. The vigorous figures that characterize German expressionism, when carefully examined, will be seen similarly to rely on the aesthetic principles and practice of traditional West African art. For Picasso and the cubists, for the German expressionists, for the participants in the jazz age, African Americans and Africans are always the exotic other, the flip side of the coin of reality. They are accessible only in Palés Matos' terms: "Esta noche me obsede la remota / visión de un pueblo negro..."

From the Eurocentric perspective the history of America is a marvelous phenomenon, from the American perspective the history of America is the history of reality plain and simple. Since Africans played the significant role in the development of civilization and culture in the Americas, it is clear that the Afrocentric perspective will foster the most fulfilling version of this history. It follows, then, that Zapata's chronicle is a wholly Afrocentric version of "lo real" and not a Eurocentric "crónica de lo real maravilloso." The tale that Ngafúa spins begins in the mythological prehistory of "Muntu," the term—generally considered to have been introduced to the mainstream of the academy by Janheinz Jahn—in Bantu philosophy for mankind in general. The opening stanza is:

> ¡Oídos del Muntu, oíd!
> ¡Oíd! ¡Oíd! ¡Oíd!
> ¡Oídos del Muntu, oíd! (6)
>
> [Ye ears of Muntu, hear!
> Hear! Hear! Hear!
> Ye ears of Muntu, hear!]

The opening epic poem tells how in this real world of mythological prehistory the Yoruba orisha (god, power, *ntr*, or *loa*) known as Shango, having fallen from grace and having being sent into exile, in turn wreaks vengeance on mankind (Muntu) by condemning them to the experience of chattel slavery and the slave trade:

¡Eléyay, ira de Changó!
¡Eléyay, furia del dolor!
¡Eléyay, maldición de maldiciones!
Por venganza del rencoroso Loa
condenados fuimos al continente extraño
milliones de tus hijos
ciegos manatíes en otros ríos
buscando los orígenes perdidos. (16)

[Eleyay, Shango's anger!
Eleyay, a raging pain!
Eleyay, curse of curses!
In a fit of embittered vengeance
the Loa condemned us to a foreign continent
millions of your children
now like blind manatees seek
their lost roots in alien rivers.]

Along with the curse there is also a promise of sure liberation in the fullness of time. The structure, then, of the novel is clearly established; the 500 or so pages of prose narrative that follow this brief (28 pages) verse introduction will relate the labors of Muntu in meeting the fate ordained by Shango with the permission of *Odumare*, the One Supreme Being, The Existing One.[2]

Charles S. Finch's penetrating study of the African basis of human mythology, *Echoes of the Old Darkland*, sheds significant light on the question of Shango, whom he presents as follows:

> Shango is the first king of the Yoruba nation of Oyo who is eventually persecuted by his own subjects and driven from the throne. In his despair, he hangs himself from a tree after which he falls into a deep hole. Eventually he ascends into the sky on a chain and becomes one of the most powerful orishas, the controller of thunder and lightning. His emblem is the axe and his zootype the ram. There are a number of curious mythic parallels between Shango and Jesus: (1) each is styled a king, (2) each suffers persecution by his people, (3) each dies by hanging, (4) each descends into the nether world, (5) each is resurrected, ascends into heaven, and is translated into a divine immortal, and (6) each exhibits a zootypical identification with the Arian Ram. This is further evidence that the Church fathers drew on long-standing, ubiquitous mythic material. (198)

Finch's major point is that Christian theology springs from a pre-existing African theological tradition. This tradition, of course, is viewed simply as "mythology" by the unenlightened Eurocentric "experts." As Finch equates this "mythology" with what he would term the Christian mythic tradition, he establishes the basis for the pivotal premise of this section of our study, namely, that for Zapata African mythology functions in exactly the same way as Christian theology. Zapata's chronicle of America is no more a chronicle of "marvelous reality" than would be a historical novel written by a Christian who believes, for example, in the kingship of Christ.

The parallels Finch discerns between Shango and the Christian Messiah are in themselves fascinating and will be considered at some length in the following chapter devoted to Quince Duncan, when the whole subject of so-called religious "syncretism" is reexamined. At this juncture the discussion must be limited to evaluating the "mythic material" used by Zapata and that on which the "Church fathers drew." Whereas Christians untrained in theological speculation would reject the very notion of a mythological basis for Christian theology, no Christian theologian would hesitate to characterize some of the content of the Bible as mythological. Roman Catholic theologians, for example, sanguinely assert that the creation story in Genesis is merely a mythological tale, a parable, an allegory, a fabulous/marvelous tale to teach a powerful truth.

Zapata's opening epic can be viewed as a Yoruba creation myth. In order to construct a truly holistic narrative, Zapata has to begin at the very beginning. If he had set himself the self-same task of retelling the history of America but from the so-called Judeo-Christian perspective, he would have begun with the Genesis account of creation. Indeed, no true Christian would write any chronicle that did not begin with Genesis, and it is not included explicitly in every Christian chronicle only because such exactness would be considered superfluous, redundantly unartistic. Zapata has to enter specifically into the world of prehistory and mythology since he understands that he is swimming against the tide, that he is, in the terms used by Vera Kutzinski, going "against the American grain." This is what Carpentier would view as entering the realm of magic, of reality that is marvelous. In Baudelaire's terms it would be taking a trip to a "Là[-bas où] tout n'est qu'ordre et beauté, / Luxe, calme et volupté."

The four remaining parts of the novel are the following: "El Muntu americano" [The American Muntu], "La rebelión de los vodús" [The *Vaudou* Rebellion], "Las sangres encontradas" [Racial Mixing], and "Los ancestros combatientes" [Fighting Ancestors]. They present in accurate historical sequence the focal points of the drama of the African-ancestored Americans' experience in the New World. "El Muntu americano" focuses on the colonial period; there then follows a presentation of the first successful Latin American revolution, the Haitian (the same revolution that sparked Carpentier's fanciful lucubrations on "lo real maravilloso). In "Las sangres encontradas," the reader's attention is brought to bear on the period of national struggles for independence. And the fifth and final part, the longest, presents the history of the African North American from the days of slavery to the period of the 1960s. All of the principal actors in this continental drama are of African origin. The "Loba Blanca" [White Wolf], the term employed in the novel to refer to the Caucasoid race, makes a brief appearance as a narrator in one of the earlier sections of the book, dealing with the nefarious slave trade, but their intervention is sidelined in the world into which it is inscribed exclusively in italics.

A work of this type lends itself intrinsically to poetic treatment, and, indeed, in an earlier essay, "*Changó, el gran putas,* una nueva novela poemática" [*Shango the Baddest SOB*, A New Poematic Novel], this author focused precisely on the novel's poetic content. We contended at that time that just as modern Eurocentric writers had turned to their classical mythological tradition for aesthetic sustenance, Zapata Olivella was seeking a kind of renewal in the mythology of traditional African civilization. However, as was indicated earlier in the preceding section of this chapter, Zapata's use of mythology is akin to the Christian's grounding in certain admittedly "mythical" elements of the Bible. For the real people, who struck Carpentier as so exotically odd, and for whom Zapata resolutely seeks to be the representative voice, the mythological element is no mere literary flight of fantasy. It is as real as are the biblical truths for a Christian.

Zapata employs four primary devices, which could be labelled *unidades* [unities] or *comuniones* [communions], to achieve the effective blend of what has been generally considered "historical" by Eurocentric scholars with what these same ideologues have inconsistently deemed merely "mythological." The characters frequently merge into each other; there is no clear distinction between the world of the living and the world of the dead, between past, present, and future. And finally, the very entities that compose the universe themselves merge from time to time into a marvelous ontological conflation. This treatment of the history of the New World is clearly Afrocentric. However, thanks to the work Gates has accomplished in analyzing Reed's *Mumbo Jumbo*, the fundamentally American dimensions of Zapata's approach have also been made manifest. (The reader may wish to refer again to the opening pages of Chapter Two.)

In the preferred language of the most in-vogue of contemporary literary theories, the critic Gates establishes a central aesthetic connection between a contemporary North American literary expression and traditional African religion/culture in both its Old World and New World manifestations. There is, furthermore, the manifestation of an important link with Latin American "magical realism" as we have presented it. For, as we have indicated in the preceding pages of this chapter, Carpentier and the Eurocentric theoreticians and artists see the quintessential American experience as unfolding in an exotic "là-bas." For the real Americans whose center is Africa, reality is not an exotic "là-bas"; it is, in Gatesian terms, "right here." Papa Legba, the Yoruba orisha, the wise one, the original Hermes, is the force through which the Eurocentric "abstraction" (in the Albert Camus sense), or more accurately "hocus-pocus" or fantasy analysis is debunked, or "deconstructed."

Papa Legba is manifested through the "Signifying Monkey." The tie between African American popular culture and traditional African culture/religion embodied, for example, in the notion that the "Signifying Monkey" is a manifestation of Papa Legba, as obvious as it may appear to be, has been sedulously ignored by the academy for the many reasons that we have already indicated. In the main, even scholars of apparent African ancestry have thought it necessary to eschew this connection as well. Its affirmation by Gates, an African American, Ivy League scholar, represents, then, a significant break with tradition in the inner circles of the academy. It is particularly poignant that Gates' analysis focuses on the clear ties between popular African American culture and Haitian *vaudou*, confirming Reed's vision as given expression to in *Mumbo Jumbo*. Gates's and Reed's "discovery" was articulated by Aimé Césaire with intense poetic force in his 1930s work that is still considered the manifesto of negritude, *Cahier d'un retour au pays natal*: "Haiti où la négritude se mit debout pour la première fois et dit qu'elle croyait à son humanité" (67) "Haiti, where Negritude stood up for the first time and swore by its humanity" (66). It must be reiterated that Carpentier "discovered" his magical realism in and through his contact with the reality of Haiti. Magical realism of Carpentier's Eurocentric mind of the late 1940s, then, exactly parallels Negritude of the Afrocentric tending minds of those young Africans who founded the movement during their student days in Paris almost two decades earlier.

Reed was clearly convinced of Haiti's central role in the development of African civilization in the Americas. He asserts through the reliable narrator that Haiti is the "miasmatic source" (64) of Jes Grew. And Jes Grew can be defined quite adequately in the terms once employed by Léopold Sédar Senghor to explain his Negritude: "La négritude est le patrimione culturel, les valeurs et surtout l'esprit de la civilisation négro-africaine" (Kesteloot 110) [Negritude is the cultural patrimony, the values and above all the spirit of Black African civilization]. It is an indefinable something that one catches and without which black cultural expressions could not be created. It comes from Haiti, so that, as Reed's narrator affirms: "When an artist happens upon a new form he shouts 'I Have Reached My Haiti!'" (64).

Gates apparently stumbled upon this incredible theoretical find, for he could not mine it adequately. He did not advance beyond portraying Legba as a Trickster standing at the crossroads between this world and the world beyond, a messenger between the two. At the level of insight into Yoruba mythology that Gates attained,

Legba is "the master of style and the stylus, phallic god of generation and fecundity, master of the mystical barrier that separates the divine from the profane world" (*Black Literature* 287). Legba by his very tricks mediates between the two worlds, two poles of the inherent, irreconcilable contradiction of the human condition. Thus, Gates asserts that "the figure of Esù can stand . . . as our metaphor for the act of interpretation itself" (287).

With superior insight Finch connects the Legba crossroads symbolism to the tradition that undergirds all of humanity's theological tradition, declaring that "The cross too was a venerable Afro-Kamitic symbol long before the emergence of Christianity and the Tree was the earliest natural type of cross. . . . That Osiris is identified with the Tree is clear from Plutarch's narrative, where a tree grows up around his coffin, emblematic of his resurrection. Iconographically, the Tree is the Tet or Djed cross, 'the backbone of Osiris,' whose raising enacts his re-arising. The cross is both a figure of the dead, i.e., those who have 'crossed over,' *and* the raising of the dead to new life" (197). Finch's discourse lifts the veil of confusion imposed by the epistemological requirements of white supremacy and leads to true, liberating enlightenment as the paragraph quoted above continues uninterrupted to establish the connection between Legba, the Christian Savior, and Shango. Neither Gates nor the particularly insightful Roger Abrahams, who authored *Man-of-Words in the West Indies*, approximated the searing clarity articulated in the following excerpt from Finch's text:

> Notably in West Africa, the crossroads is a place charged with numinous power as the point where the material and human meets the spiritual and divine. The West African guide of souls, Eshu or Legba, is the warder of the afterlife and guardian of the crossroads—the dead can only be admitted to the company of the ancestors through his intermediation. . . . the crucifixion of Jesus encapsulates the fusion of his divine and human natures, making him the Christ. . . . If the cross carrying the dying savior is not raised on the Mount of Calvary, there is no union of God and man, no dissolution and re-creation of the divine man, and therefore no hope for universal resurrection. . . . Nailing to the cross is merely one type of crucifixion. . . . Hanging from a tree or gallows [as was Shango's fate] was another. In fact, in the Book of Acts it is stated that Jesus was hanged from a gibbet. (197-98)

Finch's arguments are as convincing as they are fascinating. The kind of fundamental rewriting and rethinking, in a word, "deconstruction," that his analysis involves quickens every branch of scholarship. One of the most germane applications would be that which leads to a better understanding of the mythic content in Chinua Achebe's *Things Fall Apart*. The archetypal nature of the protagonist Okonkwo is considerably enhanced when his suicide by hanging from a tree is juxtaposed to Shango's and elucidated by Finch's enlightened theorizing.

For Gates, the literary scholar working unimpeachably within the pale of the contemporary academy, the Signifying Monkey is Legba, and is simply a Trickster and, above all, a peculiarly black American symbol of literariness. Even at this, the Gatesian level of analysis, the literary act for the black American can be construed as the ultimate act of self-assertion, rejection of the essential racist paradigm. Literature is an act of liberation, and a Trickster for an oppressed people is essentially a liberator. Fanon in his chapter "On National Culture," made it quite clear that every truly artistic expression of an oppressed native is posited necessarily on the rejection of the colonial paradigm (177-83). He had earlier on in the same book, *The Wretched of the Earth*, with inimitable clarity, characterized the colonial situation as essentially dichotomous, "Manichean" in his terms (29-36). Gates's theory is, then, quite compatible with Fanon's views, and both sets of ideas fit harmoniously into Finch's transcendental matrix.

In Zapata Olivella's work the liberator may at first sight appear to be not Legba but *Changó*. The point has to be noted that both are Yoruba "gods," (orishas, *loas*, or *ntrw*). Contemporary African-ancestored inhabitants of the New World descend from the many scores of ethnic groups that are considered native to West, Central, East, and even South Africa. It is, then, significant that "gods" from one particular group should play such a fundamental role in the culture of African-ancestored people from the entire Americas. Reed's instructive *Mumbo Jumbo* clearly roots this connection in the culture and civilization of Kemet, which was both quintessentially African and the earliest of the great civilizations developed by man. Gates, faithful to the dogmas of the Eurocentric academy, implicitly eschews this reading of Reed's text when he claims that "The closest Western relative of Esù is Hermes" (287). In spite of the growing body of scholarship presented by such thinkers as Finch, Diop, James, Martin Bernal, and Van Sertima, to mention just a few, this particular hesitancy on Gates's part is still the rule rather than the exception, even with African-ancestored scholars who work within the pale of the academy. It springs from an extremely deep-seated reflex of rejection of any theory that would appear to cast any doubt on the doctrine of white supremacy.

The new Afrocentric scholars have presented an array of impressive arguments to support their theses. Any thinker who fails to take account of these theses would be lacking in the rigor expected of the most elementary intellectual inquiry. According to the arguments presented specifically by Diop and even by the 19th century British Egyptologist E. A. Wallis Budge—a thinker who clearly had no Afrocentric axe to grind—the people of Kemet were Africans in the exact same sense in which contemporary Yorubas are Africans. Budge is still recognized as one of the leading experts on the world's most ancient sacred book, the so-called *Book of the Dead* from Kemet. And, on the basis of his knowledge of this collection of religious texts, in his *Osiris and the Egyptian Resurrection*, he comes to the conclusion that "beyond all doubt . . . the indigenous Religion of ancient Egypt was unlike any of the Asiatic Religions with which it had been compared" (1:xiii). He cites in support of his conclusion the opinion of such renowned Egyptologists as "Professor Maspero . . . E. Lefébure and . . . Professor Wiedemann" (1:xvi). A true scholar, he conducted his own field research "in the summer of 1897 [in] . . . Marawi, in the Dongola Province of the Egyptian Sûdân" (1:xvi). He continues as follows: "During subsequent visits to the Sûdân I became convinced that a satisfactory explanation of the ancient Egyptian Religion could only be obtained from the Religions of the Sûdân, more especially those of the peoples who lived in the isolated districts in the south and west of that region, where European influence was limited, and where native beliefs and religious ceremonials still possessed life and meaning" (1:xvii).

It is common for the devotees of white supremacy to obfuscate all chronological considerations and then, with duplicitous relativism, appeal to spurious but high-sounding claims of mutual influence, cross-cultural assimilation, intertextuality, and the like. With an air of secular wisdom they declare that all cultures clearly influenced one another, no one culture has the monopoly, none was first, except, of course, the Graeco-Roman—as their subtext always reads. Budge encountered and dealt with precisely this line of argumentation when he affirmed that "It may be objected that the modern beliefs and superstitions of the Sûdân and Congo-land and Dahomey are survivals of ancient Egyptian religious views and opinions, but the objection seems to me to possess no validity. The oldest and best form of the Egyptian Religion died more than 3,000 years ago, and many of the most illuminating facts for comparative and illustrative purposes are derived from the Religions of peoples who live in parts of Africa into which Egyptian influence never penetrated" (1:xvii). Budge concludes with unequivocal clarity: "Modern Sûdânî beliefs are identical with those of ancient Egypt, because the Egyptians were Africans and the modern peoples of the Sûdân are Africans" (1:xvii).

White supremacist doctrine has so distorted the reasoning mechanisms of the Western academy that it requires all of the considerable intellectual authority of a Budge to support an assertion that is little more than a truism: "Egyptians are Africans." As we have indicated earlier (in Chapter One and elsewhere) Diop and Théophile Obenga, considering the same data that were available to Maspero, Budge, and the entire academy, demonstrate convincingly that, since the thought systems and civilizations of the Sudan and of those lands that occupy the very heart of Africa (what the Bible refers to as Cush and Put respectively) were identical to the Egyptian and clearly considerably more ancient, they were the source from which Egypt sprang. All the most elaborate efforts by the white supremacist academy to demonstrate the existence of civilization outside of Africa prior to the Egyptian have met with resounding failure. Diop, then, concludes with incontrovertible clarity that not only is Africa the cradle of Homo Sapiens Sapiens, but it is the cradle of all human civilization.

James, Chancellor Williams, Yosef ben-Jochannan, Finch, Hilliard, and many others join Diop and Obenga in affirming categorically that Kemet is the source of so-called Western civilization.

Bernal is not prepared to confront the basic tenets of Eurocentrism, but in both volumes of *Black Athena* he argues with compelling elegance and an almost bewildering wealth of detail for massive Egyptian influence on so-called "classical" civilization. One of the cogently argued claims made by Bernal is "that all scholars agree that Hermes [Trismegistos] is the same as the Egyptian Thoth [Jehuti]" (1:139). He states further that "Thoth was the inventor of writing, the originator of mathematics and the master of magic spells; the divine act of speech which related the gods to each other and to men, and even the creator of the world." He is above all the "great communicator" (1:141). "Orthodox," "serious" scholars have necessarily to abjure the "wrongheaded" arguments of such "heretical," "irreverent" thinkers as Bernal. Informed by this doctrinal approach to intellectual inquiry, Gates, as indeed the typical scholar working within the pale of the academy, missed the essential, liberating link between Jehuti (Thoth) and Legba.

Zapata, an expert folklorist who has evinced a particular interest in Yoruba culture, understands that Legba and Shango are two distinct deities, or "loas" or "orishas." However, they subtly overlap in their function and role in his novel, as they do in Finch's articulation. Shango is defined for the reader in the glossary as follows:

> **Changó, Xangó** o **Sangó**: En la mitología yoruba, hijo de Yemayá y Orungán. Fue el tercer soberano del estado imperial de Oyo, cuya capital, Ife, ubicada en las cercanías del Niger, fue cuna de los Orichas, creadores del mundo. . . . Dios de la guerra, la fecundidad y la danza. (517)

> [**Changó, Xangó** or **Sangó**: In Yoruba mythology, offspring of Yemayá and Orungán. He was the third ruler of the imperial state of Oyo, the capital of which, Ife, located in the environs of the Niger, was the birthplace of the Orishas, the creators of the world. . . . God of war, fertility and dance.]

Legba is defined, in turn, as follows:

Elegba, Legba, Elegúa, Eshú, Echú, Exú: (El Poderoso). Distintos nombres para denominar al Oricha intermedario entre los difuntos y los vivos. Es imprescindible su invocación y presencia para que desciendan las demás deidades. Sin su ayuda ningún difunto encuentra el camino que conduce hacia la Morada de los Ancestros. (517)

[**Elegba, Legba, Elegúa, Eshú, Exú**: (The Powerful One). Various names used to refer to the Orisha who acts as the mediator between the dead and the living. He must be invoked and made present if the other deities are to come down. Without his help no dead person can find the way to the Land of the Ancestors.]

Quite independently of each other, Finch and Zapata Olivella arrived at a similar focus on Shango and Legba. Whereas Shango is a genuine ancestor intimately linked to the peculiar historical experience of the contemporary Yoruba people, Legba appears not to have any direct relationship to the recalled history of the tribe. This would tend to argue for an origin in more remote antiquity, an argument that is significantly strengthened by the striking similarity between the role and function of Legba and that of Jehuti (Thoth). Aylward Shorter, a Roman Catholic priest who has studied traditional African religion, and who has no Afrocentric axe to grind, places the Yoruba culture/religion in the category of "Relative Deism" in his *African Christian Theology* (105). As such, "divinities" like Shango and Legba, while clearly distinct from the One Supreme God, exercise great independence in their relationships with each other and with mankind. In this extremely complex theological system, Shango at times assumes the power of the Creator, as one of the sovereigns in the kingdom of the orishas. Clearly, too, Legba, as one of his titles (The Powerful One) indicates, enjoys considerable power as well.

The powerful Shango who rules the fate of mankind, a veritable king of the gods, is inscribed into Zapata's text as a Trickster through the very title of the work, *Changó, el gran putas*. Lewis in *Treading the Ebony Path* (85) has offered *Changó, the Great SOB* as the most appropriate English rendition of the idiomatic turn of phrase encoded therein. During the course of a lecture at Howard University in Washington, D.C. in 1983, a few months after the book appeared, Zapata offered the expression "the holy fucker" as the best English version of "el gran putas." The most accurate, if not the most elegant nor polite rendition, would be something like "Shango, the Baddest Mother-Fucker." A "putas" is a quintessential Trickster, and the great Shango, god of war, fertility and dance, is declared to be the quintessential "putas." Furthermore, it is impossible to avoid the association at the purely extrinsic, superficial level between *putas* the masculine singular form and *putas* the feminine plural form of the most common word to refer to a prostitute. Of course, the association is entirely devoid of any semantic relevance, but it is nonetheless quite real. With a poignancy intensified by the cheap shot of a rather gross pun, the principle is affirmed that, for an oppressed people, trickery is a necessary and perhaps sufficient condition for the realization of power.

Shango, like the saints in the Christian theological tradition (as was argued in Chapter One in the section on "Syncretism"), is above all an ancestor. So too are the major historical characters who enter into the world of the novel. They are all reincarnations of the most significant forebears of Africans in the Americas—the "Muntu americano." Certain of them, as a mark of their prophetic calling to be the special agents of Shango's basic mandate, bear the sign of Elegba (Legba) stamped on their flesh, entwined snakes, the sign of the crossroads, of the crossing over. These chosen ones of Elegba will, indeed, effect the liberation that will necessarily follow the long centuries of slavery and oppression imposed by Shango on his people so that they might make expiation for their major offense against him. All of these special characters, from the very earliest days of human history to the absolutely contemporary period, are rebels. Most representative of them, and one of the earliest ancestors of the distinctively American "Muntu," is

> . . . Nagó el navegante
> hijo de Jalunga
> nacido en las costas de Gafú
> biznieto de Sassandra el Grebo
> cuyas fuertes y ágiles barcazas
> exploraron el Este. (42)

> [. . . Nagó the mariner
> son of Jalunga
> born on the Gafú coast
> great grandson of Sassandra the Grebo
> whose strong swift crafts
> explored the East.]

Nagó's archetypal act of liberation (*cimarronaje*) is carried out during the first voyage of the symbolic slave ship. He is reincarnated in many forms over the time and space of the African experience of subjugation in the Americas. He ranges from being Benkos Biojo, a male leader of the African resistance in colonial Colombia, to the almost completely opposite pole. He becomes a young female North American black-power activist from the 1960s, Agne Brown, a figure clearly reminiscent of the historical Angela Davis.

The agents of emancipation in Zapata's text are, then, Trickster heroes and heroines who are bona fide *cimarrones*, rebels called specifically to be instruments for carrying out the mandate of the great Shango. Our section on *cimarronaje* as emancipation or liberation fully explored the Pan-Caribbean, Pan-African significance of this approach. The Zapata text, however, represents a more complete understanding of the Trickster figure. For, going far beyond the academic lucubrations of a Gates, it represents a conflation of Legba and Shango—as indeed was seen in Finch's presentation—and, in some sense, the wedding of theory to praxis.

□ □ □

The title of the work notwithstanding, it is Legba who exercises most of the control over the day-to-day details. The central actors of the drama are referred to consistently as the "elegidos de Elegba" [Legba's chosen ones]. It is only through Legba that Shango can become "el gran putas." Zapata, of course, enjoys the distinct advantage of his medium, he is a creator rather than a commentator. He has more latitude to enact the central traditions of his people. Thus, as custom demands, Legba is invoked at the end of the opening verse section of the novel, a section entitled significantly: "La despedida" [The Farewell], with the subtitle "Bienvenida a Elegba abridor de puertas" (29) [Welcome Legba Who Opens Doors]. As the prime empowering principle, he is invoked at the beginning of every religious activity in traditional African culture. Edward Kamau Brathwaite, one of the greatest of the contemporary Caribbean men-of-words, long before Gates and Zapata, penetrated deeply into the culture of Africans in the Americas and saw the importance of Legba, upon whom he himself has called. The most impressive of these artistic Legba rituals occurs at the close of one of Brathwaite's finest poems, "Negus," from the collection *Islands* of his trilogy, *The Arrivants*. There is no need for the scribal poet working in English to add anything to the poetic power of the following Haitian liturgical formula:

Att
Att
Attibon

Attibon Legba
Attibon Legba
Ouvri bayi pou' moi
Ouvri bayi pou' moi. . . (224)

Empowerment for an oppressed person involves rebelling and necessarily becoming a Trickster. Since the empowerer in African theological/philosophical tradition has always been Jehuti (Thoth), Hermes, Legba, the Word Force, Legba must be a Trickster as well as the communicator. Legba, the Word Force, communicates power; he, as the lines of poetry cited above proclaim, is the opener of doors, the enabler par excellence. Every end is a beginning and every beginning is an end. Brathwaite turns to Legba at the end of "Negus" just as he brings closure to his trilogy with the simple but stirring declaration of rebirth resonating with the pulsating rhythms of the carnival "Jou'vert" (opening ceremony) song (267-70). Necessarily, the very final page of Zapata's novel inscribes a new beginning with all the sense of hope that this implies. This is the space which Legba fills, he intervenes to pronounce the absolutely final words of the book. Significantly, he speaks to calm Shango's rage at the "Muntu americano" for their slow progress in the march towards liberation and complete expiation:

> —Difuntos que podéis mirar de cerca las Sombras de los Ancestros, comparad vuestros insignificantes actos con las hazañas de nuestros Antepasados y encontraréis justificada la furia de los Orichas. ¡Desde que Changó condenó al Muntu a sufrir el yugo de los extraños en extrañas tierras, hasta hoy, se suman los siglos sin que vuestros puños hayan dado cumplimiento a su mandato de haceros libres!
> ¡Ya es hora que comprendáis que el tiempo para los vivos no es inagotable! (511)

> ["You departed ones who can look closely at the Shadows of the Ancestors, compare your insignificant acts with the great deeds of our Forefathers and you will find that the Orishas' fury is justified. From the time that Shango first condemned his Muntu to suffer under an alien yoke in alien lands, to this day, centuries have passed and your fists have not yet carried out his command to set yourselves free!
> It is about time that you realize that the time allotted to the living is not inexhaustible!"]

The second person plural, used in Spain as the familiar form, is reserved in Spanish America for only the most formal occasions, most commonly in sermons. It is this high-register form that Legba employs in the final utterance of the long text. The setting is, in fact, the mythical space where the kingdom of the dead "communes," "unites" freely with that of the living. The narrator of this final act is none other than Malcolm X, describing what transpires at his funeral and at his point of passage into the Kingdom of the Dead. Through the poetry of traditional African theology, all of the heroes of the race, literally the living and the dead, are brought together in transcendental convocation. Although the recently departed Malcolm X narrates the final act, the section itself, the fifth and last, is enacted principally through the voice of Agne Brown, a young Angela Davis type who is still alive at this point. And once the barrier between the kingdom of this world and that of the world beyond vanishes, all time is compacted mythically into the eternal *nunc*; past, present, and future become one.

Legba's intervention is realized in this quintessentially revolutionary, liberationist environment. It is occasioned by the elevation into the pantheon of one of the greatest revolutionaries of the twentieth century. It occurs in the presence of such figures as Harriet Tubman, Nat Turner, John Brown, and Martin Luther King, Jr. His message is clearly addressed to those oppressed black people who still reside in the land of the living, who are still subject to the curse of sequentiality, and who are hounded by Cronus. They must achieve their liberation within the limits of an imperfect time that is not inexhaustible. It is a message of secure hope, for not only is it couched in terms that are uncompromisingly Afro-centric, but it seeks directly to inspire a continued commitment to revolutionary struggle. It conforms to Fanon's analysis and precepts proclaimed in the classic, *The Wretched of the Earth*, making *Changó, el gran putas* an essential part of the struggle for liberation, an example of "liberation literature."

Zapata Olivella dedicated almost twenty years to the writing of this text. It represented for him an entirely new kind of expression, one that arose from a conscious attempt to give voice to the cultural wealth of unlettered common folk. Lewis is one critic who understands the full import of the process that resulted in the publication of this novel. In *Treading the Ebony Path*, he insightfully entitles his chapter devoted to Zapata's literature, "From Oppression to Liberation." Indeed, the particular form of the thrust toward liberation manifested in Zapata's *Changó* is one that has emerged in at least one other very recent scribal expression in the Hispanophone Africana literary canon, in Duncan's *La paz del pueblo* (to be examined in the next chapter), a work which presents the chief protagonist as a liberator par excellence of his people, a *cimarrón* in the best sense of the term, and as well an embodiment of the orisha "*Cuminá*," a new divinity created by the neo-African Jamaican people. When popular cultural energy combines with scribal literary talent, authentic literary expression always results. It is this combination that engendered the works of a Langston

Hughes, a Nicolás Guillén, an Ishmael Reed (as Gates demonstrates), and, clearly, the combination accounts for the aesthetic success in this particular work of Zapata Olivella. Beyond doubt, the driving force of traditional African civilizations and culture has always been and continues to be the people's spirituality.

Because Zapata Olivella focused his creative imagination on the core elements of African American culture, his work is always current. More than a decade before the dramatic rehabilitation of the image of Malcolm X, a phenomenon that only the most insightful Afrocentric minds could have foreseen, the Colombian writer had inscribed his North American brother into the most privileged environment of the text. In 1992, the year that was supposed to have been marked by the celebration of European hegemony, the most significant cultural event to have occurred in the world's most powerful Eurocentric nation was centered not on Columbus but rather on Malcolm X. This must be a source of considerable satisfaction for Zapata Olivella, who had been disappointed, even sorely so, by the lukewarm reception accorded his novel in the small community of African-ancestored Colombian intellectuals.[3]

Even though the author might not have been fully conscious of the remarkable liberating power of his work—and indeed very few creative spirits capture the full extent of their contribution—he is aware that very few scholars anywhere have manifested more than a glimmer of suspicion of the overwhelming significance of this novel. *Changó, el gran putas* simply cannot be understood and appreciated within the corpus of Latin American literature, or even as an Afro-American or Hispanophone Africana work, without recourse to the elucidating connections of the type uncovered in this chapter. The best criticism is that which attains the deepest and broadest levels of explanation, while maintaining the purest and most intense cogency. This chapter, as indeed the entire book, stretches the limits of the interrelationships between various forms of African, neo-African, and non-African cultural expressions with a cogency that is hopefully compelling overall. Manuel Zapata Olivella's *Changó, el gran putas* liberates at the two basic levels, of theory and praxis. It is a work of "fighting literature" in the Fanonian sense, an integral part of the Afro-American literary canon, and as such it lays incontrovertibly legitimate claim to inclusion in the Latin American, the American, and the general Western literary canons.

5

Cuminá as *Cimarrón*

Quince Duncan is the Spanish American literary figure whose works resonate most robustly with the vibrations of those amazing connections that have been the subject of this study. He was born on December 5, 1940 in San José, Costa Rica, to a second generation Costa Rican mother, of Jamaican roots, and a Panamanian of Barbadian heritage. He grew up in Limón, a province situated on his nation's Caribbean coast that has traditionally been the seat of a vibrant African culture, the gift of Jamaicans and other West Indians who began migrating to the area towards the end of the nineteenth century. He is a trained teacher and was at one time an Anglican priest. Having earned the licentiate in Latin American Studies from the National University, he is scholar, researcher, and university professor in addition to being a full-fledged educator. The list of his publications indicates the breadth of his scholarly interests and artistic focus. However, it is in the area of creative writing that Duncan has made his most lasting contribution, a cluster of resonances generated by the interplay of four cardinal tropes: the *samamfo*, the *cimarrón*, laughter, and the river.

Duncan's *cimarrón* is not Shango but *Cuminá*, because his art is as fully Caribbean as it is fully Hispanophone, and his fictional universe is built on roots that are as deep as the very beginnings of man's self-consciousness that is articulated in the oldest and most pervasive myths of the human family. His fictional universe, indeed, reveals in all their wondrous reality the "amazing connections" both synchronically and diachronically. This chapter will focus on how the interconnectedness between the four cardinal tropes is Caribbean and African, demonstrating that the idea of *Cuminá* as *cimarrón* is a central axis of this complex.

□ □ □

The very first page of Chapter One referred to Edward Kamau Brathwaite's classic essay, "The African Presence in Caribbean Literature," in which he declared resoundingly that "everyone agrees that the focus of African culture in the Caribbean was religious" (73). Now, with the benefit of two decades of increasingly enlightened research into African civilizations and religion, the Brathwaitian formulation would have to be amended to "spiritually centered." The most fruitful approaches to, and readings of, Caribbean literature are, then, those that are themselves oriented by this centering. And, of course, it is precisely such a spiritually centered reading that yields the fullest possible understanding of Duncan's art.

The review of Duncan's published work provides useful insight into the interstices of his art. His first published creative work was a collection of short stories, *Una canción en la madrugada* (1970) [A Song in the Early Morn]. The first novel of his to see the light of day as an actual book was *Hombres curtidos* (1971) [Chastened Men]. Duncan, in Ian I. Smart's, "The Literary World of Quince Duncan: An Interview," recounted the instructive history of this book. He had rushed it to publication before he was completely satisfied with it in an effort to preempt the plagiarizing designs of a fellow Costa Rican writer (one who was, at the time, better known, considered to be white, and was ready to appropriate a black man's artistic product). Having frustrated his fellow writer's scheming, he lacked the will to revisit the work and simply moved on to his next project. Now that the original edition is out of print, the novel is effectively unavailable. *Los cuatro espejos* (1973) [The Four Mirrors] is the first of Duncan's currently available novels. The next significant creative work was another collection of short stories, *La rebelión pocomía y otros relatos* (1976) [The Pukumina Rebellion and Other Stories]. In it the *samamfo* enters Duncan's fictional universe. After this book, as Duncan reported in the interview referred to earlier, he began work on "a short story of about five pages or so. But when I sat down at my typewriter and started writing, I couldn't stop" (286). The novel *La paz del pueblo* (1978) [Peace to the People] emerged from that creative process. It is a novel that, as he himself claimed later on in the same interview, "marks a turning point in my writing" (288). This is the first of his novels (as distinct from short stories) to give voice to the *samamfo*. Constantly at the cutting edge of creativity, Duncan attempted an experiment in his next work, *Final de calle* [Dead End], a novel. Costa Rican society, like every other society in the so-called Western world, is relentlessly Eurocentric and steeped in the most pervasive and perverted racism. Duncan decided to use this evil as grist for the mill of his art and set himself the goal of writing a novel in which all overt reference to the African presence would be deliberately suppressed. He understood that this would be a necessary and perhaps, too, sufficient condition for attaining the highest acclaim in Costa Rican literary circles. His sociological analysis was flawless, for the novel, purged of "blackness" and submitted anonymously, won the very prestigious Premio Editorial Costa Rica [Costa Rica Publishing House Award] in 1978. The following year it was given the equally prestigious Aquileo Echeverría literary award. There is obviously no mention of the *samamfo* in this racially sanitized work. With *Kimbo* (1990), the latest novel to date, the protagonist is once more a "hijo del samamfo" [son of the *samamfo*].

The first appearance of the *samamfo* comes at the end/beginning, that is, in the text of the very last story of *La rebelión pocomía y otros relatos*, in the tellingly titled tale, "Los mitos ancestrales" [The Ancestral Myths]. And this beginning/end occurs aptly on the very first page of this final short story. The action recounts allegorically the history of colonization in Africa as Duncan reconstructs an African mythology based on his erudite contact with African philosophy and religions. Thus in 1976, at the very moment that Manuel Zapata Olivella, his Colombian counterpart, was wrapped up in his struggle to find an appropriate African-centered creative voice, a process that lasted almost two decades, the Costa Rican had already begun to articulate a deeper understanding of the African heritage. It would be just seven years later that Zapata Olivella would publish his magnificent *Changó, el gran putas*, discussed in Chapter Four. The principal voice in the Duncan short story, that of the first-person narrator, emanates from the *samamfo*, where the principal character resides. This place is defined briefly in a footnote as: "Espíritu y herencia de los antepasados" (*La rebelión* 73) [Spirit and inheritance of the ancestors]. There can be no doubt about the legitimacy of this character's status as a "hijo del samamfo," for he declares expressly: "Y nos ejecutaron a los dos, a mi valiente hijo y a mí, en la plaza pública, el día quinto, cuando para pena mía, el lunes encabezó la semana" (81) [And they executed us both, my valiant son and myself, in the public square, on the fifth day, when to my embarrassment, the week began on a Monday].

The Carpentier inspired discourse could be used in the analysis of this work, but, as was pointed out in Chapter Four, that discourse misses the essential creative thrust of African-centered fiction. The narrative is bewilderingly complex because it respects the fundamental values of ancient and traditional African approaches to reality. It unites this world and the other in a marvelous unity, a fictional universe which resembles that of the magical realists and the critical realists. The sure guidepost for the reader's orientation takes the form of the main character's passionately declared fidelity to the *samamfo* in the closing/opening lines of the story and the entire collection: "Pero yo he contado la historia del Samamfo. Solo yo. Yo he adorado a Nyambe, y lo he encarnado en el Pueblo" (91) [But I have told the tale of the *Samamfo*. I alone. I have worshipped Nyambe, and I have made him incarnate in the People]. In this respect the protagonist here exactly prefigures Pedro, the main character of *La paz del pueblo*, for the latter, too, can be essentially defined by his fidelity to the *samamfo* and to a higher power, "god," "orisha," "*ntr*," or "*loa*," whom he terms significantly *Cuminá* rather than Nyambe, and whom he, too, makes incarnate in the *pueblo*. In the pivotal interview already referenced, Duncan explains the source and meaning of the term *samamfo*, confirming the preceding exposition:

> I found it in some book on African culture. I had been searching for a word that would express this idea we have at home that the spirits of our ancestors are alive, present all the time there with you. I well remember hearing my grandparents talking about the older people just as if they were still there. They really were there, the only problem was that they were, you know, still in Jamaica. . . . Well, the ones that had died in Costa Rica would be considered to be around. And, well anyway, I remember many times, for example, at night when we arrived home after a walk through the dark, an animal or something might go by and the comment would be: "Your grandmother walk with you to protect you." So the spirits of the ancestors are here constantly with you. I couldn't find any way of expressing this in either Spanish of English until I ran across that term *samamfo*, which said exactly what I wanted to say. (290)

Once he discovered the appropriate line of approach and label, Duncan would from then on create a fictional universe that exactly matches the real world of his formative years, by centering his narrative in the *samamfo*. His words cited above make it quite clear that his narrative seeks to replicate not some fantasy world, a "là" or "là-bas" of "luxe, calme et volupté," but rather the most solid, and hence most mundane, reality he has experienced. The creative process for Duncan is a search for roots, a grounding experience, not a flight of fancy, a flight from reality.

Carpentier's search for roots in a novel like *Los pasos perdidos* [The Lost Steps] is a bookish, literally escapist, adventure that ends in dismal failure. In fact, the fundamental frustration enunciated in the final declaration of Carpentier's main character contrasts with the strong sense of fulfillment and purpose that radiates from the "hijo del samamfo." The two protagonists are polar opposites;

Duncan's finds himself, the other finds that his personal search for the environment in which meaning and liberation can occur is, in the terms of the existentialists, "voué a l'echec," condemned inexorably to failure. The Carpentier alter ego seeks salvation in the escape from the shackles of temporality, a state that he knows, as he affirms, to be per se achievable: "Aquí puede ignorarse el año en que se vive, y mienten quienes dicen que el hombre no puede escapar a su época" (286) [Here it is possible for someone not to know what year it is, and anyone who says that man cannot escape from his historical moment is a liar]. But, whereas others can attain this nirvana, it is absolutely inaccessible to him, as he admits:

> Pero nada de esto se ha destinado a mí, porque la única raza humana que está impedida de desligarse de las fechas es la raza de quienes hacen arte, y no sólo tienen que adelantarse a un ayer inmediato, representado en testimonios tangibles, sino que se anticipan al canto y forma de otros que vendrán después, creando nuevos testimonios tangibles en plena consciencia de lo hecho hasta hoy. Marcos y Rosario ignoran la historia. El Adelantado se sitúa en su primer capítulo, y yo hubiera podido permanecer a su lado si mi oficio hubiera sido cualquier otro que el de componer música—oficio de cabo de raza—. (286)

> [But none of this is meant for me, because the only race of humans that cannot free itself from dates is the race of the creative spirits, and not only do they have to push forward to the immediate past, represented through tangible testimonies, but, indeed, they anticipate the shape and form of other testimonies that are still to come, creating new realities that fully reflect what has existed up to that point in time. Marcos and Rosario know nothing of history. The Point Man operates in the opening chapter of history, and I could have stayed on there with him if my occupation had been any other than that of composing music—the occupation of a leader of the pack—.]

He is the quintessential romantic, a lonely rebel who, with supreme egotism, glories in his uniqueness, even when the very distinctiveness is the enormity of his unspeakable pain. This is the same persona who proudly declares his splendid suffering separation from the pack in Charles Baudelaire's "L'Albatros" from his signature collection, *Les fleurs du mal*: "Lui, naguère si beau, qu'il est comique et laid!" [He, once so fine, how comical and ugly he has become!]. The final stanza proclaims:

> Le Poëte est semblable au prince des nuées
> Qui hante la tempête et se rit de l'archer;
> Exilé sur le sol au milieu des huées,
> Ses ailes de géant l'empêchent de marcher. (20)
>
> [The poet is like the prince of the skies
> Who haunts the storm and mocks the arrow flying;
> Exiled to the ground amidst the derisive cries,
> His giant's wings impede his very walking.]

He is the same tragic Sisyphus envisaged by Albert Camus, who presents an effete declaration of supposed superiority over his absurdity through the arrogance of his privilege as a thinking subject.

On the contrary, Duncan and, later, Zapata Olivella seek to immerse themselves in the black pack, to plunge themselves into the very essence of things, the very core of reality. As was the case with the central persona of Aimé Césaire's *Cahier d'un retour au pays natal / Return to My Native Land*, escape is the furthest thing from their mind. "Take me as I am. I don't adapt to you" (86), is the defiant declaration of this proud rebel (*cimarrón*), manifesting a self rooted in reality, and one that thrusts basically toward solidarity with the oppressed group rather than toward singularity. Negritude for the Cesairean poetic figure is very personal, it is "my Negritude" (116) as it is redolent of the stuff of reality. It is

> . . . not a speck of dead water
> on the dead eye of the earth
> my Negritude is neither a tower nor a cathe-
> dral
>
> it thrusts into the red flesh of the soil
> it thrusts into the warm flesh of the sky. (116)

It is ultimately

> flesh of the flesh of the world
> panting with the very movement of the world
> Tepid dawn of ancestral virtues. (118)

The communion with the group involves communion with ancestral values. In Carpentier's scheme of things the central organizing self cannot do like El Adelantado of *Los pasos perdidos* (basically a marginal character) who "operates in the opening chapter of history." For Duncan and Zapata, to enter into oneself is to enter into the self of the community and to enter not merely into the "opening chapter" but rather to transcend the partitioning into "chapters."

In *La paz del pueblo*, which was published two years after *La rebelión pocomía y otros relatos*, there is an evolution in the definition of *samamfo*. The term appears in a glossary at the end of the book, rather than in a footnote, and is defined as a "palabra de origen ashanti que significa lugar o estado en que se encuentran los muertos, o los espíritus de los antepasados" (192) [word of Ashanti origin which signifies the place or state in which the dead find themselves, or the spirits of the ancestors]. The *samamfo* first surfaces in that novel early in the plot in an environment that is especially significant. An unidentified, and hence archetypal, grandfather is conversing with his equally unidentified, and hence equally archetypal, grandchild as follows:

> —Abuelo y . . . ¿cómo es eso del cielo y del infierno?
> —Eso es cuando termine todo. Al final, después del juicio. Pero por ahora nadie se muere, hijo: simplemente volvemos al samamfo. (24)
>
> ["Grandfather and . . . how does this business about heaven and hell go?"
> "That's when it's all over. At the end, after the judgement. But for now nobody dies, son: we simply return to the *samamfo*."]

Furthermore, the function of the *samamfo* in the novel recalls that of Legba in Zapata Olivella's *Changó*. It is a dynamic living presence, activating all beings, maintaining a constructive continuity between them. La señora Mariot, one of the important secondary characters in the novel, undertakes as a young girl an act of rebellion that prefigures the fundamental Promethean-Osirian, *Changó/Cuminá*, rebellion-liberation act of the main character, Pedro Dull (this will be developed more fully further on). Duncan makes significant use of the artistic devices developed or employed by other Latin American fiction writers. In this sense he is more of a stylist than Zapata. There is thus much of the vaunted Latin American critical realism in Duncan's works. According to the convention of this, the preferred style of many of the successful contemporary Latin American novelists, the progeny of Faulkner, there must be certain moments when the narrative is, albeit fleetingly, grounded in certitude. One such moment occurs precisely with the narration of La señora Mariot's youthful but defining act of *cimarronaje*. The text reads: "Ese fue el motivo de su decisión. Aconsejada por quién sabe qué oculta fuerza del samamfo, que la hizo capaz del supremo acto de la rebelión" (132) [That was the reason for her decision. Counseled by who knows what hidden force of the *samamfo*, which made her capable of the supreme act of rebellion].

It is through the agency of the *samamfo* that the primal connectedness between La señora Mariot and Pedro is established. Pedro is, in fact, her daughter Sitaira's lover, and the text in another orienting moment makes this relationship quite manifest to the reader, immediately prior to the older woman's offer of herself to the young Pedro. The offer was accepted and its consummation is pointedly recorded in part as follows:

> Te acordarás de ella, de sus convulsiones, de la alegría de su entrega, de su fanática fidelidad al samamfo, y del espasmo final seguido por un leve comentario:
> —Ya una está vieja, pero talvez . . . talvez . . . (169)
>
> [You will remember her, her convulsions, the joy with which she gave herself, her fanatical fidelity to the *samamfo*, the final spasm and then the casual remark:
> "I'm old now, but maybe . . . maybe . . .]

The text underscores this event, one of primevally mythical significance, by suspending the chronological order, by, indeed, transcending the shackles of sequential existence, situating the action in the realm of the African "sous-réalité" [substratum reality]. In this, Duncan coheres with the creative tradition of the negritude writers, a tradition envisioned by Jean Paul Sartre as an

Orphic plunge into the very hell of the African condition to rescue the Eurydice of wholeness, that is, the liberating holism of pristine African values. The device the author employs for manifesting this particular grounding in the transcendence of his cultural heritage is the use of the future tense to narrate a past action, indeed, a recollection. The same stylistic device has been used by other contemporary Latin American writers. Students of the field will undoubtedly recall immediately Carlos Fuentes's novel, *La muerte de Artemio Cruz* [The Death of Artemio Cruz], itself quite clearly heavily indebted to Faulkner's *As I Lay Dying*. Notwithstanding this inescapable evidence of intertextuality, it would be absurd to set the limits of interpretation of Duncan's or Zapata's work purely within the Eurocentric matrices of magical realism, critical realism, the novel of the boom, the new novel, modernism, postmodernism, etc. etc.

The fact that this is a *samamfo* event legitimizes analytical penetration into the deeper Afrocentric resonances. And, certainly, the keen critic, fully informed about the African cultural heritage, will discern an almost sacralizing tone in the description of the event. The text thereby signals its awareness that its intertextual base is none other than humankind's most fundamental and earliest narrative, the corpus of primordial myths. In this case it is the myth of the son-consort, the self-sacrificing vibrant young liberator-victim. For the Yoruba people, as Zapata Olivella reveals in his novel, this myth is actualized in the story of Shango's father-brother Orungán, the son-consort of Yemayá—and Shango himself is a hero whose violent death is ultimately a self-immolation for the benefit of his people. For the ancient Africans from Kemet, it is enshrined in the multiplicity of narratives around Heru (Horus) and Wosir (Osiris) the son/brother-consort of Auset (Isis). Indeed, not only is the figure of Wosir conflated with that of his and Auset's son, Heru, but "the [very] Egyptian name of Osiris, ASAR or WOSIR, means 'begotten of Isis'" (Finch 181). The Greeks, thousands of years later, grappling with the unspeakable complexity of these mythical narratives, reduced the immense beauty of the Heru/Wosir-Auset-Set tragic tangle to the story of Oedipus-Jocasta-Creon. They thereby severely limited the power of the mythical narrative, but made it more comprehensible and "human," in their eyes at least.

The protagonist of Duncan's *Los cuatro espejos*, Charles McForbes, also participates in the primevally significant act of mating with an older woman, Engracia, who is a form of the earth mother and whose legitimate spouse, as was the case with La señora Mariot, had passed his prime. The street language of African-ancestored North Americans is replete with what must be considered references to this myth, albeit vaguely intuited across the fog of the past five hundred years of brutalization by Europeans. For it can be compellingly argued that the particular neo-African culture of black Americans has, with uncanny accuracy, sensed the essential mythological function of such primordial and "high-culture" figures as Heru/Wosir, Shango's father-brother Orungán, and Oedipus. Indeed, what is ultimately the defining and certainly the most dramatic characteristic of all of these mythical heroes—and, thanks to Sigmund Freud, this is poignantly true for Oedipus—is roundly proclaimed in the big MF term that is evoked with such power and such unrelenting frequency in the day-to-day world of many contemporary Africans in America.[1]

The eponymous protagonist of the novel *Kimbo* is, too, a servant of his *pueblo*, like Pedro Dull, and, to some considerably lesser extent, Charles McForbes. Indeed, Kimbo achieves the fullest possibilities of the role, for he literally gives up his life for his people (*pueblo*). And Kimbo is also pointedly identified in the text as a "hijo del samamfo" (122). Duncan, ever the artist on the move, presents in this novel a significantly more evolved *samamfo*. This work was published as one of the thirtieth anniversary (1989) titles of the prestigious Costa Rica Publishing House, but was first completed in 1982 and then reworked by 1985, and, amazingly, carries a 1990 publication date in the most official place of the copyright page. The definition given for *samamfo* in the glossary is the following:

> Espíritu y herencia de los Ancestros. En el samamfo están los valores y tradiciones del pueblo. Es la memoria colectiva de la raza-cultura que pasa de generación a generación y que se actualiza en los ritos religioso-seculares del

> pueblo, en sus luchas, en sus experiencias. Los Ancestros nunca han abandonado a sus herederos. (153)
>
> [The spirit and inheritance of the Ancestors. It is in the *samamfo* that the values and traditions of the people reside. It is the collective memory of the race-culture that passes on from generation to generation and that is actualized in the religio-secular rites of the people, in their struggles, in their experiences. The Ancestors have never abandoned their heirs.]

This particular definition is quite close to Duncan's articulations in the 1985 interview, and so the trajectory Duncan's thought has taken aligns it more solidly with Zapata Olivella's, whose 1983 novel placed the destiny of African-ancestored Americans, and by extension that of the entire race, squarely in the hands of the ancestors (the "gods" or *ntrw*). The Zapata text proclaims a peculiar and powerfully proactive presence of these beings, especially Shango, with the declaration: "¡Desde que Changó condenó al Muntu a sufrir el yugo de los extraños en extrañas tierras, hasta hoy, se suman los siglos sin que vuestros puños hayan dado cumplimiento a su mandato de haceros libres!" (511) [From the time that Shango first condemned his Muntu to suffer under an alien yoke in alien lands, to this day, centuries have past, and your fists have not yet carried out his command to set yourselves free!]. Liberation is the certain result, and, in fact, the very purpose for which the suffering was imposed. However, according to the Zapata reading of black history (as was demonstrated earlier), Shango only becomes the liberator through the agency of Legba. Legba's role in the Zapata text is played by the *samamfo* in Duncan's.

In both the Zapata and the Duncan texts the thrust towards liberation is the fundamental driving force. The central Duncan protagonists are liberators, *cimarrones*, who resemble in every respect the multitude of characters in Zapata's novel that are marked with the sign of Legba and are utterly dedicated to the work of liberation. Duncan, however, does not highlight the part played by Legba—who is a version of Hermes, who is himself a version of Jehuti (Thoth); and Jehuti was the agent, facilitator, empowerer divinity in ancient Africa. Rather, Duncan focuses on the contemporary human manifestation of the liberator/*cimarrón* figure, so much so that his messianic and hence "syncretic" dimension appears to be privileged.

Our discussion in Chapter One showed that whereas the term "syncretism" was common currency in the scholarly discourse on American culture and civilization prior to the explosion in Afro-centric scholarship that has been triggered by Molefi Asante's *Afrocentricity: Towards a Theory of Social Change* (1980), it now needs to be reassessed. For it is becoming increasingly impossible to ignore the claim inscribed in the title of Cheikh Anta Diop's fundamental *The African Origin of Civilization*, and expressly articulated in the following celebrated lines from the eighteenth century French scholar Constantine Francis Chassebeuf de Volney:

> There [in Black Africa, or African Ethiopia as he would have put it] a people, now forgotten, discovered, while others were yet barbarians, the elements of the arts and sciences. A race of men now rejected from society for their *sable* [polite for "black"] *skin and frizzled* [polite for "nappy"] *hair*, founded on the study of the laws of nature [the Kemetic *ntr* appears to be the etymon of the Latin root "*natura-*"], those civil and religious systems which still govern the universe. (Cited in Jackson *Man, God, and Civilization* 205)

The concept of "syncretism" was posited on the unsubstantiated white supremacist assumption that so-called Judaeo-Christian values were diametrically opposed and superior to African ones. The historical data resoundingly reject this assumption. The messiah element in the *cimarrón* results not from an aping of European religious thought, but rather from a fidelity to an African philosophico-theological tradition that is literally the "mother" of all human cultures and civilizations.

Duncan's first fully developed *cimarrón* figure is, indeed, *La paz del pueblo*'s Pedro Dull, who is clearly a messiah figure. This role is definitively inscribed into the text by the official religious voice of a pastor of the Christian church. The voice proclaims Pedro's messianic role in a "sermón sin sentido" [a sermon without meaning] that occurs at a key point in the development of the action. The pertinent text reads as follows:

> Jugando, esperaban. Como si esa noche fuese a nacer el mesías. Como si aquel sermón sin sentido, tantas veces predicado por el pastor "De entre mi pueblo levantaré a uno —dice el Señor— le quitaré el corazón de piedra y le daré uno de carne, y será la liberación de muchos y la gloria del pueblo". Cuando el pastor decía eso, los hombres se miraban unos a otros sin entender nada. (184)
>
> [As they played, they waited. As if on that night the messiah were to be born. As if that sermon without meaning, preached so many times by the pastor "From among my people I will raise up one," says the Lord. "I will take away his heart of stone and will give him one of flesh, and he will be the liberation of many and the glory of his people." When the pastor would proclaim this, the men would look at one another, not understanding anything.]

The sermon is only temporarily "sin sentido," for its meaning, although hidden from the official man of God, becomes quite clear to the people (*pueblo*)—who in the final analysis constitute the core of the work's universe—just three pages later, on the very final page of the text:

> Los hombres ya no esperaban nada. De pronto entendieron la obstinada predicación del pastor, y estaban seguros de que él mismo no lo entendería jamás. Y vieron con toda claridad, en el profundo silencio de la madrugada, el silencio del medio día. (Cuminá danzaba la paz del pueblo). (187)
>
> [The men did not wait for anything else. They immediately understood the pastor s insistent preaching, and they were sure that he himself would not ever understand it. And they saw in all clarity, in the deep silence of the early morning, the noontime silence. (Cuminá danced his peace to the people).]

The style chosen by Duncan to encode his message, as we indicated before, is one that calls for very attentive, active readers, who are co-creators. Only this kind of reader will appreciate the richly epiphanous nature of the passage just cited. It declares Pedro's full transformation into a messiah figure, as announced by a spokesman of the prestige Euro-Christian church. But this spokesman is incapable of understanding the fully African nature of Pedro's messiahhood, which attains its climax only when Cuminá (a truly neo-African "god," "*ntr*," or orisha, for he was invented by Africans from Jamaica who practice Christianity) dances his *Peace to the People*.

The fullness of meaning of the two passages last quoted is realized only when they are linked to yet another that appears in the text just a few lines before the last quote: "La señora Mariot estaba pensando en Pedro y Pedro estaba pensando en las grandezas del samamfo, en la pasión que despierta la naturaleza en función sexual, en la tara del tiempo, en Cuminá, doblado en los bananales" (186) [La señora Mariot was thinking about Pedro and Pedro was thinking about the greatness of the *samamfo*, about the passion that nature arouses as a function of sexuality, about the counterweight of time, about Cuminá, bent over in the banana fields]. *Cuminá* is a New World orisha, an ancestor of Jamaican Africans, and, most significantly, one elevated to the pantheon by Duncan's creative intelligence under the guidance of the *samamfo* (Legba).

The term *cuminá* is defined in the glossary of *La paz del pueblo* as simply "dios" [god, *ntr*]. It is clearly a Hispanicization of "Kumina," just as *pocomía* is Duncan's Spanish language version of "Pukumina." In the study, *Central American Writers of West Indian Origin: A New Hispanic Literature*, we affirmed that Kumina and Pukumina were household terms to most Jamaicans at least, if not to many other Caribbean people. We indicated that Leonard Barrett, whose work on Caribbean and other Afro-American cultures is well-recognized, traced the etymology of "Kumina" as follows: "The word comes from two Twi words: *Akom*—'to be possessed,' and *Ana*—'by an ancestor'" (48). It is one of the many lexical items from the Twi language of the Ashanti people that remain in the everyday speech of present-day Jamaicans. Kumina for him, then, is a folk religion of some of those Africans who have become natives of Jamaica. It is related to myal, which can be considered the benign counterpart to obeah (insofar as there is any real distinction between the two in the popular mind). "Kumina," Barrett also reports, originally referred to the "rigorous dance" which accompanied the myal—"being in a state of possession"—ritual. "Kumina" can refer also to the actual service in which the dance of possession is the central act. On the other hand, Pukumina is for Barrett the Afro-Christian syncretic sect which, of the three principal ones in Jamaica, is the most African in its rituals and beliefs. We brought closure to our discussion asserting that "Cassidy and LePage explain that the obviously related form 'pocomania,' was established by a false Hispanicizing of a probably African form 'pu+kumona.' What emerges from all this is that the terms Kumina and Pukumina exhibit the phonological dynamism that frequently characterizes the most widely used lexical items, and that they are clear samples of Africanisms in popular Jamaican speech" (48).

The passage from *La paz del pueblo* that was last quoted further demonstrates Duncan's intuitive understanding of the deepest levels of the central mythos of mankind, again, one that was first articulated in the art and literature of Kemet. For in the text, Pedro enters into one important part of the role of the son-consort who fecundates his earth mother in the natural sexual way and then proceeds to fecundate mother earth ritually by watering her with his blood, his life's blood. The rite can only be effected fully through the actual death and dismemberment of the virile young liberator. This is entirely what the Wosir (Osiris) myth is about; he was murdered and dismembered by his brother Set, his polar opposite. Set, of course, is the etymon of our Satan, the diametrical opposite of goodness and liberation. Duncan's version of the myth respects the realities of the sociohistorical context, for the most important arena of struggle and the real focus of liberation for the West Indian Costa Rican population (of principally Jamaican provenance) has to be the banana plantation.

One of the more important precursor short stories to *La paz del pueblo* is the lead and title work of the collection, *La rebelión pocomía y otros relatos*. This collection, published in 1976, is still Duncan's latest in the short-story genre, and it must be recalled that the closing/opening "*relato*" of the book is the pivotal "Los mitos ancestrales." The main character of "La rebelión pocomía" is also a liberator inspired by Cuminá. This rebel figure, Jean Paul, is the precursor to Pedro Dull, for he, too, leads West Indian Costa Rican banana workers in industrial action against the exploiting plantation owners. His precursorship parallels that of the biblical John the Baptist to the Christian Messiah. He is a John (Jean), whom the text connects quite explicitly to his biblical namesake: "En el entierro habló Jean Paul, como otrora hablara un Bautista en el desierto" (9) [Jean Paul spoke at the funeral in the manner in which that other John once spoke in the wilderness]. Jean's identification with his prototype is more complete, however, than is Pedro Dull's, for Jean attains the fullest level of sacrificial service to his people; he actually gives up his life. His completeness is echoed in the latest liberator, Kimbo, of *Kimbo*, for this hero—-Heru (Horus)—as well actually gives his life for the good of the people.

Duncan is quite painstaking in his development of the messianic imagery with respect to Kimbo. In the final pages of the text, one of the reliable narrators definitively inscribes Kimbo's messiahhood declaring: "Sí, él devuelve las esperanzas. No murió en vano. Vuelve de su tumba y el mundo va a creer su palabra" (144) [Yes, he brings back our hopes. He did not die in vain. He will come back from his grave, and the world will believe his word]. Just as was indicated with the text that was cited earlier with reference to the "sermón sin sentido," Duncan, who was schooled in the Christian theological tradition, deliberately gives a biblical tone to his text. Within the constraints of the short-story format, Duncan has cloaked Jean Paul in an analogous biblical aura. It is a matter of significance that Charles McForbes of *Los cuatro espejos* is the only major protagonist of the "black experience" novels who clearly does not enter into the paradigm in any substantive sense. He is, however, a representative of the conflict between the Eurocentric and the Afrocentric worlds, as was most certainly the unnamed hero of "Los mitos ancestrales."

Nicolás Guillén, Cuba's poet laureate of the twentieth century, has given to the world an archetypal liberator figure in his poem "Elegía a Jesús Menéndez" [Elegy for Jesús Menéndez] (The poem was discussed at some length in Chapter Four). In life and in art, this Jesús—and Guillén is not above punning on the obviously profound significance of his given name—traveled the same path as Duncan's Jean Paul, Pedro Dull, and Kimbo. The Cuban Jesús wages his battles not on the banana plantation but in the canefield. He, like Kimbo in Duncan's fictional universe, like Wosir/Heru and

Shango in the universe of African mythology, like the Christian Messiah, returns from the tomb to anchor the hope of his people liberated through his suffering and death, declaring: "—He vuelto, no temáis" (Guillén 1: 436) [I have returned, have no fear]. One of the most important of the symbols with which Shango is associated, and which in a sense define him—as it was for Zeus and Min (a much earlier Kemetic deity)—is the lightning bolt, the "gran relámpago bruñido" of the Guillén poem. Shango is known simply as the "god" of thunder. The Guillén text therefore makes the same kind of "amazing connections" as do the various Duncan texts, and, of course, the Zapata Olivella text to which reference has been made before.

Frantz Fanon, as our discussion in Chapters Three and Four has highlighted, made it clear that the colonized person can achieve fullness of being only in the crucible of a holistic liberation, one that entails as a necessary and, in fact, sufficient condition the overcoming of sociopolitical oppression. Fanon extolled as an exemplary *cimarrón* the Rebel character from the play by his fellow Martinican, Césaire, *Et les chiens se taisaient* [And the Dogs Were Silent]. Fanon developed a coherent theoretical framework for his position, and his discourse includes the language of metaphor. One of the most poignant of his metaphors is laughter. In The *Wretched of the Earth*, he describes the second of the three phases in the development of a full-blown revolutionary consciousness in part as follows: "We spew ourselves up; but already underneath laughter can be heard" (179). Janheinz Jahn, one of the early but still much respected commentators on neo-African literature, reporting in *Muntu* on the tenets of a peculiarly Bantu philosophy, asserts that "'man' has not only the power of the word, but also the power of laughter. Laughter is a special kind of flowing; in neo-African poetry it is repeatedly associated with a river" (139).

Duncan's views on the question of laughter were specifically elicited and proffered in the interview referred to earlier. He declared that

> When you hear black people laugh . . . well, let us take, for example, the case of a play written by another author from Limón, based on Joaquín Gutiérrez's

> *Puerto Limón*. The author presents the situation of the complete breakdown of the system for those engaged in the banana industry on the Atlantic coast. After all those years of labor, the company is suddenly leaving and there is nobody to sell bananas to. . . . The black man starts laughing, whereas the Spaniards carry on with their "¡Ay! ¿Qué vamos a hacer?" and all those lamentations. The black man's laughter erupts at that final moment [of *La paz del pueblo*] when this character, Sitaira, sees that an alliance has been formed, that there is a ray of hope. (288)

The very final sentence of *La paz del pueblo* is precisely: "Pero todos oyeron a lo lejos una carcajada de mujer que venía del río" (187) [But everyone heard in the distance a peal of woman's laughter coming from the river].

The peals of Sitaira's triumphal laughter literally flow from the *samamfo*, for she has already been immolated in the prime of her female fecundity, and she has returned to the waters of life. She shares with her mother, La señora Mariot, the role of earth mother, assuming all the raw vitality and beauty, as well as her mother's physical fecundity. Duncan has shaped her character in conformity with the most pristine state of the mythos, when the female was the sole creative force and hence the only adequate sacrificial victim. Mother and daughter both are quite clearly specially associated with the *samamfo*. The daughter's laughter coming forth from the river—the actual water and blood, for she had been murdered, immolated, there in the river—affirms the advent of the new liberator and hence sacrificial victim, Pedro, the male *cimarrón*. Pedro, the newly formed liberator is, then, like Wosir, the symbolic son of his consort Sitaira, and, indeed, the consort of his mother figure, la Señora Mariot. But, he is still a liberator in formation, not ready as yet for the fullness of the role. It is rather Sitaira whose blood waters the water—not precisely the earth. He will evolve, however, into Kimbo, and he was prefigured in Jean Paul. Consciously or unconsciously, Duncan has homed in on all of the rich dimensions of the fundamentally African mythos and has creatively echoed the articulations of Fanon and Jahn. The same laughter and the river are evoked powerfully in the finale of Guillén's pivotal poem "Llegada" [Arrival]: "nuestra risa madrugará sobre los ríos y los pájaros" (1: 116) [our laughter will rise up early over the rivers and the birds].

Jahn's commentary on the confluence of laughter and river, which we discussed in Chapter Two, was supported by exhaustive reference to the texts of African-ancestored writers from the Americas: the Ecuadorian Adalberto Ortiz, the Cuban Marcelino Arozarena, the North American Paul Vesey, Césaire, and, of course, Guillén. And it would be impossible not to evoke the following opening strophe of Langston Hughes's classic poem:

> I've known rivers:
> I've known rivers ancient as the world and older than the
> flow of human blood in human veins. (4)

Hughes's verse, as does Duncan's prose, resonates with mankind's oldest and surest symbols of fertility, water and blood. And, once the right line of approach has been identified, the interpretation deepens and expands considerably. Thus Nelson Estupiñán Bass's classic novel, *El último río*, translated as *Pastrana's Last River*, contributes significantly to the exploration of the trope, for José Antonio Pastrana's last river is, in fact, the alluring female protagonist, the flower of Ecuadorean womanhood, Ana Mercedes. The laughter element is not included in either Estupiñán or Hughes, and, correspondingly, Duncan, at other epiphanous moments, strikes the deep chord of laughter (even in its less intense form, the smile) without evoking the river. One important instance of this is precisely the absolute finale of *Los cuatro espejos*: "Una sonrisa profunda iluminó el color de mi piel" (163) [A deep smile illumined the color of my skin]. The novel essentially told the tale of a black man's struggle to come to terms with his blackness. Duncan explained that the *sonrisa* was inscribed into the text at that significant final moment to signal Charles's (the main protagonist) success in his quest, to indicate that Charles was again at "peace" with himself. "Even when he . . . doesn't know exactly what he is going to do, he at least has learned to accept himself: 'This is me,' you see" (289). Kimbo utters a final "word" to his wife an instant before he is immolated in accord with the established twentieth century American ritual—he is gunned down by a rogue policeman. The "word," we are told in the text, "Fue una sonrisa linda. . . . Nunca le había visto sonreír así" (148) [It was a beautiful smile. . . . I had never seen him smile like that].

According to Henry Louis Gates's reading of the mythos, laughter is fundamental to the human enterprise, for signifying is the core of all art, and signifying is Legba's basic activity. Legba is the Signifying Monkey. And, as was fully explored in the opening section of Chapter Two, laughter is a central element of the ethos of the West Indian "man-of-words," to use Roger Abrahams's preferred terminology. Duncan's approach to laughter is rooted, then, in his African cultural heritage, which itself undergirds his fundamental West Indianness.

□ □ □

Quince Duncan, a West Indian Costa Rican, is a man of two worlds, as the epigraph from A. Sivanandan that he uses for "Los mitos ancestrales" proclaims: "On the margin of European culture... the 'coloured' intellectual is an artifact of colonial history... He is a creature of two worlds, and of none" (73). The preceding analysis shows Duncan's artistic activity to revolve around the process of resolving the conflict of the colonized person. The artistic task is an act of *cimarronaje*. It consists essentially for him in the affirmation of his West Indianness as a neo-African cultural manifestation. Indeed, the novel *Los cuatro espejos* is a dramatization of this conflict, for Charles McForbes, while not being a deliberately fashioned alter ego, mirrors Duncan's life experience in some important ways. Like Duncan he is a trained priest of the Anglican faith, who, after a period of exercising his priesthood in rural and African West Indian Limón, departs definitively for the capital city, San José, a modern Western urban center. Here, the confrontation literally assumes crisis proportions, as one morning Charles awakes to find that he is unable to see the color of his face in the mirror. The novel ends, as was indicated earlier, in an epiphanous moment that is clearly a metaphor for success. A success, it has been argued, that is manifested through the novelist's artistic growth in *La paz del pueblo* and *Kimbo*.

The case of the novel *Final de calle* is particularly instructive in this regard. The circumstances out of which it sprang have already been discussed in this chapter. Bereft of reference to the West Indian Costa Rican experience, the novel is, nevertheless, consistent with Duncan's neo-African aesthetic. It is essentially an existential novel heavy with the burden of man's fundamental absurdity, so poignantly symbolized in the very title, *Final de calle* [Dead End]. This is the only one of Duncan's novels that plumbs entirely without relief the depths of pessimism. By so doing, the author gives indirect but unequivocal expression to his rejection of the Eurocentric, hegemonic, and, of course, racist ethos of the Costa Rican cultural establishment.

Along with his fellow Costa Rican, Eulalia Bernard, a poet, and the Panamanians, Gerardo Maloney and Melvin Brown, also poets, and Carlos Guillermo Wilson, poet, novelist, and short story writer, Duncan has created a very impressive Central American West Indian literature. It is, indeed, a "New Hispanic Literature" and at the same time a very Caribbean/West Indian expression. The four central tropes, namely, the *samamfo*, the *cimarrón*, the river, and laughter have been shown to be linked to the neo-African core of Caribbean creativity. The themes of the plantation, interracial love, and the journey, along with the four tropes, are sufficient to make for a profound "West Indianness" in Duncan's literature. It is clear that Duncan, Bernard, Maloney, Wilson, Brown, and others, authors of Anglophone Caribbean heritage, have begun to create a literature in Spanish that is essentially similar in form and content to the Anglophone literature emanating from the region. The similarity, which can be labelled "West Indianness," is based on an essential thread of homogeneity that runs through all Caribbean cultures, and hence all Caribbean literary expressions: in English, French, Spanish, Dutch, and their corresponding Creoles, especially in Papiamento (a Portuguese-based Creole of the Dutch-speaking Caribbean) and the Creole language of Haiti.

The four central symbols have been developed for an artistic universe in which the plantation is paramount. Charles McForbes's second wife Ester is a white/mestizo woman, a solid member of the San José upper class. The theme of black-white love runs through both *La paz del pueblo* and *Kimbo*. It is a theme that was of some importance to the white/mestizo Panamanian and Costa Rican writers who, before Duncan and his "group," began to concern themselves artistically with the experience of West Indian Central Americans. Such mainstream authors as Panama's Joaquín Beleño C., and Costa Rica's Joaquín Gutiérrez, Fabián Dobles, and Carlos Luis Fallas can be legitimately considered the precursors of the Duncan "group" (Smart, *Central American* 13-34).

According to George Lamming of Barbados, one of the Caribbean's best known novelists, the theme of the journey is one of the most explicit principles of communality in the literature of the region. All the major Caribbean works, in Lamming's view, are stories of a voyage of some type. He identifies various phases in the journey metaphor: the original journey, Columbus, the Middle Passage, etc.; the migration from a rural to an urban environment, depicted in such novels as *Jane's Career* (1914) and *The Harder They Come* (1980), by the Jamaicans H.G. DeLisser and Michael Thelwell respectively, as well as in *La Rue cases-nègres* (1950) by the Martinican, Joseph Zobel; the interior journey, the problem of self-realization, as in *Minty Alley* (1936), *A Brighter Sun* (1952), and *A House for Mr. Biswas* (1961), by the Trinidadians C.L.R. James, Samuel Selvon, and V.S. Naipaul, respectively; the journey into new exile in the metropolitan centers, as in Selvon's *The Lonely Londoners* (1956); finally there is the journey of reaffirmation, the journey back to Africa, either real or symbolic. This phase is best appreciated in Brathwaite's *The Arrivants*.

Charles McForbes made several journeys back and forth between the two worlds before undertaking the final Orphic journey of "reaffirmation" back to the Limón of his neo-African West Indian roots. He had already undertaken the "journey within," from country (Limón) to town (San José), as well as the "interior journey" of self-realization, rising above the limits of his original immediate socioeconomic circumstances. In *La paz del pueblo* as well as in *Kimbo*, the journey theme is central. In both novels the protagonists attain their full dimension as liberator/*cimarrón* by journeying back to the sites of struggle and sacrifice.

The question of language is the most important one for any "word soldier," and certainly it must be so for the "man-of-words in the West Indies" (Abrahams). The question impinges in a particularly poignant way on the creativity of Duncan and his "group." It could be argued that the non-West Indian precursors fail to penetrate the inner reaches of West Indian literature precisely on the basis of language. Beleño is the precursor who comes the closest to mastering the speech of his subjects, but he never quite does (Smart, *Central American* 36-40). With Duncan the very language of narration is West Indian. It is fully Hispanic, for it is Spanish, but it exudes a peculiar and authentic Anglophone West Indian flavor. This is done first and foremost through the use of what Stephen Henderson, in *Understanding the New Black Poetry*, called "mascon" terms, described as "Certain words and constructions [which] seem to carry an inordinate charge of emotional and psychological weight, so that whenever they are used they set all kinds of bells ringing, all kinds of synapses snapping, on all kinds of levels" (44). Duncan's narrative is charged with such terms as: *yuca, bofe, cho!, obeahman, dopí, pocomía, Cuminá, Hermano araña*, and *Kimbo*. The second mechanism through which the authentic West Indian flavor is generally inserted is the use of an artistic bilingualism. In Duncan's prose this technique is not used in any significant way. However, it is in Maloney, Brown, Bernard and Wilson. It is clearly a technique that lends itself more to verse, and, indeed, Duncan prefers to write his poetry—still unpublished—in English.

In summation, it can be affirmed that Quince Duncan's literature is one of the richest and most exciting cultural products of the Caribbean region. *Cimarronaje* is at the center of his art, it is a quintessentially West Indian *cimarronaje*. And the most fundamental defining symbol of this *cimarronaje* is the peculiarly West Indian orisha, *Cuminá*.

Epilogue

The archetypal African-in-America protagonist of Aimé Césaire's *La tragédie du roi Christophe* [The Tragedy of King Christophe] posed two questions in answer to which he proclaimed prophetically:

> sentez-vous la douleur d'un homme de ne savoir
> pas de quel nom il s'appelle? A quoi son nom
> l'appelle? Hélas seule le sait notre mère l'Afrique! (37)
>
> [do you know the pain a man feels not knowing
> what name he goes by? What his name calls
> him to? Alas only our Mother Africa really knows!]

If only Mother Africa knows the answer to the two questions, it is reasonable to conclude that she, like a good mother, has shared her knowledge with her children and imbued them with the power and the obligation to communicate that knowledge to the rest of humanity. Armed with that knowledge, some of Africa's children, once voiceless in the hallowed assemblies of the "Western" academy, have undertaken the task of giving a legitimate name to the area of studies that many scholars were once happy to call "Afro-Hispanic Literature and Culture." In keeping with the spirit of Césaire and my findings reported in the preceding chapters, I am proposing that this area of studies be renamed "Hispanophone

Africana Literature and Culture."

Many voices from the community of Spanish-speaking peoples resident in the United States have expressed a distinct preference for their group to be referred to with the term "Latino" over "Hispanic" or even "Hispano." They argue that "Hispanic" and "Hispano" conjure up images of Spain and hence Europe, whereas "Latino" evokes Latin America, that is, itself. For the countless millions of African-ancestored people who continue to endure the hellish racism of Latin American society, that distinction is utterly without meaning. For the scholars who know that the "Latin" of "Latin America" is directly connected to the Latin of Rome, as in "Graeco-Roman," the distinction is, at best, frivolous. The roots of, the resonances and associations conjured up by, "Latino" are quintessentially European, connected to the very bedrock of so-called Western civilization, the veritable "classical" world. On the other hand, as our discussion in Chapter Two and throughout this book made clear, the roots of, the resonances and associations conjured up by "Hispanic" are profoundly African. We empathize with the ardent emotions of those who would privilege "Latino" over "Hispanic," but reason dictates that we reject their position.

The term "Africana" is a noun that can be used as an adjective. It is clearly, then, per se, much more "substantive" than "Afro," the prefix form of the adjective "African." Chapter Two and Chapter One focus specifically on arguments that established the "African-ness" of *hispanidad*, that is, the quality of being Hispanic. Therefore the combination of "African" with "Hispanic" is ultimately a tautology, but one that we must tolerate if we are to live in this current world. And, "African" is the redundant element, since it is contained in "Hispanic." The label "Afro-Hispanic," far from signaling that *hispanidad* has an African core, suggests rather the opposite, that *hispanidad* is fundamentally European, and that there is a subspecies of it that has as its differential factor an exposure to African exotica.

The term "Afro" as in "Afro-American" has, in any case, fallen out of favor with the self-appointed guardians of political correctness in the linguistic realm of contemporary North American society. It has gone the way of "colored," "Negro," and even

"Black," and has been replaced by "African" as in "African American," because some self-conscious purists piously argue that reverential respect for Mother Africa prohibits the shortening of "African" to the prefix "Afro." This argument, it appears to us, is one of the heart rather than the head, for the term "European" itself is normally reduced to the prefix form "Euro-," as in "Euro-American" for "European American." By very definition there is absolutely no stigma associated with this particular prefix form, which, furthermore, is the absolute analogue of "Afro-." Indeed, if the ardent defenders of Mother Africa's honor wanted unimpeachable correctness in the generation of an "o" prefix for the sacred "African" term, they would have to propose the form "Africo-" rather than "Afro-" on analogy with such terms as: "Graeco-Roman" for Grecian Roman, "Americo-Liberian" for "American Liberian," "Hispano-Romance" for "Hispanic Romance," and "Franco-Prussian" for "French-Prussian."

The term "Anglophone" is defined in the *Webster's Ninth New Collegiate Dictionary* as: "consisting of or belonging to an English-speaking population" (86). The exactly analogous "Francophone" has the meaning "consisting of or belonging to a French-speaking population" (489). Scholars in the field of literature and culture of Spanish and Portuguese expression sorely need the terms "Hispanophone" and "Lusophone." Surely, is it just a matter of time before these legitimate lexical items will be recorded in all English dictionaries. We have opted for "Hispanophone Africana" rather than "African Hispanic"—a term that would presumably be more politically correct in the current North American academy—or the more linguistically orthodox "Africo-Hispanic." For, in our view, whereas any expression that combines "African" with "Hispanic" would be tautologous, the expression "Hispanophone Africana" is least consistent with white supremacist ideology. This latter expression resoundingly proclaims that *hispanidad* is but one of the manifestations of *africanía* (African culture and civilization) by assigning to the African element the substantive function, and to the putative European one the subordinate, qualifying, function.

Immutability is perfection. Until such time as we have attained perfection, we humbly claim the right to tinker with our basic terminology.

□ □ □

The Trinidad and Tobago saying, "After one time is two time," expresses a firm determination to reverse an unfavorable state of affairs occasioned by the speaker's leniency in dealing with those who would do him harm. It articulates pithily and powerfully the mood of the colonized intellectual elite in the Americas at the dawning of the second five hundred years of hegemonic European presence. Enough is enough, "masa day done," "our day has come." In the spirit of Legba, this epilogue is simply a beginning. In the spirit of the historical moment, the conclusion of the first five hundred years of death and destruction for most of us in the Americas is simply a beginning of the second five hundred years of liberation and fullness of being.

Our first chapter ended with the declaration that the thrust to deconstruction was of more profound significance than even Jacques Derrida suspected it could be. All psychologically and culturally healthy persons of African ancestry need to undertake this deconstruction of the governing paradigms of so-called Western civilization, for these paradigms are posited on the destruction of African civilizations and are founded consciously and unconsciously on untruths or half-truths. Our text has referred to a series of thinkers whose central tenets constitute an articulation of this principle: Frantz Fanon, Selwyn Cudjoe, Kortright Davis, Patrick Taylor, Asa Hilliard, Ivan Van Sertima, George G. M. James, Cheikh Anta Diop, Théophile Obenga, Yosef ben-Jochannan, John G. Jackson, Chancellor Williams; the list is extremely long. Our text seeks to be added to the canon of emancipatory writing. It has focused on the realm of Hispanophone Africana letters. This is precisely the realm from which the most potent post-1992 voices will emerge.

The 1492 experience has been the root of much evil, not only for the Americas, but for the world. If, as many scholars hold, the Enlightenment was the fundamental shaping element of modern human civilization, then the 1492 experience gave birth to the Enlightenment. The 1492 experience "begot" the Atlantic slave trade and the plantation system. These in turn breathed life into capitalism and spawned, as C.L.R. James in *The Black Jacobins* and Eric Williams in *Capitalism and Slavery* have argued compellingly, both the industrial revolution and the French revolution. And the world as we know it today, divided into First, Second, and Third, into North and South, into a tiny but powerful white Western minority versus an immense, powerless majority, sprung directly from these cataclysmic societal processes.

Martin Bernal, as we pointed out in Chapter Three, provides the nuts-and-bolts evidence of one of the heinous and very representative evils perpetrated by the Enlightenment, namely, "The Fabrication of Ancient Greece 1785-1985." In the words of Cheikh Anta Diop, ideology prevailed over the scientific method. To put it simply, there was no way the European intelligentsia would be allowed any other preoccupation but that of justifying slavery and the slave trade, the goose that was laying abundant eggs of pure gold. The ideology of white supremacy was specifically created by the "enlightened ones" as the only antidote to the naggings of both a moral and an intellectual conscience.

Over and over again in the preceding pages, we have attempted to make the case for the necessity to deconstruct the Eurocentric hegemonic worldview that has shaped us all. We have combated white supremacist ideology in the specific battlefield of Hispanophone Africana literary studies. We have engaged in the deconstruction of the prevailing white supremacist ideologically based paradigms by constructing an African-centered analysis of specific literary works produced by African-ancestored writers from Latin America. Through this analysis we have sought to move these works from the dark margins, to which they have been relegated by Eurocentric literary scholars, to the wonderful new center of focus. We have shown that since this center is attained through a purified or liberated epistemology, that is, one not conditioned by the need to justify the unacceptable, it is necessarily richer, wider, and deeper than the current center of focus for the academy.

Our text has sought to present coherently and cogently all of the scholarship that validates our defiant declaration at this momentous historical juncture: "After one time, is two time."

❐ Notes ❐

Chapter One

1. See, for example, the works by Leonard Barrett, Alfred Métraux, and Lydia Cabrera listed in "Works Cited."

2. This is cited in John G. Jackson, *Man, God and Civilization* 205. It is taken from Volney's *The Ruins of Empire*. Volney, of course, was an eighteenth century French aristocrat, and it would be naive to expect that the views contained in this much quoted passage reflected the entirety of his thought.

3. The works of these authors are listed in "Works Cited."

4. Consistent with the mythology that has had to pass as science in the reconstituted academy, the explanation is offered with a straight face that the black Madonna of Czestochowa owes her blackness simply to the effect of the smoke from the millions of candles that have been burned before her over the hundreds of years. Any one with a modicum of common sense and good faith will be forced to reject this explanation as absurdly ex post facto. Was the Madonna, then, a white one for the first century; and why didn't they have the respect to clean the soot from the face of the revered icon?

5. This is offered, obviously, as a common sense judgment rendered by someone who is neither a theologian nor a biblical scholar.

6. In my own daughter's 5th grade social sciences text, *The Growth of Civilization*, a work prepared by the Social Science Staff of the Educational Research Council of America, with a 1982 copyright, I came upon the following:

> Until a few years ago, people thought that civilization first appeared in Egypt. Then scholars learned about Sumer. Now they believe that Egypt was the second civilization, not the first. (129)

Offering a bald assertion of this nature without any commentary offends grievously against the multiculturalism of the 1990s in the United States academic environment. Above all, it is simply sloppy scholarship. Indeed, it is almost pure propaganda.

□ □ □

Chapter Two

1. There is an entire group of black scholars who diligently eschew the connections with Africa. They find this the most appropriate way to assert the validity of the North American black experience and its right to exist in contemporary society on a par with the corresponding white experience.

2. Cited by Lilyan Kesteloot 110. Senghor—from Senegal—along with Césaire—from Martinique—and Léon Gontran Damas—from French Guiana—founded the literary movement they called "Négritude." This movement was the fruition of the literary ferment which affected them as young students in Paris in the early 1930s.

3. Quoted in V.S. Naipaul, *The Middle Passage* (81), from a local newspaper, *The Trinidad Guardian*.

4. We have, indeed, beginning on page 52, cited almost verbatim from pages 65-69 of our book *Nicolás Guillén, Popular Poet of the Caribbean*, with the permission of the University of Missouri Press. Copyright © 1990 by the Curators of the University of Missouri.

5. A "wannabe" is someone who wants to be (wanna be) what he is not.

6. I refer, of course, to the sonnet that ends with the quintessentially baroque tercet:

no sólo en plata o víola troncada
se vuelva, mas tú y ello juntamente
en tierra, en humo, en polvo, en sombra, en nada.

[not only turns to silver or plucked violet, but you and it together become earth, smoke, dust, shadow, nothing]. (*The Penguin Book of Spanish Verse* 213)

7. Starting on page 70, we have been citing verbatim from our article, "The Trickster *Pícaro* in Three Contemporary Afro-Hispanic Novels." We are grateful to the editors of the *Afro-Hispanic Review* for the necessary permissions.

8. On the question of the Manichean colonial world, see Fanon (29-36). And on the matter of how this relates to artistic activity, see Fanon's pivotal chapter, "On National Culture," setting forth the ideas which would later be elaborated by Amilcar Cabral into the Dialectical Theory of Identification (especially 177-83).

□ □ □

Chapter Three

1. Carpentier is highly regarded by literary scholars who have addressed the question of Guillén's peculiar contribution to Western art. Roberto González-Echevarría, for example, in his piece "Guillén as Baroque: Meaning in *Motivos de son*," claims that "Carpentier's *Concierto barroco* is in many ways one of the most perceptive pieces of criticism on Guillén's poetry and a clarification of its vast genealogy and progeny" (306). For, he argues, because the "inclusive" Baroque aesthetics created a space for the exotica that was and continues to be the peculiarly American, "The speech of blacks in Góngora's poetry is like the presence of Inca or Aztec deities on church friezes" (305). All of this is true and useful, as far as it goes. However, the central thesis of my book is that this line of approach is incomplete. In fact, I have suggested the following in "Popular Black Intellectualism in Gerardo Maloney's *Juega vivo*": "In the exclusively Hispanic literary context, Maloney may be termed a practitioner of the baroque 'conceptismo,' and his art may be seen as simply a remanifestation of a secular Peninsular tradition. Such a vision would be inordinately narrow, and the claim of being derived exclusively from the baroque would be just as tendentious as the claim that the baroque itself derives exclusively from the secular African tradition which both preceded it in time and with which it had considerable contact. To appreciate fully Maloney's art, one has to place it in an African context, not exclusively obviously, but squarely and solidly" (46).

2. In January 1996, the Trinidad and Tobago government, under Basdeo Panday—that nation's first prime minister of East Indian descent—decreed March 30 a national holiday to celebrate the anniversary of the 1951 repeal of British colonial legislation outlawing the practice of the Spiritual Baptist (Shouter) faith. It was the 1951 event that Lovelace used as the historical base for *The Wine of Astonishment*.

3. This information is taken from the "cronología" [chronology] given by both Angel Augier, in *Nicolás Guillén obra poética 1920-1958*, and Nancy Morejón, in *Recopilación de textos sobre Nicolás Guillén*. In the same spirit of flagrant expansionism, the United States government manipulated the internal political situation in Gran Colombia so that the province of Panama would successfully secede in 1903. The first act of the government of the newly "independent" nation, and in the real sense the primary purpose for which it was created, was the signing of the Hays-Bunai treaty ceding "in perpetuity" to the United States a strip of land ten miles wide that cut through the very center of the new nation. This was for the purpose of constructing the Panama Canal.

4. See Ian I. Smart, "The African Heritage in Spanish Caribbean Literature," 23.

5. Gerardo Maloney, *Juega vivo* 19. For more on this topic see Smart, *Central American Writers of West Indian Origin* 28.

□ □ □

Chapter Four

1. Walcott is, of course, employing his characteristically beautiful, densely poetic, and eminently Caribbean language. Only those of us raised in a region where common folk persist in the infuriatingly hypercorrect linguistic practice of renaming the banana with the more "proper" term *fig*, taken directly from the colonizers' lexical repertoire, can appreciate Walcott's rich irony.

2. The passage beginning on the previous page with "It follows. . ." and ending at this point is taken from my article, "*Changó, el gran putas* as Liberation Literature,." which was published in the *CLA Journal*, Volume 35 (1991) 15-30. Several lines from this article have also been quoted on pages 128-29, 135-37, and 138-41. I am grateful to the editors of the *CLA Journal* for their permission to use these quotes.

3. This became abundantly clear during the intense sessions of the special Seminar on Afro-South American Studies, funded by a pilot grant from the Ford Foundation and organized in conjunction with Howard University, that was held in a retreat center not far from Bogotá during April, 1986. Manuel Zapata Olivella was one of the many distinguished South American intellectuals of African ancestry who attended the Seminar.

□ □ □

Chapter Five

1. "MF," of course, is a polite form of "mother-fucker."

❑ Works Cited ❑

Abrahams, Roger D. *The Man-of-Words in the West Indies: Performance and the Emergence of Creole Culture.* Baltimore: The Johns Hopkins University Press, 1983.

Achebe, Chinua. *Things Fall Apart.* Greenwich, Connecticut: Fawcett, 1959.

Arreola, Juan José. *Confabulario.* 4th ed. Mexico City: Fondo de Cultura Económica, 1966.

---. *La feria.* 3rd ed. Mexico City: Mortiz, 1966.

Arriví, Francisco. *Máscara puertorriqueña.* Río Piedras: Editorial Cultural, 1971.

Asante, Molefi Kete. *Afrocentricity: The Theory of Social Change.* Buffalo, New York: Amulefi, 1980.

Augier, Angel. *Nicolás Guillén.* Instituto Cubano del Libro, 1971.

Azuela, Mariano. *Los de abajo.* 1916. Reprint. Mexico City: Fondo de Cultura Económica, 1960.

Barrett, Leonard. *The Rastafarians: Sounds of Cultural Dissonance.* Boston: Beacon, 1977

Baudelaire, Charles. *Les fleurs du mal.* Paris: Gallimard, 1964.

---. *Petits poèmes en prose (le spleen de Paris).* Paris: Garnier-Flammarion, 1967.

ben-Jochannan, Yosef. *African Origins of the Major "Western Religions."* New York: Alkebu-Lan, 1970.

Bernal, Martin. *Black Athena: The Afroasiatic Roots of Classical Civilization.* 2 vols. New Brunswick, New Jersey: Rutgers University Press, 1987, 1991.

Bernard, Eulalia. *Ritmohéroe.* San José: Costa Rica, 1982.

Brathwaite, Edward. *The Arrivants.* London: Oxford University Press, 1973.

---. "The African Presence in Caribbean Literature." *Daedalus* 103.2 (1974): 73-109.

Budge, E. A. Wallis. *Osiris and the Egyptian Resurrection.* 2 vols. 1911. Reprint. New York: Dover, 1973.

---. *The Gods of the Egyptians.* 2 vols. 1904. Reprint. New York: Dover,

1969.

Cabrera, Lydia. *El monte: Notas sobre las religiones, la magia, las supersticiones y el folklore de los negros criollos y del pueblo de Cuba.* 4th ed. Miami: Universal, 1975.

Captain-Hidalgo, Yvonne. *The Culture of Fiction in the Works of Manuel Zapata Olivella.* Columbia: University of Missouri Press, 1993.

Carpentier, Alejo. *Écue-Yamba-Ó.* 1933. Reprint. Havana: Arte y Literatura, 1977.

---. *El reino de este mundo.* 2nd ed. Mexico City: Cía General de Ediciones, 1967.

---. *Los pasos perdidos.* 7th ed. Mexico City: Cía General de Ediciones, 1969.

Césaire, Aimé. *Cahier d'un retour au pays natal Return to my Native Land.* Trans. Emile Snyder. Paris: Présence Africaine, 1971.

---. *Et les chiens se taisaient.* Paris: Présence Africaine, 1956.

---. *La tragédie du roi Christophe.* 2d ed. Paris: Présence Africaine, 1970.

Chandler, Wayne B. "The Moor: Light of Europe's Dark Age." *African Presence in Early Europe.* Ed. Ivan Van Sertima. New Brunswick: Transaction, 1985. 144-75.

Cobb, Martha K. "Afro-Arabs, Blackamoors and Blacks: An Inquiry into Race Concepts through Spanish Literature." *Blacks in Hispanic Literature: Critical Essays.* Ed. Miriam DeCosta. Port Washington, New York: Kennikat, 1977. 20-28.

Cudjoe, Selwyn R. *Resistance and Caribbean Literature.* Athens: Ohio University Press, 1980.

Davis, Kortright. *Emancipation Still Comin': Explorations in Caribbean Emancipatory Theology.* Maryknoll, New York: Orbis, 1990.

Del Río, Angel. *Historia de la literatura española.* Rev. ed. Vol 1. New York: Holt, 1963.

Díaz Sánchez, Ramón. *Cumboto.* Santiago, Chile: Editorial Universitaria, 1967.

Diop, Cheikh Anta. *Civilization or Barbarism: An Authentic Anthropology.* Trans. Yaa-Lengi Meema Ngemi. Eds. Harold J. Salemson and Marjolijn de Jager. New York: Hill, 1991.

---. *The African Origin of Civilization: Myth or Reality.* Ed. and trans. Mercer Cook. New York: Hill, 1974.

Duncan, Quince. *Final de calle.* 2nd ed. San José: Editorial Costa Rica, 1979.

---. *Kimbo.* San José: Editorial Costa Rica, 1989.

---. *La paz del pueblo.* San José: Editorial Costa Rica, 1978.

---. *La rebelión pocomía y otros relatos.* San José: Editorial Costa Rica,

1976.
---. *Los cuatro espejos*. San José: Editorial Costa Rica, 1973.
---. *Una canción en la madrugada*. San José: Editorial Costa Rica, 1970.
Estupiñán Bass, Nelson. *Bajo el cielo nublado*. Quito: Cultura Ecuatoriana, 1981.
---. *El último río*. Quito: Cultura Ecuatoriana, 1966.
Fanon, Frantz. *The Wretched of the Earth*. Trans. Constance Farrington. 2d ed. Suffolk: Penguin, 1970.
Faulkner, Raymond O. *A Concise Dictionary of Middle Egyptian*. Oxford: Griffith Institute, 1962.
Felder, Cain Hope. *Troubling Biblical Waters: Race, Class and Family*. Maryknoll, New York: Orbis, 1989.
Finch, Charles S. lll. *Echoes of the Old Darkland: Themes from the African Eden*. Decatur, Georgia: Khenti, 1991.
Friedemann, Nina S. de. "Perfiles sociales del carnaval en Barranquilla (Colombia)." *Montalbán* [U Católica Andrés Bello, Caracas] 15 (1984): 127-52.
Fuentes, Carlos. *La muerte de Artemio Cruz*. 4th ed. Mexico City: Fondo de Cultura Económica, 1968.
Gallegos, Rómulo. *Doña Bárbara*. 32nd ed. Buenos Aires: Losada, 1975.
Gates, Henry Louis, Jr., ed. *Black Literature and Literary Theory*. New York: Methuen, 1984.
---. *The Signifying Monkey: A Theory of African-American Literary Criticism*. Oxford: Oxford University Press, 1988.
González Echevarría, Roberto. "Guillén as Baroque: Meaning in *Motivos de son*." *Callaloo* 10 (1987): 302-17.
Goodison, Lorna. *I Am Becoming My Mother*. London: New Beacon, 1986.
Guillén, Nicolás. *Obra poética 1920-1972*. 2 vols. Havana: Instituto Cubano del Libro, 1972, 1973.
Henderson, Stephen. *Understanding the New Black Poetry: Black Speech and Black Music as Poetic References*. New York: Morrow, 1972.
Hill, Errol. *The Trinidad Carnival: Mandate for a National Theatre*. Austin: University of Texas Press, 1972.
Hughes, Langston. *Selected Poems*. New York: Knopf, 1959; New York: Vintage-Random, 1974.
Jackson, John G. *Introduction to African Civilizations*. 2nd ed. Secaucus, New Jersey: Citadel, 1974.
---. *Man, God, and Civilization*. New York: Carol Publishing Group, 1990.
Jahn, Janheinz. *Muntu: The New African Culture*. Trans. Marjorie

Grene. New York: Grove, 1961.

James, C.L.R. *The Black Jacobins: Toussaint L'Ouverture and the San Domingo Revolution.* 1938. Reprint. New York: Vintage-Random, 1963.

James, George G. M. *Stolen Legacy.* 1954. Reprint. San Francisco: Richardson, 1985.

Johnson, Lemuel A. "The Dilemma of Presence in Black Diaspora Literature: A Comparativist Reading of Palacios' *Las estrellas son negras.*" *Afro-Hispanic Review.* 1.1 (1982): 3-10.

Keita, Lancine. "African Philosophical Systems: A Rational Reconstruction." *The Philosophical Forum* 9 (1977-78): 169-189.

Kesteloot, Lilyan. *Les écrivains noirs de langue française: Naissance d'une littérature.* 4th ed. Brussells: L'Institut de Sociologie, 1971.

Kutzinski, Vera M. *Against the American Grain: Myth and History in William Carlos Williams, Jay Wright, and Nicolás Guillén.* Baltimore: The Johns Hopkins University Press, 1987.

La vida de Lazarillo de Tormes. Ed. R. O. Jones. Manchester: Manchester University Press, 1963.

Lamming, George. *In the Castle of My Skin.* New York: Collier, 1970.

Lane-Poole, Stanley. *The Story of the Moors in Spain.* 1886. Reprint. Baltimore: Black Classic Press, 1990.

Lewis, Marvin A. *Treading the Ebony Path: Ideology and Violence in Contemporary Afro-Colombian Prose Fiction.* Columbia: University of Missouri Press, 1987.

Llerena Villalobos, Rito. *Memoria cultural en el vallenato: Un modelo de textualidad en la canción folclórica colombiana.* Medellín: Centro de Investigaciones Facultad de Ciencias Humanas U. de A., 1985.

Lovelace, Earl. *The Dragon Can't Dance.* London: Deutsch, 1979.

---. *The Wine of Astonishment.* London: Deutsch, 1982.

Lumpkin, Beatrice. "Africa in the Mainstream of Mathematics History." *Journal of African Civilization* 2.1-2 (1980): 68-77.

Maloney, Gerardo. *Juega vivo.* Panama City: Formato 16, 1984.

Mbiti, John S. *African Religions and Philosophy.* New York: Anchor-Doubleday, 1970.

McCray, Walter Arthur. *The Black Presence in the Bible.* 2 vols. Chicago: Black Light Fellowship, 1990.

Métraux, Alfred. *Voodoo in Haiti.* Trans. Hugo Charteris. New York: Schocken, 1972.

Morejón, Nancy. *Recopilación de textos sobre Nicolás Guillén.* Havana: Casa, 1974.

Naipaul, V. S. *Miguel Street.* London: Deutsch, 1959; Middlesex, England: Penguin, 1971.

---. *The Middle Passage*. London: Deutsch, 1962; Middlesex, England: Penguin, 1969.

---. *The Mimic Men*. London: Deutsch, 1967; Middlesex, England: Penguin, 1969.

Obenga, Théophile. "African Philosophy of the Pharonic Period 2780-330 B.C." *Egypt Revisited*. 2d ed. Ed. Ivan Van Sertima, ed. and trans. Habib Sy, Elizabeth Clement, and Irene d'Almeida. New Brunswick: Transaction, 1989. 286-324.

Orloff, Alexander. "Time outside of Time: The Mythological Origin of Carnival." *Carnival: Myth and Cult*. 2nd ed. Worgl, Austria: Perlinger, 1981. 15-30.

Ortiz, Adalberto. *Juyungo*. Buenos Aires: Americalee, 1943; Barcelona: Seix Barral, 1983.

Palacios, Arnoldo. *Las estrellas son negras*. 2nd ed. Bogotá: Revista Colombiana, 1971.

Pascal, Blaise. *Pensées*. Ed. Jacques Chevalier. Paris: Gallimard, 1936; Paris: Livre de Poche, 1962.

Quevedo, Raymond (Atilla the Hun). *Atilla's Kaiso: A Short History of Trinidad Calypso*. St. Augustine, Trinidad: UWI Extra Mural Studies, 1983.

Rashidi, Runoko. "Africans in Early Asian Civilizations: A Historical Overview." *African Presence in Early Asia*. Eds. Ivan Van Sertima and Runoko Rashidi. Rev. ed. New Brunswick, New Jersey: Transaction, 1988. 5-52.

Reed, Ishmael. *Mumbo Jumbo*. New York: Doubleday, 1972.

Richards, Henry J. *La jornada novelística de Nelson Estupiñán Bass: Búsqueda de la perfección*. Quito: El Conejo, 1989.

Rivera, José Eustacio. *La vorágine*. 13th ed. Buenos Aires: Losada, 1972.

Sarmiento, Domingo F. *Civilización y barbarie*. 8th ed. Buenos Aires: Austral, 1951.

Senghor, Léopold Sédar. *Liberté l: Négritude et humanisme*. Paris: Seuil, 1964.

Shorter, Aylward. *African Christian Theology—Adaptation or Incarnation*. Maryknoll, New York: Orbis, 1977.

Smart, Ian I. *Central American Writers of West Indian Origin: A New Hispanic Literature*. Washington, D.C.: Three Continents, 1984.

---. "*Changó, el gran putas* as Liberation Literature." *CLA Journal* 35 (1991): 15-30.

---. *Nicolás Guillén, Popular Poet of the Caribbean*. Columbia: University of Missouri Press, 1990.

---. "Popular Black Intellectualism in Gerardo Maloney's *Juega vivo*." *Afro-Hispanic Review* 5.1-3 (1986): 43-47.

---. "Quince Duncan." *Dictionary of Literary Biography. Volume*

145: Modern Latin American Fiction Writers. Second Series. Ed. William Luis and Ann González. Detroit: Gale, 1994.

---. "Religious Elements in the Narrative of Quince Duncan." *Afro-Hispanic Review* 1.2 (1982): 27-31.

---. "The African Heritage in Spanish Caribbean Literature." *The Western Journal of Black Studies* 5 (1981): 23-31.

---. "The Literary World of Quince Duncan: An Interview." *CLA Journal* 28 (1985): 281-298.

---. "The Trickster *Pícaro* in Three Contemporary Afro-Hispanic Novels." *Afro-Hispanic Review* 7. 1-3 (1988): 49-51.

Taylor, Partick. *The Narrative of Liberation: Perspectives on Afro-Caribbean Literature, Popular Culture, and Politics*. Ithaca: Cornell University Press, 1989.

The Penguin Book of Spanish Verse. Middlesex, England: Penguin, 1956.

Valdés-Cruz, Rosa E. *La poesía negroide en América*. New York: Las Américas, 1970.

Van Sertima, Ivan. *They Came before Columbus*. New York: Random, 1976.

---. and Runoko Rashidi, ed. *African Presence in Early Asia*. Rev. ed. Brunswick: Transaction, 1988.

Walcott, Derek. *Dream on Monkey Mountain and Other Plays*. New York: Farrar, 1970.

Webster's Ninth New Collegiate Dictionary. Springfield, Massachusetts: Merrian-Webster, 1988.

Williams, Chancellor. *The Destruction of Black Civilization: Great Issues of a Race from 4500 B.C. to 2000 A.D.* Chicago: Third World, 1976.

Williams, Eric. *Capitalism and Slavery*. 1944. Reprint. New York: Capricorn, 1966.

Wilson, Carlos Guillermo. *Chombo*. Miami: Ediciones Universal, 1981.

Zapata Olivella, Manuel. *Changó, el gran putas*. Bogota: Editorial Oveja Negra, 1983.

---. *Las claves mágicas de América*. Bogotá: Plaza & Janes, 1989.

Zenón Cruz, Isabelo. *Narciso descubre su trasero: El negro en la cultura puertorriqueña*. 2 vols. Humacao, Puerto Rico: Furidi, 1974, 1975.

Index

Abrahams, Roger D., 54-56, 85, 131, 165, 168
Abydos, 17, 30
Achebe, Chinua, 65
African American, 5, 11, 12, 45, 47, 56, 60, 85, 92, 117, 118, 129, 130, 142
African-ancestored Americans, 62, 128, 156
African-ancestored writers, 9, 43, 47, 78, 164, 173
African-centered analysis, 43, 173
African culture, civilization, 3, 43, 51, 52, 55, 58, 115, 117, 129, 139, 145, 146, 149, 155, 172
African theological tradition, 79, 127, 148, 157
African theology, 140
Africana, 2, 4, 6-8, 14, 69, 70, 101, 113, 141, 142, 170, 172, 173
africanía, 171
Africanness, 31, 170
African mythology, 115, 127, 148, 162
African roots, 4, 5, 94
African spirituality, 3, 6, 79, 82
Afro-American, 31, 46, 47, 52, 106, 142, 143, 159, 170
Afro-Antillean, 7, 37, 121, 123
Afro-Christian, 99, 159
Afro-Cuban, 7, 37, 116, 121, 123
Afro-Hispanic, Hispanist, 2, 6, 68, 75, 84, 114, 169, 176
Afroasiatic, 25, 87
Afrocentric, 2, 4, 8, 9, 42, 52, 65, 77, 95, 116, 117, 125, 129, 130, 133, 136, 141, 142, 154, 157, 161
Afrocentricity, 3, 93, 117, 157
americano, 35, 116, 117, 137
Americas, 3, 6, 7, 11, 27, 29, 30, 33, 38, 42, 47, 69, 77, 90, 91, 93, 96, 104, 105, 111, 117, 119, 125, 130, 132, 138, 139, 164, 172, 173
ancestor worship, 28
Ancient Greece, 88, 89, 173
Andalusia, 64, 65
Anglican, 145, 165
Anglophone, 101, 102, 113, 166, 168, 171
Antar, 66
Aquileo Echeverría literary award, 147
Arabic, 63, 65, 67, 68
Argentina, 32
Arozarena, Marcelino, 124, 164
Arreola, Juan José, 3, 8, 54
Arriví, Francisco, 60
artistic bilingualism, 168
Asante, Molefi Kete, 13, 117, 157
Ashanti, 152, 159
Asiatic, 41, 105, 133
Atilla (see Quevedo, Raymond)
Atom, 49-51, 55
Augier, Angel, 100, 106, 177

Auset (Isis), 8, 17, 26, 154
Averroes, 63
Azuela, Mariano, 35
Aztecs, 90

Babylon, 24, 40
Ballagas, Emilio, 123
banana plantation, 160, 161
Bantu philosophy, 52, 125, 162
Barbados, 101, 167
barbaric, barbarism, 5, 14, 28, 32, 33, 35, 36, 38, 66, 77, 94, 105
baroque, 74, 84, 176, 177
Barrett, Leonard, 11, 159, 160, 175
Baudelaire, Charles, 46, 65, 118
beguin, 95
ben-Jochannan, Yosef, 13, 89, 135, 172
Bernal, Martin, 13, 14, 87-89, 91, 133, 135, 173
Bernard, Eulalia, 166, 168
Bible, 4, 16, 21, 22, 27, 39, 40, 127, 128, 134
Black Muslims, 67
Black Stalin, 111
black-white love, 167
bomba, 84
Bouckman, 119
Brathwaite, Edward Kamau, 11, 13, 53, 139
Brazilian candomble, 11
Brown, John, 141
Brown, Melvin, 166
Budge, E. A. Wallis, 4, 16, 18, 25, 26, 30, 31, 133, 134

Call-response, 96
Camus, Albert, 129
Canaan, 21, 22
canboulay riots, 96
Cantar de Mio Cid, 67
cante hondo, 64
Capitulation, 101, 107
Captain-Hidalgo, Yvonne, 114
Caribbean, 2-4, 6, 7, 11, 45, 54-57, 59, 65, 79-87, 89-95, 97, 98, 100, 102-07, 109-11, 113, 114, 120, 121, 123, 138, 139, 145, 146, 159, 166-68, 176, 178
Caribbean culture, 7, 55, 81, 84, 95, 98, 100, 105, 111
Caribbean literary hermeneutics, 84
Caribbean literature, 11, 45, 81, 84, 94, 107, 110, 146, 178
Caribbean unity, 90, 92, 93, 105, 111
carnival, 6, 7, 29-31, 54, 65, 93-98, 100, 103-05, 139
Carpentier, Alejo, 7, 8, 31, 84, 102, 115-21, 123, 127-30, 148, 150, 177
Cartey, Wilfred, 64
castellano, 67
Caucasoid, 67, 128
Caucasus, 39
Césaire, Aimé, 7, 48, 58, 91, 110, 130, 162, 164, 169
Chandler, Wayne B., 13, 63
chantwells, 96
Chile, 32
Chinese, 39, 41
choteo, 57, 60, 103
Christ, 16, 19-29, 31, 42, 80-82, 127, 131
Christian, 6, 16, 18-21, 24-28, 31, 62-64, 79-82, 90, 91, 99, 109, 111, 127, 129, 131, 136, 137, 157, 158, 160-62
Christology, 81
Christophe, Henri, 110, 119, 120, 169
cimarrón, 6, 7, 69, 77, 79, 82, 110, 113, 141, 145, 146, 151, 157, 162, 163, 166, 168
cimarronaje, 6, 69, 72, 73, 79, 81, 83, 90, 95, 104-06, 108, 111,

138, 153, 165, 168
circum-Caribbean, 7
civilization, 1-5, 8, 13, 14, 19, 23-25, 30, 32-36, 38-41, 43, 49-51, 62, 64, 69, 77, 87-89, 91, 117, 125, 128, 130, 132, 134, 135, 157, 170-73, 175
classical, 171
Cobb, Martha K., 65, 66
Colombia, 2, 8, 29, 36, 65, 70, 93, 94, 102, 103, 106, 113, 138, 177
colonial authorities, 99
colonial machine, 104
colonial paradigm, 77, 132
colonial situation, 96, 132
colonial status, 106
colonization, 32
colonized person , 162
Columbus, 42, 90, 106, 142, 167
Communist Party, 108
compartmentalization, 97
comuniones, 129
Congo, 93, 98, 101, 134
consort, 154, 160, 163
Costa Rica, 2, 8, 45, 113, 145, 147, 149, 155
Council of Ephesus, 25
creation, 18, 39, 40, 48-51, 127, 131
Creole, 89, 97, 166, 167
critical realism, 153, 154
Cro-Magnon, 39
crossroads, 51-54, 130, 131, 137
Cruz, Celia, 111
cuatro, 102
Cuba, Cuban, 2, 53, 93, 94, 97, 102, 106, 111
Cubena (see Wilson, Carlos Guillermo)
Cudjoe, Selwyn R., 6, 81, 94, 113, 172
Cuminá, 7, 141, 145, 146, 149, 152, 158-60, 168, 169
Cush, 39, 40, 134

Damas, Léon Gontran, 91
Darío, Rubén, 34, 107
Dark Ages, 66
Davis, Angela, 138, 140
Davis, Kortright, 6, 79-83, 87, 90-93, 105, 106, 109, 110, 113, 172
deconstruct, deconstruction, deconstructive, 15, 43, 119, 129, 172, 173
Del Río, Angel, 67
Dendera, 30
Derrida, Jacques, 31, 43, 172
Dialectical Theory of Identification, 77, 107, 176
Díaz Sánchez, Ramón, 69, 74
Diop, Cheikh Anta, 5, 13, 14, 39-41, 87, 89, 91, 117, 133-35, 172, 173
Duncan, Quince, 2, 7-9, 45, 59, 106, 109, 113, 127, 145-49, 151-58, 161-68; *Final de calle*, 147, 166; *Kimbo*, 147, 155, 161-63, 165-68; *La paz del pueblo*, 141, 147, 149, 152, 158-60, 163, 166-68; *La rebelión pocomía y otros relatos*, 147, 148, 152, 160; *Los cuatro espejos*, 147, 155, 161, 164, 165

Earth mother, 155, 160, 163
Ecuador, 9, 61, 69, 104
Eden, 26, 39, 40
Egypt, 1, 12, 17, 19, 21, 22, 26, 30, 40, 88, 133, 134, 175
Egyptologist, 1, 4, 16, 133
El Cid, 66
emancipation, 6, 80, 83, 90, 95, 96, 104, 105, 109-11, 138

Enlightenment, 2, 33, 37, 64, 88, 131, 173
Epiphany, 72, 100
Esmeraldas, 104
Essenes, 18
Estupiñán Bass, Nelson, 7, 9, 61, 104, 164
Esu, Esu-Elegbara (see also Legba), 48, 50-55
Ethiopia, 13, 40, 91, 157
Euphrates, 39, 40
Eurocentric, 4, 11, 14, 23, 27, 29, 31-33, 37, 40, 42, 43, 51, 52, 77, 78, 84, 85, 87, 94, 97, 103-05, 107, 117, 120, 125, 127-30, 132, 142, 147, 154, 161, 166, 173
European, 23, 25, 27, 29, 32-38, 42, 46, 66, 68, 69, 88, 95, 117, 118, 120, 133, 142, 157, 165, 171-73
existentialism, existentialist, 7, 54, 55, 150

Fanon, Frantz, 6, 57, 70, 72, 77, 81, 84, 94, 107, 115, 132, 162, 163, 172, 176
Faulkner, Raymond O., 1
Faulkner, William, 8, 153, 154
Felder, Cain Hope, 13, 39
female fecundity, 163
fighting literature, 94, 115
fighting phase, 107
Finch, Charles S. 111, 7, 26, 87, 89, 127, 131, 133, 135, 136, 154
flamenco, 6
Francophone, 101, 172
French, 13, 38, 46, 48, 52, 66, 97, 101, 102, 157, 166, 172, 173, 175, 176
French Creole, 97
Freud, Sigmund, 155
Friedemann, Nina S. de, 29
Fuentes, Carlos, 8, 37, 154

Gallegos, Rómulo, 37
García Márquez, Gabriel, 35, 102
Gates, Henry Louis, Jr., 5, 6, 11, 13, 45-49, 51-54, 68, 69, 77, 85-87, 118, 129-32, 135, 138, 139, 142
Genesis, 21, 22, 24, 39, 40, 50, 88, 127
German expressionism, 125
Gihon, 39, 40
giving fatigue, 60, 103
Golden Age, 76
Góngora, Luis de, 74
Gonzalo de Berceo, 24
Goodison, Lorna, 7, 110
go-go, 93, 105
Graeco-Roman, 63
Greek, 2, 13, 21, 50, 88
Grenada, 94, 101
Grimaldi, 39
guaguanco, 84
Guillén, Nicolás, 2, 7, 8, 31, 57, 58, 60, 76, 81, 83, 86, 93-95, 99, 100, 103, 104, 106-11, 113, 124, 142, 161, 162, 164, 176, 177
Guirao, Ramón, 123

Haiti, 47, 48, 53, 119, 120, 130, 167
Haitian Revolution, 117, 120
Haitian vaudou (voodoo), 11, 47
Ham, Hamitic, 24, 40
Harlem Renaissance, 121, 123
Hebrew, 21, 50, 66-68
hegemonic, 85, 105, 166
Henderson, Stephen, 168
hermeneutics, 84-86, 89, 91
Hermes, 129, 135, 139, 157
hero, heroine, 66, 98, 106, 108,

109, 111, 138, 154, 161
Herskovits, Melville, 11
Heru (Horus), 8, 17, 25, 26, 154, 161
Heru/Wosir, 155
Hill, Errol 49-51, 86, 98, 99
Hilliard, Asa, G. 111, 89
Hispanic, 2-6, 14, 24, 25, 33, 45, 62, 64, 66, 68, 70, 75, 77, 83, 84, 159, 166, 168, 170-72, 176, 177
hispanidad, 170, 171
Hispano-Romance, 66, 67, 171
Hispanophone, 2, 4, 6-8, 69, 70, 101, 113, 141, 142, 146, 171, 172
Hispanophone Africana, 2, 4, 6-8, 69, 70, 113, 141, 142, 170, 171, 172
Hispanophone Caribbean, 113
hoodoo, 53
Hughes, Langston, 107, 142, 164
humor, 5, 57, 60

Iberian Peninsula, 5, 62, 66, 67
Incas, 90
indianista, 37
indigenista, 37
Islam, Islamic, 5, 25, 50

Jackson, John G., 4, 13, 19-21, 23, 24, 26, 38, 62, 157, 172, 175
Jackson, Richard L., 8, 114
Jahn, Janheinz, 52, 55, 58, 123, 162, 163
Jamaica, 84, 101, 149, 159, 160
James, C. L. R., 109, 120, 167, 173
James, George G. M., 13, 49, 51, 87, 89, 91, 117, 133, 135, 172
jarchas, 67, 68
jazz, 105, 124, 125
Jehuti (Thoth), 17, 135, 136, 139, 157
Jes Grew, 46, 47, 84, 130
Jethro, 17, 21
jitanjáfora, 124
John the Baptist, 160
Johnson, Lemuel A., 72
Jones, R. O., 56, 68
jou'vert, 139
Judaeo-Christian, 157
Judeo-Christian, 16, 18

Kaiso, 7, 84, 86, 93-98, 100-02, 105
Keita, Lancine, 89
Kemet, 1, 4, 9, 26, 27, 49, 51, 75, 82, 87, 97, 132, 133, 135, 154, 160
Kemetic, 7, 8, 17, 50, 157, 162
Kesteloot, Lilyan, 48, 130, 176
King, Martin Luther, Jr., 106, 141
Kingdom of the Dead, 140
Kmt, 1
kora, 64
Krishna, 19, 20
Kumina, Pukumina, 11, 105, 159, 160
Kunene, Mazisi, 95
Kutzinski, Vera M., 31, 94, 95, 100, 127

Là, là-bas, 46
Lamming, George, 167
Lane-Poole, Stanley, 62-65, 67, 76
Latin American literature, 3, 32, 107, 114, 142
Latin American revolution, 12
Latino, 171
laughter, 5, 52-54, 57-60, 76, 145, 162-66
Lazarillo de Tormes, 68, 72, 76
Legba, 5, 6, 48, 51, 53, 54, 59, 79, 129-32, 135-40, 152, 156, 159,

165, 172
Lewis, Marvin, A., 114, 136, 141
liberation, 6, 79, 81, 141
liberation literature, 114, 115, 126, 178
Llerena Villalobos, Rito, 7, 65, 102
loa, 48, 53, 125, 126
logos, 50, 51
Lovelace, Earl, 7, 97, 99, 103, 177
Lumpkin, Beatrice, 13, 63
Lusophone, 171

Mackandal , 119
magical realism, 7, 116, 117, 129, 130, 154
Malcolm X, 79, 106, 140, 142
Maloney, Gerardo, 7, 59, 60, 84, 110, 166, 168, 177, 178
mamaguy, mamaguyer, 59, 61, 103
man-of-words, 54, 131, 168
Mandingo, 64
Manichean, 77, 96, 132, 176
marimba, 104, 105
Mariological, 24
Martinican, Martinique, 47, 56, 57, 162, 167
marvelous reality, 118-21
mas', 99
Mass, 16, 19, 40
Massey, Gerald, 91
Mayas, 90
Mbiti, John S., 11, 13, 45
McCray, Walter Arthur, 4, 13, 21-23
Mediterranean, 67
Memphis, Memphite Theology, 49, 50
merengue, 95
Mesopotamia, 39, 40
messiah, messiahhood, 21, 22, 109, 127, 157, 158, 159, 161, 162
Métraux, Alfred, 175
Mexican, 3, 35-37, 54
Midian, 17
Mighty Sparrow, 76
Min, 162
modernism, 154
modernismo, 34, 35
Moor, 62
More, Beny, 111
Morejón, Nancy, 106, 177
Mother Africa, 170, 171
mozárabe, 66, 67
Muntu, 52, 58, 125, 126, 128, 140, 156, 162
muwassahas, 66
myal, 159
Mystical Body of Christ, 28, 82
mythology, mythos, 7, 26, 41, 51, 52, 69, 126-28, 130, 135, 148, 162, 175

Naipaul, V. S., 55, 56, 167, 176
national culture, 77, 132, 176
national literature, 94, 115
negrismo, 117
negrista, 7, 37
negritude, 7, 37, 47, 91, 92, 102, 117, 130, 151, 154
neo-African, 5, 7, 52, 53, 55, 58, 83, 105, 141, 142, 155, 159, 162, 165-167
New Testament, 18
New World, 4, 11, 15, 27-30, 34, 46, 52, 69, 79, 90, 100, 128, 129, 132, 159
Nicaragua, 107
Nile, 2, 40, 41, 49, 50
Nile Valley School, 41
Nipponese, 39, 41
noble savage, 33, 118, 119
North American, 12, 45-47, 58, 75, 102, 107, 113, 114, 128, 129, 138, 142, 164, 171, 176
Northeast Africa, 26
nous, 50, 51

ntr, *ntrw*, 48, 53, 125, 132, 156, 157
Obeah, 159
Obenga, Théophile, 12, 45, 50, 89, 134, 135, 172
Oedipus, 155
Old Kingdom, 50
Old World, 23, 46, 129
Olmecs, 90
Olodumare, 48
oppressed people, 69, 70, 132, 137
oppression, 91, 137, 141, 162
oral literature, orality, 45, 92, 97, 101
oral poetry, 84, 93
orisha, 48, 53, 125, 129, 136, 141, 159, 169
Orloff, Alexander, 97
Orphic, 154, 167
Ortiz, Adalberto, 8, 58, 69, 71, 74, 164
Ortiz Fernández, Fernando, 11
Orungán, 135, 154, 155
Oshun, 15, 123
Osirian, 17, 30, 152
Osiris (see Wosir)
Our Lady of Czestochowa, 26

Paella, 64
Palacios, Arnoldo, 8, 69, 73, 74
Palés Matos, Luis, 7, 121
Palestine, 231
Pan-African, Pan-Africanism, 46, 51, 52, 92, 138
Panama, 93, 102, 106, 110, 177
Pan-Caribbean, 2, 6, 81, 84, 86, 100, 103, 109, 138
PaPa LaBas, 46
Papa Legba, (see Legba)
Papiamento, 167
Paris, 48, 62, 91, 130, 176
Pascal, Blaise, 2, 53
Pedroso, Regino, 124
picardía, 71-73
picaresque novel, 5, 77
pícaro, 5, 6, 54, 68-72, 74, 75, 77, 176
Picasso, Pablo, 124, 125
picong, 55, 57, 60
Pishon, 39, 40
plantation, 74, 109, 110, 160-62, 166, 167, 173
Platt Amendment, 106
plena, 84, 15
Port-of-Spain, 56, 65
Portugal, 31
posmodernismo, 35
postcolonial, postcolonization, 32, 81, 106
postmodernism, 107, 154
praise song, 66
Premio Editorial Costa Rica , 147
Promethean, 152
Ptah, 49-51, 55
Puerto Rican, 60, 61, 121, 123
Puerto Rico, 84, 122
Put, 13, 38, 53, 76, 84, 119-21, 134, 157, 173

Quetzalcoatl, 19, 20, 42
Quevedo, Raymond (Atilla), 7, 86, 93, 101

Ra, 55
racism, racist, 5, 33, 35, 37, 38, 40-42, 63, 71, 72, 77, 88, 91, 132, 142, 147, 166, 170
Radicalization, 107, 108
Rashidi, Runoko, 13, 41
Rastafarianism, 11
realism, 7, 42, 116, 117, 130, 153, 154
rebellion, 98, 99, 117, 128, 147, 152
Reed, Ishmael, 46, 47, 84, 118, 130,

142
Reid, Vic, 110
reggae, 84, 95, 100
Relative Deism, 136
resistance, 81, 98, 105, 106, 109, 111, 117, 138
resurrection, 16, 17, 19, 20, 24, 30, 99, 131, 133
Revitalization, 107
revolution, 35, 36, 117, 119, 120, 128, 173
revolutionary consciousness, 162
revolutionary literature, 94, 115
Richards, Henry J., 105
river, 40, 58, 61, 73, 145, 164, 166
Roaring Twenties, 121
Roman Catholic(ism), 3, 4, 12, 24, 25
romanticism, 7, 33, 118
Rome, 19, 26, 29, 31, 170
rumba, 64, 84, 123, 124

Sacrificial victim, 163
saints, 4, 27, 28, 82, 137
Saint Barbara, 15, 29
samamfo, 145, 147-50, 152-56, 159, 163, 166
santería, 11
Sarmiento, Domingo F., 5, 32-35, 37, 38, 85, 87
Sartre, Jean Paul, 154
saviors, 19, 20, 26
scribal literary, literature, 14, 84, 111
secular humanism, 12
self-affirmation, 93
selfhood, 82, 83
Senghor, Léopold Sédar, 47, 91, 102, 130
Set, 8, 17, 18, 26, 30, 68, 72, 77, 89, 119, 124, 127, 140, 147, 154-56, 160, 168
Shango, 6, 7, 11, 15, 27, 29, 79, 96, 97, 109, 123, 125-27, 131, 135-38, 140, 146, 154, 156, 162
Shorter, Aylward, 136
Signifying Monkey, 5, 11, 46, 47, 48, 51, 52, 77, 85, 129, 132, 165
signifying, 5, 11, 46-48, 51, 52, 60, 69, 77, 85, 132, 165
Sisyphus, 151
slave trade, slavery, 80, 82, 89, 91, 95, 97, 120, 125, 128, 137, 173
slave ship, 138
Smart, Ian I., 59, 104, 107, 110, 167, 168, 178
smartman, 54, 57, 59, 103
son, 7, 17, 20, 22, 23, 47, 58, 66, 69, 71, 84, 93-95, 100-02, 105, 114, 117, 130, 138, 148, 152, 154, 160, 163, 169, 177
son-consort, 154
sonero, 100
sous-réalité, 7, 153
Spain, 3, 31, 33, 39, 56, 62-65, 68, 69, 72, 76, 98, 106, 140, 170
Spiritual Baptist (Shouter), 99, 177
St. Thomas of Aquinas, 12
St. Vincent, 55, 101
stickfight, stickfighting, 30, 96
Sumer, Sumerian, 21, 40, 175
syncretic, syncretism, 4, 15, 29, 32, 37, 103, 160

Table of Nations, 21, 24, 40
Tallet, José Z., 123, 124
Taylor, Patrick, 6, 81, 113, 172
The 1492 experience, 173
The Blessed Virgin Mary, 24
The Existing One, 55, 126
The Gambia, 64
The Holy Qur'ān, 49
The Penguin Book of Spanish Verse, 176

theology of liberation, 79
Thomistic, 52
Thoth (see Jehuti)
Tigris, 39, 40
Toussaint L'Ouverture, 109
traditional African religions, 28
traditional African spirituality, 79
Trickster, 5, 6, 45, 46, 51, 53-55, 62, 68-71, 74, 75, 77, 79, 130, 132, 136-39, 176
Trinidad and Tobago, 7, 11, 30, 55, 60, 84, 86, 93-96, 99, 102-04, 173, 177
Tubman, Harriet, 141
Turner, Nat, 141

United States, 34, 40, 53, 106, 122, 124, 170, 175, 177

Valdés-Cruz, Rosa E., 97, 123
vallenato, 7, 65, 86, 102-04, 114
Van Sertima, Ivan, 4, 12, 13, 42, 88, 89, 117, 133, 172
Vargas Llosa, Mario, 8
Venezuela, 37, 69, 102
Volney, Constantine, 13, 91, 157, 175
Vulgar Latin, 66

Walcott, Derek, 120, 178
warrior element, warriorhood, 30, 97, 98
water and blood, 163, 164
Webster's Ninth New Collegiate Dictionary, 171
West Africa, 64, 131
West African art, 125
West Indian(ness), 6, 82, 165
West Indian Central Americans, 167
West Indian Costa Rican, 160
Western academy, 2, 15, 35, 63, 68, 88, 89, 134
Western civilization, 25, 43, 69, 87, 135, 170, 172
white supremacist, 4, 7, 14, 40, 63, 68, 85, 88, 97, 120, 134, 157, 171, 173
white supremacy, 2, 105, 120, 131, 133, 134, 173
Williams, Chancellor, 13, 38, 135, 173
Williams, Eric, 120, 173
Wilson, Carlos Guillermo (Cubena), 83, 110, 166, 168
Wolof rice, 64
word, 12, 17, 18, 23, 50, 52, 58, 67, 76, 80, 92, 97, 124, 132, 137, 139, 149, 159, 162, 165
Word Force, 139
Wosir (Osiris), 8, 17, 26, 154, 160

Yemayá, 135, 154
Yoruba, 5, 6, 27, 48, 50-52, 69, 77, 97, 125-27, 129, 130, 132, 135, 136, 154

Zapata Olivella, Manuel, 2, 3, 8, 106, 109, 113, 114, 128, 136, 141, 142, 148, 151, 154, 162, 178; *Changó, el gran putas*, 7, 75, 114, 136, 141, 142, 148
Zenón Cruz, Isabelo, 122
Zeus, 162